THE POWER OF
THE PRESS?

LOUIS HEREN

THE POWER OF THE PRESS ?

ORBIS · LONDON

First published in Great Britain
by Orbis Publishing Limited, London 1985

Phototypeset by Falcon Graphic Art Ltd,
Wallington, Surrey
Printed in Great Britain
by Biddles Limited, Guildford

ISBN 0–85613–608–5

CONTENTS

EARLY TIMES

The human race has for centuries had an apparently insatiable appetite for news. The first newsletters were circulated throughout the Roman Empire as early as the fifth century BC, and the first known newspaper publisher was Julius Caesar, who launched the *Acta Diurna* in 60 BC. His hand-written wall newspaper, posted daily in the Forum, was, however, limited to official announcements. Newspapers as we know them were impossible before Gutenberg invented printing in Mainz in 1450. The first primitive efforts were known as newsbooks, occasional publications which were printed in a number of European cities. They regularly pirated each other's news items (a practice which continues today) but helped to spread among the public the custom of reading the news rather than hearing it by word of mouth. Without this pirating the development of newspapers would have been slower than it was.

The first weekly and daily newspapers appeared in Germany in the early 1600s. The delay was due in part to high production costs and widespread illiteracy, but also partly to harsh censorship. A free press was not tolerated because the rulers instinctively knew that it would be dangerous. The publication of all domestic news was prohibited in Switzerland, which could explain why in later years the *Neue Zürcher Zeitung* became famous for its foreign news service. Britain was the first country to abandon censorship, in 1693, more than two hundred years after Caxton set up his press in London.

The *Daily Courant* appeared in London nine years later, but the publisher did not take any chances. No original reporting was attempted. Britain's first daily newspaper was filled with extracts from Continental papers. This was surprising because some of the journalists of the period, who wrote pamphlets or for periodicals, had little respect for authority. They were natural nonconformists and crusaders, and thrived on controversy. Jonathan Swift (1667–1745) was the greatest polemical journalist of his time and probably the world's first editorial writer. Daniel Defoe (*c.*1660–1731) was a hack in that he wrote millions of words, but an inspired hack. Defoe is mainly remembered for *Robinson Crusoe* (1719) and *Moll Flanders* (1722), but he was a first-rate reporter. To quote Harold Nicolson: 'he had endless curiosity and a passion for facts, and was faithful to what he saw. He used his eyes and described what they told him without bias or rancour. His uncalculating love of liberty shines through all he wrote. What more can one ask of any reporter?' What indeed. Defoe was the father of modern reporting, and memorials to him should be erected in every press club.

Another pioneer was Richard Steele (1672–1729), who launched the *Tatler* in 1709. He found many of his gossipy news items and most of his reading public in London's new coffee houses. They were frequented by the *literati* and men-about-town as well as politicians and merchants, and their popularity was a sign of social change. Britain was moving from the post-Restoration period into the Age of Enlightenment, and the excitement was communicated to readers all over the country by Joseph Addison (1672–1719), who wrote about morals and manners for the *Tatler*, and its successor the *Spectator* which he founded with Steele in 1711. The latter (originally a daily and not to be confused with the 'radical' weekly of the same name founded more than a century later) was a runaway success. It sold about 4000 copies a day, half as much again as the total circulation of all other papers. This was an extraordinary achievement. Printing techniques were still primitive and distribution by stagecoach slow, but success was assured by its entertainment value. The historian Thomas Babington Macaulay (1800–59) said that Addison 'effected a great social reform'. He also proved that the press had another function apart from publishing political and commercial news. Popular journalism – admittedly of a superior kind – was created before the arrival of the 'serious' press.

Various functions of modern journalism were beginning to emerge, and one can only speculate on what would have happened if development had continued unimpeded. It might well have paralleled the great expansion of the American press after the War of Independence (1775–81), but the government took fright and in 1712 imposed the first stamp tax on newspapers. Swift lamented that 'Grub Street is dead and gone.' Grub Street, described by a later journalist, Dr Johnson (1709–84), as 'much inhabited by writers of small histories, dictionaries, and temporary poems; whence any mean production is called *grubstreet*', was not destined to flourish and prosper. On the other hand, Swift was precipitate in his judgment.

The late Lord Francis-Williams wrote in his book *Dangerous Estate: The Anatomy of Newspapers* that British newspaper history of the next 150 years reflected the ruling class's fears of an expanding newspaper-reading public. The purpose of the stamp tax, which was not abolished until 1855, was to keep the press on a leash; to tame it if it could not be suppressed; and if all else failed to ensure that the price of newspapers should at least confine their circulation to the 'responsible' middle and upper classes. The tax killed some papers, including the *Spectator*, and while total sales continued to rise the rate of growth was greatly reduced. The tax had at least one unforeseen consequence; it fuelled the revolutionary fervour in the American colonies where newspapers were also taxed. Another consequence was that even successful newspapers could not make a profit, and had to accept bribes to survive. Much of the British press was corrupted by government and party subsidies until the commercial success of a London paper, *The Times*, enabled Thomas Barnes (its editor from 1817 to 1841) to assert its editorial independence. The stamp tax also stifled the radical press and was later to inhibit the growth of

[8]

newspapers connected with the Chartist and nascent trade-union movement.

The stamp tax was not the only obstacle dropped in front of the press; the politicians' passion for secrecy was such that the reporting of Parliament was declared to be a breach of privilege. The struggle which followed was bizarre. Doorkeepers at Westminster were bribed to admit reporters chosen for their retentive memories, who without the help of notes memorized the main points of the debates. When the screw was turned further the *Gentleman's Magazine* employed Dr Johnson in the late 1730s to rewrite its reporter's efforts in the form of debates in the senate of a fictitious country, Lilliputia. The decisive battle was fought by John Wilkes (1727–97), the agitator and reformer. It is hard to imagine a more unlikely hero. Wilkes, a profligate, belonged to a secret fraternity infamous for obscene orgies. He fought and lost the 1754 election in the Berwick-upon-Tweed constituency (despite bribing a sea captain to land a shipload of opposition voters in Norway) but was subsequently elected Member of Parliament for Aylesbury in Buckinghamshire. In 1762 he founded the political weekly the *North Briton*, and after attacking the King's Speech was arrested on a general warrant and dispatched to the Tower of London. The Lord Chief Justice ordered his release on the grounds that the arrest was a breach of parliamentary privilege, and general warrants – which did not name the person or persons to be arrested – were declared illegal.

Wilkes was then expelled from Parliament for printing obscene literature, and was declared an outlaw for failing to stand trial. On his return from the Continent, where he had spent four years pursuing 'amorous delights', he was elected and expelled four times, and again imprisoned. All this and his radical political programme made him a popular hero, especially among small trades-men and the growing number of skilled and literate workmen. The main planks of his radical programme, including electoral reform by way of suppression of 'rotten boroughs' and the extension of the franchise to the 'lower orders', were not enacted until after his death; but he won a famous victory against censorship when as an alderman of the City of London he defied the ban on parliamentary reporting in his *Middlesex Journal*. The freedom of the press was increased, and government and Parliament made more accountable. They continued, and still continue today, to avoid the scrutiny of the press whenever possible, but they could no longer hope to ignore the press and the people.

Wilkes was also the London representative of Boston's 'Sons of Liberty', and a champion of the colonial cause during the American Revolution. One wonders what the straight-laced New Englanders thought of his libertine behaviour, but he had his admirers among those who fought for the freedom of the American press.

The first printing press to be imported into the American colonies arrived in Cambridge, Massachusetts Bay Colony, in 1638. Two more were shipped to Boston and Philadelphia within a few years, and the first American newspaper appeared in 1690. The publisher of *Publick Occurences Both Foreign and Domestick*, Benjamin Harris, was an unpleasant character. In England he had edited a sheet publicizing rumours (started by the rascally Titus Oates) of a fictitious Popish Plot, which led to judicial persecution of Roman Catholics. Afterwards he was sentenced to the pillory and imprisonment for printing seditious pamphlets. He emigrated to Boston after his release, and earned a footnote in history by publishing the first newspaper in the New World. Not for the last time was the cause of journalism to be advanced by a scoundrel. *Publick Occurences* was to have been a three-page monthly – the fourth page was left blank, presumably for private correspondence – but was suppressed after the first issue. Whether or not the colonial governor was aware of Harris's activities in England, he and others in authority, like their political masters in London, regarded newspapers as dangerous. Fourteen years were to pass before the appearance of the next newspaper, the *Boston News-Letter*. This survived because it supported the Tories, and others quickly followed.

It was an inglorious beginning, but the honour of American journalism was saved by the runaway apprentice, Benjamin Franklin (1706–90). He fled from Boston to Philadelphia in the early 1720s, and after a few years of jobbing printing bought the *Universal Instructor in all Arts and Sciences: and the Pennsylvania Gazette*. The front page of this eccentric paper was devoted to the serialization of *Chambers's Cyclopaedia*. It had begun with 'A', and Franklin reckoned that it would take about 50 years to reach 'Z'. No doubt appalled by the prospect, Franklin dropped the cyclopaedic serial, 'spiked' another written by Defoe and reduced the masthead to the *Pennsylvania Gazette* (1729). It quickly became the liveliest newspaper in the colonies, and the best-written because Franklin wrote most of it. The *Gazette* was so successful that the usual four-page issues had to be increased to six and occasionally eight pages to accommodate the advertising. Franklin could have become history's first press baron, but after 18 years as publisher (1730–48) he sold the paper to an English immigrant and devoted his remaining years to public affairs, diplomacy and science.

Most of the early American newspapers were run by postmasters who had access to foreign newspapers and distributed their own, free, through the mails. Standards were not high. They were generally four-page weeklies, and the average circulation was about 500. This was sufficient to attract advertising because copies were read more than once, being passed from hand to hand. Among the advertisements for patent medicines and ship sailings were notices offering rewards for runaway slaves, apprentices and bonded servants.

A great deal of the news was pirated from the London papers. They took between four and eight weeks to cross the Atlantic, and the transmission of news from one colony to another could be even slower. Post riders took one week to cover the distance between Boston and New York, and two in winter.

The physical isolation of those then small towns partly explains why little colonial news was published but, more significantly, the colonists were more interested in Britain than in each other. The colonies were still British possessions, and London was the seat of power. Parliamentary and other political news frequently led the early American papers, although the French and Indian wars were the best running story in the 1750s. Editorial comment was rare until the Stamp Act kindled the flames of revolution.

The War of Independence was also the battlefield for press freedom, and the first shot in the early skirmishes was fired in 1734 when John Zenger of the *New York Weekly Journal* was tried for criminal libel. He had exposed in the paper the personal extravagances of the colonial governor and the inefficiency of his administration. His lawyer, Andrew Hamilton, saw wider implications and told the jury that their duty was to serve the cause of liberty:

> Your upright conduct this day will not only entitle you to the love and esteem of your fellow citizens, but every man who prefers freedom to a life of slavery will bless and honour you as men who have baffled the attempt of tyranny and by an impartial and uncorrupt verdict have laid a noble foundation for securing to ourselves, our posterity and our neighbours, that to which nature and the laws of our country have given us a right – the liberty of exposing and opposing arbitrary power, in these parts of the world at least, by speaking and writing – truth.

The jury found Zenger not guilty after that inspiring if breathless plea, and the verdict encouraged other newspapers to take up the struggle.

The *Boston Gazette* led the campaign against the Stamp Act, and a grand jury rejected an indictment against it for libel. The colony's House of Representatives then declared that: 'the Liberty of the Press is a great Bulwark of the Liberty of the People. It is therefore the incumbent Duty of those who are constituted the Guardians of the People's Rights to defend and maintain it'. This was probably the first guarantee of press freedom. The Revolutionary statesman George Mason incorporated another in the Virginia Constitution of 1776, and it was enshrined in the First Amendment to the US Constitution in 1791 – not that the amendment was always respected in the early years.

Massachusetts, which had been most vocal in the struggle for independence, tried to continue the stamp tax. State printing contracts were denied to publishers of opposition papers by sanctimonious Bostonians who only a few years earlier had declared that their duty was to defend and maintain a free press. Elsewhere printers and editors were fined or imprisoned under the Alien and Sedition Acts. They were pardoned by Thomas Jefferson when he became President (1801–09), but even that paragon and advocate of press freedom was not prepared to take the press into his confidence when negotiating the Louisiana Purchase of 1803. The reason on this occasion was obvious, the success of the deal with the French government depending upon complete secrecy. With the passing years the freedom of the press became inviolate. Genuine conflicts of interest such as this became less of a problem than in Britain and elsewhere because of the constitutional guarantee.

There were other reasons. Independence meant more than severing ties with the mother country. Freedom and independence became articles of faith. The white American of the post-Revolutionary generation knew that he was as good as the next man, if not better. No less important, the open frontier offered an escape if society became too constraining. All anyone had to do was to join one of the wagon trains which crossed the mountains and floated on rafts down the Ohio River. In 1787, the year of the Constitutional Convention, 900 flatboats were seen floating westwards. An official report estimated the number of migrants at 18,000 men, women and children (equal to the population of Boston at the time). There was no way of imposing a governing elite despite the Federalists who believed that the United States should become a kind of republican Britain. And wherever the wagon trains went, printers followed.

In the early decades of the nineteenth century the number of newspapers increased from about 200 to more than 1000. Most of them were weeklies, although the first daily, the *Pennsylvania Evening Post,* appeared in 1783. It was a miserable half-sheet, or two pages, and was written, printed and hawked on the streets by the owner, Benjamin Towne, who was a genuine pioneer but once again not a man to be included in a pantheon of great journalists. He had toadied to the British when they reoccupied Philadelphia during the Revolutionary war, and was indicted for treason a year after he had launched the *Post.* If Towne was not to be admired, his contemporaries have been forgotten. Perhaps because of the explosion of titles (many more in the US than in Britain), editorial standards were lower than across the Atlantic. The *Belfast News-Letter,* which was first published in 1737, remains a mine of information for historians of the period. Much of the information available about the emigration of the Scots-Irish, as Ulstermen are known in the United States, came from its files. The *Glasgow Herald,* the oldest surviving national daily newspaper in the English language, was launched in the same year as Towne's *Post,* but its first issue is still a good read. It had the inestimable advantage of starting its long life with a great scoop, the official dispatch announcing the Versailles treaty which gave the United States its official independence, but it reflected the superiority of British journalism at the time.

Frank Mott, the author of *American Journalism: A History of Newspapers in the US from 1690 to 1940,* wrote that this was the dark age of political journalism. He was a bit unfair. The Constitution provided a framework for the young republic, but the direction in which it was to move was still bitterly contested. The press divided along party lines and hence suffered from a lack

[12]

of objectivity. That said, the new publishers and editors could be as swash-buckling as any frontiersman. They were often scurrilous and frequently corrupt. No doubt there were extenuating circumstances, but it was remarkable that in a country which had produced great political philosophers, men such as Jefferson who wrote the Declaration of Independence and the founding fathers who drafted the world's greatest written Constitution, not a single publisher or editor had emerged with enough vision to see the proper place of the press in a democratic and rapidly changing society. The same was more or less true in Britain, where the Industrial Revolution was well under way, and the struggle for parliamentary reform had begun.

There were intelligent journalists in both countries, but their horizons were limited not only by their collective past but by technical and economic factors. William Caxton, who set up the first press in England in 1477, would still have recognized the presses they used, and circulations were small. Even if literacy had been more widespread it would have been difficult to cope with increased demand. News-gathering techniques were primitive, the telegraph had not been invented and distribution outside the main cities was too slow for such a 'perishable' product as newspapers. Many years would pass before inventions would come to the rescue, but the dark age began to recede in Britain when Thomas Barnes was appointed editor of the London *Times* in 1817, and in the United States when James Gordon Bennett I launched the *New York Herald* in 1835.

There could not have been two men or newspapers more different. Both were great journalists who reported as well as edited. Both wanted to get to the truth, but Barnes worshipped anonymity and even the paper's short notice announcing his death did not mention that he was the editor. Bennett, on the other hand, was a megalomaniac. Barnes's prime concern was to reflect and create public opinion; or to be more precise, the opinion of the emerging middle classes and in so doing influence government proceedings. Bennett, a Scottish immigrant, created a newspaper primarily interested in crime and scandal. But both recognized that they could only succeed by first asserting editorial independence. Between them they created modern journalism, and they became the world's first press barons.

A pause for definition. The press barons, or press lords as they were generally known in Britain, where most of them were elevated to the House of Lords, were the men who controlled the chief means of mass communication for more than a century. To own a newspaper was not sufficient to win the accolade. The press barons were involved in shaping and producing their papers, and their ranks included editors as well as proprietors. Lord Northcliffe was a press baron, but not the 1st Lord Thomson who owned more newspapers but boasted that he only read the balance sheets. Arthur Hays Sulzberger of the *New York Times* is a baron, but not Samuel Newhouse whose chain of newspapers was run only for profit. Press barons are now an endangered species, but not only because of advances in media technology. Television has yet to prove that it can replace the Gutenberg press, and is unlikely to do so in the foreseeable future.

The barons created and developed modern newspapers, and I can think of few other fields of human endeavour where individuals played such important and decisive roles. They made up the rules as they went along. They marched in step with events, and frequently led the way. The earlier generations thrived in an age of unprecedented economic expansion and great political and social change. Indeed, change would have been slower and probably more costly without them. Many of these barons made vast fortunes, but few were in it only for the money. With one or two exceptions, they loved their creations and with a passion denied to leaders of other industries. There is one good reason for this: the newspaper industry is like no other. Automobile companies are larger and more complex organizations, but their only function is to stamp out identical cars year after year until a new model is designed and introduced. Newspaper companies produce a new model every night. Decisions are made at speeds which would horrify manufacturers of other products. An editor may have only a few minutes to decide which story will lead the front page; I can remember some well-argued and constructed editorials in the London *Times* which were written in about half an hour. The average issue of *The Times* contains some 150,000 editorial words (about half the length of Tolstoy's *War and Peace*) and before the introduction of photo-composition most of them were written between the hours of 4 p.m. and 8 p.m. The Sunday edition of the *New York Times* contains many more, but has more time to prepare them.

The reason for this frenetic activity is that newspapers have no control over their basic raw material, news. Norman Mailer, the writer and journalist, once said that writing for newspapers is like running a revolutionary war. You go into battle not when you are ready but when the action presents itself. A romantic view, but journalism is a romantic calling, not least because much of the news is unpredictable. The best-organized newspapers can be caught unawares, and they do not survive if it happens too often. This can create enormous tensions, especially in Britain where newspapers are a highly competitive industry. This calls for a special breed of men and women who would not be happy in predictable 'nine-to-five' jobs. In the old days, some publishers were in touch with their offices day and night; many editors spent 12 hours or more a day at their desks. John Delane, who succeeded Barnes as editor of the London *Times*, rarely left the office before dawn.

Newspaper publishers flourished in many parts of the world, but the barons were largely a phenomenon of the English-speaking world. This was because editorial independence was first established in Britain and the United States, and freedom has deeper roots in the English-speaking countries, including the

[14]

old British Commonwealth. Newspapers helped to extend that freedom because a free press and democracy are indivisible. One cannot survive without the other, and the press barons played a vital role in the development of both.

Not that they were thanked for their services. Newspapermen have rarely been liked because of the nature of their vocation. They believe in the public's right to know, and, despite obeisances to the theory of a free press, authority still thinks otherwise because the free dissemination of information weakens its control over events. It comes in many guises, benign, elitist, ideological and just plain stupid. It resides in Downing Street and the White House, the Foreign Office and the State Department, in board rooms and trade-union offices – wherever decisions are made. The craving for secrecy is especially strong in Britain, which still clings to its Official Secrets Act. The hard left of the Labour party demands public accountability but hates the press more than any Tory backwoodsman. The United States has its constitutional guarantee of press freedom and the Freedom of Information Act, but news management is a fine art in Washington.

The old press barons were not above criticism, to put it mildly. Their behaviour was often outrageous, but of course they lived in a robust age, and other pioneers – industrialists and empire-builders, for instance – were no better. Many had political axes to grind, objectivity was not a common virtue, and their claim to serve the public interest could be spurious. A few were megalomaniacs who believed that they and not elected politicians best represented the people. They believed that they could dictate events and make and unmake governments. The belief was largely false, and one object of this book is to establish that they did not wield such power.

This is not to suggest that they were without influence. That they controlled the flow of news and (to quote the notable eighteenth-century American lawyer Andrew Hamilton) 'exposed and opposed arbitrary power' made them a force to be reckoned with, but they had little success when they tried to impose their own arbitrary will. The news they published could help to make or unmake governments, but the personal view of the press baron could not. For instance, President Lyndon Johnson decided against running for re-election in 1968 because the press accurately reported the horrors of the Vietnam war and mounting opposition at home. The reporting of the Watergate scandal by two young reporters of the *Washington Post* led to the resignation of President Richard Nixon. The news was the decisive factor, not the opinions expressed in editorials. If the press has any power it is as a conduit of news, and not as the voice of those who run it.

Obviously it is not as clear-cut as that. The selection of news, a prerogative of press barons, can distort – but not for long. The multiplicity of news sources, including news agencies, rival newspapers and now television and radio, prevents gross distortion. Reporting can be distorted by the personal attitudes of journalists (even if they claim to be proud of their objectivity), or if their relationship with politicians and makers of news becomes too close. All well-trained journalists are aware of the pitfalls, but the pressure to conform can become irresistible when, as during the Kennedy Administration, independent or troublesome reporters were put in the doghouse – that is, denied access to information.

Then there is the larger problem. As I have written elsewhere, journalists are supposed to be concerned with truth, but what is truth? Keats said it was beauty, and that was all you needed to know, but that was not much help when I was a young foreign correspondent. I quickly discovered that facts, let alone truth, could be elusive. I could not always witness the events I was expected to report, and eye-witnesses more often than not were unreliable. There were no press boxes at 'summit conferences' or in Cabinet rooms, and official spokesmen had axes to grind or interests to defend. Wars were easier to report than politics. I just had to walk or ride towards the sound of gunfire, but what I reported was often only one tiny segment of what was happening. Unless there was a major advance or retreat, I still had to depend largely upon official versions of what had happened and in war truth is said to be the first casualty. I gradually learned that the best I could hope to achieve was to write an honest if incomplete report, one man's version of events, and leave the rest to further investigation or history.

In the early years of the press barons, news-gathering techniques were not as developed as they are today, and resources were limited. There were no foreign correspondents before the London *Times* sent its first men abroad in the early nineteenth century, and news was pirated from foreign newspapers. Bennett of the *New York Herald* kept a fast cutter which sailed out to meet ships from Europe to collect the newspapers before his competitors. There were no news agencies to provide impartial reports against which the contents of newspapers could be checked. Competition provided some kind of balance in the big cities, but not in smaller towns. Only the press barons could evolve and impose ethical standards; only they were in a position to understand the true functions of the press, and nobody said it better than the London *Times* in 1852. After being rebuked for in effect waging a guerrilla war against authority, it said:

> The first duty of the press is to obtain the earliest and most correct
> intelligence of the events of the time, and instantly, by disclosing them, to
> make them the common property of the nation. The statesman collects his
> information secretly and by secret means, he keeps back even the common
> intelligence of the day with ludicrous precautions until diplomacy is beaten in
> the race with publicity. The press lives by disclosures: whatever passes into
> its keeping becomes a part of the knowledge and history of our times; it is

[16]

daily and for ever appealing to the enlightened force of public opinion – anticipating, if possible, the march of events – standing upon the breach between the present and the future, and extending its survey to the horizon of the world . . . The duty of the journalist is the same as that of the historian – to seek out the truth, above all things, and to present to his readers not such things as statecraft would wish them to know but the truth as near as he can attain it.

A little more prosaically C.P. Scott of the *Manchester Guardian* said that there were two sides to a newspaper. It was a business like any other, but it was much more than a business: 'It has a moral as well as a material existence and its character and influence are determined by the balance of these forces.' Adolph Ochs of the *New York Times* saw his first duty: 'to give the news impartially, without fear or favor, regardless of any party, sect, or interest involved', and the paper still proudly carries the slogan 'All the News That's Fit to Print'. Ebenezer Syme of the *Melbourne Age*, who was threatened by physical violence and advertising boycotts, said: 'We shall go on as we have begun, calling a spade a spade.'

Not all of the press barons shared these high ideals or displayed such courage. The antics of William Randolph Hearst earned the press a bad name. Lord Rothermere was primarily interested in making money and defending it against enemies conjured up by a fevered imagination. Lord Northcliffe went mad, and Colonel Robert McCormick drew up plans to repel a British invasion from Canada, the threat of which existed only in his mind. Nevertheless, most of them were imbued with the spirit of independence, and took the news to the people. Arguably, for all their foibles and prejudices, some of them better served the cause of a free press than did two of the world's greatest newspapers more recently. Geoffrey Dawson of the London *Times* ignored the principles established by his own newspaper when, in the 1930s, he censored the dispatches of his correspondents in Germany because they disclosed facts which could have turned public opinion against the appeasement policy he and the British government espoused. Similarly in 1961 Orvil Dryfoos of the *New York Times* censored reports that President John Kennedy was preparing, clandestinely and unconstitutionally, to invade Cuba. Both men believed that they were acting responsibly, but history might have been different if they had been honest with their readers instead of providing 'such things as statecraft would wish them to know'.

I prefer the attitude of Wilbur Storey of the *Chicago Times* who said 'print the news and raise hell.' Alas, he also said 'when there is no news, send rumours'. It is impossible to defend all the press barons, but, good and bad, they all helped to write the history of journalism and to extend the freedom of the press.

BARNES AND DELANE

Thomas Barnes (1785–1841), according to Leigh Hunt, might have made a name for himself in literature had he cared much for anything beyond his glass of wine and his Fielding. The English essayist and poet must have regretted that remark after his friend became the editor of *The Times* and history's first press lord; but Barnes was very much a Henry Fielding character in his youth, a 'Tom Jones' rather than a 'Joseph Andrews'. He wined and wenched with robust enthusiasm, and even when he became editor drank large measures of gin at his desk. He lived with another man's wife, who was said by Disraeli to be like a pantomime dame, but Barnes was devoted to her. Oliver Woods and James Bishop said in their *The Story of The Times* that he was a man of both eighteenth and nineteenth centuries. His education and background inclined him to the manners of the eighteenth century and the Age of Enlightenment. His creative vision and instincts were deployed ahead of their time to conjure up a world which men could not know by experience but could only descry through the exercise of their imagination – a world of steam, of machines, of vast migrations of peoples, of democracies and empires. He was thus well-equipped to report and comment upon the transformation of the known world.

Barnes was educated at the Blue Coat school, Christ's Hospital, as a charity boy, where the future *literati* Leigh Hunt and Charles Lamb were contemporaries, and at Pembroke College, Cambridge. But he gave up reading law to join Hunt's circle, to which Keats and Shelley belonged – which was itself a manifestation of the changing times. Hunt, the son of an American Loyalist who returned to Britain after the Revolution, was once imprisoned for describing the Prince Regent (later George IV) as 'a fat Adonis of fifty'. He attracted politicians as well as writers and artists, and Barnes must have found their company enjoyable and useful. He became a drama critic and political reporter for *The Times*, and was appointed editor in 1817 when he was 32.

The Times was founded in 1785, the year of Barnes's birth, by John Walter (1739–1812), a former coal merchant and Lloyd's underwriter bankrupted by American privateers who sank or seized many of the ships he had ensured. Looking about for a new venture to pay off his creditors, he chose a new printing process known as logography. Printing had hardly changed since it was invented by Gutenberg more than 300 years earlier, and logography promised a great leap forward. Complete words and syllables instead of single letters were cast in one piece of type. The process was invented to print lottery tickets, but Walter believed that it could be used for general printing. Despite encouragement by Benjamin Franklin (at this time the American Minister in

Paris) whose inventive mind was attracted to logography, Walter eventually abandoned the process. He then had to decide what to do with his printing press, and like so many printers before him chose to launch a newspaper. The first issue of *The Times* (under the name of the *Daily Universal Register* for the first three years) appeared on 1 January 1785. It was the conventional sheet folded once to make four pages and was indistinguishable from London's other eight morning papers.

Because of the competition and the stamp tax Walter had to take bribes to make a living and received a government subvention of £300 a year. He was also awarded a printing contract, and in return gave general support to the government and published paragraphs written by officials. Two were critical of the Prince of Wales (not yet Prince Regent) and his brother the Duke of York, and Walter was sued for libel and sentenced to an hour in the pillory and two years in Newgate. The pillory was remitted but Walter spent 16 months in prison. A member of his editorial staff, William Coombe, was also imprisoned for debt but continued to work for *The Times* until the tipstaffs caught up with him. It was a seedy beginning, and by 1803 the paper was in a bad way with circulation down to about 2000 when his second son, John Walter II, took over. However, he could not have chosen a better time to take charge. War is hell but it sells newspapers, and Napoleon was on the march.

John Walter II (1776–1846) was probably not the first British publisher to recognize that the press could not be free unless it was economically independent, but he was the first to do something about it. The unprecedented social and political change brought about by the Industrial Revolution demanded objective and comprehensive reporting. He was determined to be independent of bribes and government subsidies. In retrospect it seems that Walter had a predetermined plan; that was unlikely, but the steps taken had a logical progression. He developed his own news service, especially abroad, where his father had made a start in breaking the Post Office monopoly of foreign news. The French Revolution had been reported in *The Times* under an eight-decker headline, and some notable scoops were scored. When Napoleon blockaded the Channel, smugglers had been employed to bring back the dispatches.

The younger Walter appointed the paper's first staff foreign correspondent, Henry Crabb Robinson, who covered the fall of Danzig and the Treaties of Tilsit (1807) and the retreat of the British forces from Corunna two years later. The foundation was laid of the finest foreign news service in the world for at least a hundred years. This was afterwards recognized by Lord Castlereagh, the Foreign Secretary, who was obliged to consult it for the latest news: 'Will Mr Walter have the goodness to tell him if he has received any intelligence of the reported defeat of the French near Dresden?'

The circulation steadily increased, but the old hand presses could still only print 250 sheets an hour and even in those days printers were resistant to change. Walter experimented until he heard that a German, Friedrich Koenig, had invented a steam press and had failed to interest his own countrymen. In 1814 the press was smuggled piece by piece into Printing House Square and secretly assembled in an empty room to avoid Luddite interference. On the night of 28 November the printers were asked to stand by for a late foreign story while the edition was run off in the new press room. He then announced to his astonished employees that 'The Times is already printed – by steam'. The first Koenig press printed 1100 sheets an hour, and with the help of two English inventors, Augustus Applegath and E.A. Cowper, the run was raised to 4000 an hour within a few years. The age of mass circulation newspapers was dawning.

Walter employed university graduates instead of Grub Street hacks to improve the editorial content of the paper, and The Times began to earn its reputation as the newspaper written by gentlemen for gentlemen. Walter was also determined to make journalism an honourable and well-paid calling, and his writers were treated as colleagues. They ate together, and according to the official History of The Times, the venison and beef served in the 'Private House' (Walter's handsome town residence attached to the office) were exceptional and the quality of the turbot still more praiseworthy. Not all the university men were suitable, but some good writers were attracted. William Hazlitt worked as the drama critic after Walter decided to publish critical reviews – another first – instead of paid-for complimentary puffs. The essayist wrote: 'I would advise any one who has an ambition to write, and to write at his best, in the periodical press, to get if possible a situation in The Times newspaper, the editor of which is a man of business, and not of letters.'

Hazlitt was right. Walter was a printer, a born executive and not a journalist. There was no editor in the modern sense although Crabb Robinson became a kind of chief sub-editor after his adventures abroad. He said that Walter hovered in the background as he and another writer put the paper together on the dining-room table. This gentlemanly amateurism became ludicrous as the paper developed and Walter, tired of 'living over the shop', built a country house for himself in Berkshire. Having created the first British newspaper to free itself of bribes and government subsidies, he needed a strong personality to take over from him as by now he wanted to run for Parliament. And so it was that in 1817 Thomas Barnes was appointed editor, and given editorial independence. Barnes created 'The Thunderer', and under his direction it became one of the very few newspapers ever to change the course of history.

Barnes was not Walter's first choice as editor because he was regarded as a political radical. Only after his offer of the job was turned down by the poet, Robert Southey, did Walter overcome his reservations. Barnes, however, was not a radical despite the company he kept. He was a constitutionalist, a reformer rather than a revolutionary, and a practical idealist. He was humane and enlightened, and battled doggedly for political reform. He also consistently supported the underdogs of his age – the Catholics, the Dissenters (Non-Conformists) and the new industrial working class. Unlike his fiery contemporary William Cobbett (1763–1835), the political journalist and essayist, Barnes had no political ambition. He avoided the delights of London society whenever he could, and insisted upon anonymity – a tradition observed by his successors for 150 years. But despite the absence of bylines, Barnes demanded forcible writing with 'a little of the devil in it'. *The History of The Times* records him as saying that:

> Newspaper writing is a thing *sui generis*; it is in literature what brandy is in beverages. John Bull, whose understanding is rather sluggish – I speak of the majority of readers – requires a strong stimulus. He consumes his beef and cannot digest it without a dram; he dozes composedly over his prejudices which his conceit calls opinions; and you must fire ten-pounders at his densely compacted intellect before you can make it comprehend your meaning or care one farthing for your effects.

Barnes had a similarly low opinion of some of the aristocratic politicians, and, devoid of any ambition except to produce a good newspaper, reported and commented on their activities with objectivity and great gusto. He was sceptical of their ability to understand what was happening beyond Parliament, un-reformed and un-representative, and their grand town and country houses. Napoleon had been defeated, and it was a period when to Elie Halévy (1870–1937), the French historian: 'It seemed as if English politics would henceforth conform to the Continental pattern, and that for the future there would exist in England, instead of the historic parties, only these two – the party of the revolution and the party of the counter-revolution.'

The danger was greatest in the north where the postwar industrial slump had coincided with rising food prices due to the 1815 Corn Law. *The Times* reported that the people were half-starved. The Lancashire cotton spinners and weavers went on strike, mass demonstrations were held in many towns and a man was shot dead when thousands attacked a Manchester mill. These were not only food riots but part of the growing campaign for parliamentary reform, and the government became increasingly worried when plans were announced to hold a mass demonstration in Manchester. Lord Sidmouth, the Home Secretary, instructed the Lord-Lieutenant to take all measures necessary for the preservation of law and order. Barnes sent John Tyas to cover the story, a young reporter described as 'a gentleman of talent and education'. As Woods and Bishop noted in their *The Story of The Times*, Barnes was the only editor of a national newspaper who had the perspicacity, the news sense, and in all probability the resources to do so. In 1819 it took four days to get a message back and forth between London and Manchester. His decision proved more than justified. The Peterloo Massacre that year was a turning-point for *The Times*, as it was for the country.

A public meeting was held in St Peter's Fields, an open space in the middle of the city of Manchester, and whoever coined the name Peterloo had a dramatic sense of history. The original intention of the organizers was to advocate parliamentary reform and elect a 'shadow' Member of Parliament for the unrepresented people of Manchester. The magistrates held this to be subversive, and the organizers, anxious to avoid trouble, dropped the election. Nevertheless, the magistrates called for military assistance, and a brigade of horse, foot and guns was drawn up in the side streets, a large component of which consisted of relatively-untrained yeomanry cavalry.

Tyas reported that the demonstrators carried banners bearing such inscriptions as 'Annual Parliaments, and Universal Suffrage' and 'No Corn Law'. A group of women carried red flags, one inscribed 'Let us die like men, and not be sold like slaves'. His report continues:

> The Reformers who had up to this time arrived in the field demeaned themselves becomingly, though a posse of 300 or 400 constables, with the Boroughreeve at their head, had marched in a body into the field about 12 o'clock, unsupported by any military body to all outward appearance. Not the slightest insult was offered to them . . . the people . . . crying 'Let us keep peace and order'.

Tyas stood on the platform with the main speakers, and had a clear view of what took place. He estimated that about 80,000 people had gathered when the yeomanry trotted into the field to arrest Henry Hunt, the main speaker. Hunt said that he would willingly surrender to any civil officer with a warrant, at which point Tyas reported:

> . . . a cry was made by the cavalry. 'Have at their flags.' In consequence, they immediately dashed not only at the flags which were in the wagon, but those which were posted among the crowd, cutting most indiscriminately to the right and to the left in order to get at them. This set the people running in all directions, and it was not until this act had been committed that any brickbats were hurled at the military. From that moment the Manchester Yeomanry cavalry lost all command of temper . . . a man within five yards of us in another direction had his nose completely taken off by a blow of a sabre.

The cavalry took about ten minutes to clear the field, leaving behind about a dozen dead and 420 wounded.

Tyas was arrested and spent the night in prison where he completed his report. It was late in arriving in London, but in the next issue of *The Times* seven out of the twelve editorial columns were devoted to Peterloo. This feature included an editorial, reports from other papers and Tyas's story which was headed: 'Express from Manchester. Just as our paper was going to press, we received from the gentleman deputed by us to report the proceedings at Manchester, the following account . . .'

The Times's coverage was a sensation. Thundering on, the editorial hammered home: 'the dreadful fact, that nearly a hundred of the King's unarmed subjects have been sabred by a body of cavalry in the streets of a town of which most of them were inhabitants, and in the presence of those Magistrates whose sworn duty it is to protect and preserve the life of the meanest Englishman.' Tyas had greater effect because his report was comprehensive, objective and calm. Of his arrest, for instance, he wrote: 'It is only justice to the man who apprehended us to state that he did everything in his power to protect us from ill-usage, and showed us every civility consistent with his duty.' The use of the editorial 'we' to the very end must have been particularly effective. It was not just an individual but *The Times* itself speaking. A storm of protest was raised, public meetings were held and subscription lists opened for the victims. The cause of parliamentary reform became a national issue overnight, and Barnes a power to be reckoned with. A few days later he was invited to the Home Office where most members of the Cabinet had gathered. Little was said, but it was clear that Barnes was warned to mind his step. He was not deterred, and continued to campaign for reform until the great Reform Bill was finally enacted in 1832.

Britain avoided revolution for a number of reasons, not least emigration to the United States, Canada, Australia and New Zealand. Emigration began as early as the 1590s. About 250,000 people left in the seventeenth century, and more than 1,500,000 in the eighteenth. Between the First Reform Bill and the First World War more than 16 million departed. Most of them were attracted by the prospect of free land or opportunity denied to them at home. In the early years, according to the American historian, Carl Bridenbaugh, many were vexed and troubled Englishmen who did not like or understand the changes which were transforming England.

Emigration was a fortunate safety valve, and the Reform Bill set the country on a new course despite the continued agitation for universal suffrage by the Chartists. They were the ideological descendants of the seventeenth-century republican and democratic groups known as the Levellers and the Diggers. The latter were early agrarian communists, but the programme of the former, preserved in pamphlets written by John Lilburne (*c.* 1614–67) and others, could have been a preliminary draft of the US Constitution. The Chartists had a militant wing which tried to capture Newport, Monmouthshire; they were routed and the leaders were transported to Australia. Others fled to the United States, among them William Carnegie whose son, Andrew, became the great ironmaster and philanthropist. Chartism disappeared after the repeal of the

Corn Laws in 1846 and the introduction of Lord Shaftesbury's factory reforms, but the great stabilizing factor was the new middle classes – and *The Times*, as (to quote Woods and Bishop again) the aristocrats who still largely dominated Parliament now also had to take account of the marshalling of middle-class opinion by Barnes and *The Times*. This powerful but largely unorganized group of people from the emergent classes was, broadly speaking, in favour of reform and opposed to violence. Sir Robert Peel, then in his second term as Prime Minister, summed up the paper's record in these words: 'The great, principal, and powerful advocate of Reform – *The Times* newspaper.' The paper had become 'The Thunderer'.

The nickname 'The Thunderer' was earned by an editorial which urged the country to 'thunder for reform', and it stuck when Barnes successfully campaigned for other causes. One or two were surprising. For instance, along with the London mob and the radicals he supported the sluttish Queen Caroline, Consort of George IV. Her trial for adultery, which Barnes covered himself, was sensational and doubled the circulation of the paper to 15,000. Actually Barnes had no sympathy for the royal sinner, but was determined to embarrass George IV – partly because of the King's opposition to Catholic Emancipation. This was of immense importance to Ireland, and the then Prime Minister, the Irish-born Duke of Wellington, was prepared to abolish the penal laws against Catholics. The support of *The Times* was essential because of opposition within the Tory party, and the Iron Duke made a deal with Barnes. Information was made available on an off-the-record basis which produced a number of scoops, and the Emancipation Bill was enacted in 1829.

This did not mean that the government, Tory or Whig, could buy *The Times* with information. Barnes would only campaign for reforms or programmes he believed in, and as a consequence shifted his support from one party to another. He was never the creature of any party, and in 1834 the Whigs were furious when he attacked their new Poor Law Bill, which he condemned as degrading to honest paupers and families seeking temporary relief. They swore revenge, and after the ploy of subsidizing a rival newspaper had failed materially to affect *The Times*'s circulation, they took the drastic step in 1836 of reducing the stamp tax from fourpence to one penny. The theory was that papers with inferior resources would compete against *The Times* and reduce its influence if the cover prices were drastically reduced. It also looked like a liberal measure; after all the tax had been imposed in the first place to stifle the press. This move also failed and meanwhile *The Times* had grown relatively fat during Barnes's editorship, with regular advertisement supplements. The Post Office still distributed stamped newspapers free – more to the disadvantage of *The Times*'s thinner competitors. Barnes then reduced its price from seven-pence to fivepence, and circulation rose dramatically.

Barnes's authority also increased, and not only because of climbing sales.

Faithful to the Walter tradition, the news service and printing techniques were constantly being improved. Reporters on assignment outside London were provided with fast coaches, and were expected to write their stories as they were whirled towards the office at speeds of more than 12 miles an hour. Charles Dickens, who reported for the *Morning Chronicle*, remembered racing *The Times* post-chaise from Exeter, and having to bribe the post-boys to keep up. Dispatches from Paris were delivered within 22 hours, and an overland route was developed with the Waghorn agency to hasten messages from the Far East. As the Suez Canal was not completed until 1875, before then ships arrived at Suez and the messages were sent overland to Cairo, forwarded by sea to Marseille and then galloped through France to the Channel ports. It was always quicker than the regular mail. The paper's official history recalls that in 1840 dispatches sent from China on 3 July, from Singapore on 13 August and Bombay on 1 October all reached *The Times* at three o'clock on the morning of 11 November and filled eight columns of that morning's issue.

This was the true power of *The Times*. It is worthwhile remembering that the 1840s saw the beginning of the second Empire established by Britain after the loss of the American colonies. Britain was the first foreign power to establish itself in Hong Kong and what came to be known as the Treaty Ports in China. Singapore, the greatest entrepôt port in Southeast Asia, had been established by Stamford Raffles, and in India the East India Company was creating the greatest imperial possession in history. Much depended upon the earliest arrival of news – political, diplomatic and above all commercial – from these far-flung possessions, and *The Times* scooped all competitors, including the government and the great trading companies. Arguably the development of the British Empire depended to some extent upon the news service of *The Times*. Certainly the reputation it established for omniscience depended as much upon the early dispatches from faraway places as upon Barnes's ability to treat with successive British governments on equal terms. There were no competitors, neither journalistic, commercial nor official; it was unchallenged until the telegraph and subsequent methods of rapid and cheap communication opened the field to all comers.

This extraordinary communications network, made possible by the commercial acumen of John Walter II and his business managers, was presided over by Barnes. And unlike some press barons who came after, he still remained essentially modest – no illusion of grandeur, no trace of megalomania. The power and the glory belonged to *The Times*, and not to its editor. Only once did he emerge from the editorial shadows, when in 1834 King William IV dismissed Lord Melbourne and his Whig government and called on Wellington and Peel to form a new Administration. It was the last time the royal prerogative was exercised and although the concept of a constitutional monarchy had yet to be fully established Wellington was aware of the dangers. The Tory majority in

Parliament was precarious, a general election in the near future was inevitable, and he knew that the party had to win the support of public opinion if it was to survive.

This meant *The Times*. Intermediaries approached Barnes, who set his terms: the adoption of Church and local government reforms, no weakening of the Reform Bill and no change in foreign policy. He was in fact demanding what amounted to a bi-partisan policy. John Walter, who was then Member of Parliament for Berkshire, knew that the Tory left wing was suspicious of Wellington and suggested that Peel, who was to become Prime Minister, should make a popular declaration with the aim of 'correcting wrong opinions and inculcating right ones'. The declaration amounted to a party manifesto, the first in British history, and Barnes edited it. Known as the Tamworth Manifesto, because Peel addressed it to the electorate of his Staffordshire constituency (which included Tamworth), it pledged in the words of Barnes that the Reform Bill was 'the final and irrevocable settlement of a great constitutional question'. There was to be no going back. Lord Lyndhurst, one of the intermediaries, said: 'Barnes is the most powerful man in the country'. A slight exaggeration, but he helped to set Britain on the path to full democracy.

It was to be Barnes's last great achievement. His health began to fail after years of grinding work and a lifetime of good living. On 6 May 1841, before undergoing an operation, he wrote a will leaving all his possessions 'unto my dear wife or reputed wife Dinah Mary Mondet', and died the following day. He was 55, and even in death anonymity was maintained. As already mentioned, there was no official obituary.

John Delane (1818–79) was only 23 when he succeeded Barnes in 1841, and his appointment smacked of nepotism. He had worked on the paper for only one year, but his father was business manager of *The Times* and a neighbour of Walter. Delane must have been surprised by the appointment because he burst into the office of his friend, the publisher William Blackwood, shouting, 'What do you think has happened? I am the editor of *The Times*.' But Walter knew his man, for Delane had grown up in the company of journalists and had been trained by Barnes. However, Walter returned temporarily to Printing House Square to supervise things but it was not long before he transferred complete control to the new editor. Delane was not only a born journalist, but he had also inherited Barnes's sources of information, and before the year was out he announced that Peel intended to repeal the Corn Laws. This was a major scoop of historical importance, and the Tory press dismissed it as fabrication. The reaction of the Members from the 'shires' was such that the government resigned, but Peel was quickly returned when the opposition failed to form a new government and the Corn Laws were duly repealed.

This was only the beginning. Delane was more of a reporter than an editorial writer, and spent a great deal of time in the society of the men who made decisions or were party to them. He published a secret proposal of the Tsar of Russia to partition Turkey, and followed it up with an exclusive on the Anglo–French ultimatum offering peace or war to the Russians. The ultimatum was sent via Paris, and the Tsar first read about it in *The Times*. Both government and opposition were incensed, and the opposition leader, Lord Derby, was very angry. The young Delane responded with a declaration of policy:

> We hold ourselves responsible not to Lord Derby or the House of Lords, but to the people of England, for the accuracy and fitness of that which we think proper to publish. Whatever we conceive to be injurious to the public interests, it is our duty to withhold; but we ourselves and the public at large are quite as good judges on that point as the leader of the Opposition, whose object is not to serve the State, but to embarrass the Ministry.

This was the mood of the paper as it prepared to cover the Crimean War (1854–56). Thomas Chenery, a future editor, was sent to Constantinople as the anchor man. General Ferdinand Eber, a Hungarian freedom fighter, and Charles Nasmyth, a young army officer on sick leave from India, were appointed as roving correspondents. Both were dashing *condottieri*, and Nasmyth, neglecting his journalism, took charge of the Turkish defence of Silistria where the Russians were beaten back. William Howard Russell, the first man to become a professional war correspondent, was attached to the British forces. Russell was a larger-than-life figure who had reported Irish affairs and the short Schleswig-Holstein campaign. He was well known in London's literary society, and before his departure Dickens, Thackeray and other members of the Garrick gave him a farewell dinner at the club.

It was the first systematic attempt of a newspaper to provide comprehensive coverage of a major war, but Delane was not satisfied. He had to see it for himself, and travelling overland he witnessed the first landings in the Crimea and interviewed the army commanders. He returned to London appalled by the awful condition of the British troops, many of whom were suffering from cholera and other fevers, and forewarned of the tragedy which was to come.

It was fortunate both for the country and the paper that Delane sent Russell to cover what was to prove one of the worst disasters in British military history. War correspondents were to become the stars of journalism, but none was to shine more brightly than this Irish prototype. He had all the qualities required: a colourful pen, courage, tenacity and the determination to get the story come what may. He immediately offended the higher command with his dispatches describing the terrible conditions suffered by the troops during the first winter. Despite the intense cold, he was forbidden to camp within the army lines and his tent was pulled down. He was completely ostracized, but he found his way to Balaclava to report the Charge of the Light Brigade. Here is an excerpt:

> Lord Lucan, with reluctance, gave the order to Lord Cardigan to advance upon the guns, conceiving that his orders compelled him to do so. The noble Earl, though he did not shrink, also saw the fearful odds against him . . . The whole brigade scarcely made one effective regiment. . . . As they passed towards the front, the Russians opened on them from the guns in the redoubt on the right, with volleys of musketry and rifles. They swept proudly past, glittering in the morning sun in all the pride and splendour of war. We could scarcely believe the evidence of our senses! Surely that handful of men are not going to charge an army in position? Alas, it was too true – their desperate valour knew no bounds, and far indeed was it removed from its so-called better part – discretion. They advanced in two lines, quickening their pace as they closed towards the enemy . . . At the distance of 1200 yards the whole line of the enemy belched forth, from 30 iron mouths, a flood of smoke and flame, through which hissed the deadly balls. Their flight was marked by instant gaps in our ranks, by dead men and horses, by steeds flying wounded or riderless across the plain. The first line is broken, it is joined by the second, they never halt or check their speed an instant; with diminished ranks, thinned by those 30 guns, which the Russians had laid with the most deadly accuracy, with a halo of flashing steel above their heads, and with a cheer which was many a noble fellow's death-cry, they flew into the smoke of the batteries . . . We saw them riding through the guns . . . to our delight we saw them returning . . . when the flank fire of the battery on the hill swept them down, scattered and broken as they were. Wounded men and dismounted troopers flying towards us told the sad tale – demi-gods could not have done what we had failed to do . . . At 11.35 not a British soldier, except the dead and the dying, was left in front of these bloody Muscovite guns.

This was Russell's most famous dispatch, but his greatest service to the country was to report the horrors of the next winter and the appalling state of the men's rations, clothing, accommodation, and medical services. Even the generals who had served in the Peninsular War some 40 years earlier admitted that they had never seen anything like it. The hospitals were horrifying, especially after cholera broke out again. The men died unattended, reported Russell: 'There they laid just as they were gently let down upon the ground by the poor fellows, their comrades, who brought them on their backs from the camp with the greatest tenderness, but who were not allowed to remain with them. The sick appeared to be tended by the sick, and the dying by the dying.' The inefficiency of the army command in London and the Crimea, and the failure to provide elementary health care was killing off the British army.

Nearly 80 per cent of all deaths during the war was caused by disease.

Russell's reports and Chenery's description of the conditions at the base hospital at Scutari, which had no nurses or dressers, horrified the nation, and Delane appealed to his readers to help. Thousands of pounds were received, and Florence Nightingale was persuaded to help. She sailed for Scutari with 38 nurses and a representative of *The Times* as her almoner. His instructions were to give her all the help and money she required. A second *Times* man, W.H. Stowe, was also sent out to help, but contracted cholera. He was refused admission to the military hospital and died.

The government questioned the authenticity of reports in *The Times* and tried to belittle its fund, which had risen to £20,000. It also threatened to stop Russell's rations. Delane counter-attacked, writing:

> The full value of every ration shall be repaid, and the churls who represent a
> generous country shall not have one farthing to charge to the historian of the
> war . . . It was but the other day another representative of the *Times*
> clothed a regiment which had been sent utterly unprovided by the War
> Department to rot away in the trenches before Sebastopol.

His relentless attacks in the editorial columns forced the government to resign, and led to wide-ranging reforms of the War Department and the medical services.

This in itself was a considerable victory, and another example of the power of *The Times*, but the consequences were much wider and more fundamental. As Woods and Bishop observed in their *The Story of The Times*, what angered the government was the form in which Delane's attack was launched. Delane, like Barnes, was waging a class war – not a class war in the Marxist sense, but a war of the new middle classes against the old landed aristocracy. Although the Reform Bill had established these classes in politics, large oases of power, of which the army was one, were still left to the aristocracy. In the conduct of the Crimean War, the middle classes found themselves looking on, powerless. Once again, it was the function of *The Times* to organize middle-class opinion, so that it might become an effective force in government.

The paper went from strength to strength. In the first 15 years of Delane's editorship the circulation rose from 20,000 to nearly 60,000, or more than three times the combined circulation of the other London papers. Annual dividends climbed from £17,000 to £50,000, an immense sum of money in those days and the shareholders would have received more if Delane had not attached so much importance to news coverage. Communication costs alone were more than most other newspapers spent on their entire news service. The special road expresses involving the change of carriage and horses at each posting station, the dromedaries crossing the Suez isthmus, the pigeon post from Paris to Boulogne, the chartered ships across the English and St George's

Channels, and later the special trains, were all essential to maintain the paper's position as the best newspaper in the world. But by 1846 they cost £10,000 a year, and the advent of the telegraph did not make communications any cheaper – only faster and more competitive.

Russell continued to be the star correspondent, and when he covered the Indian Mutiny in 1858 he was paid £600 a year and full expenses. He was at the relief of Lucknow, and investigated the rumours of atrocities against British men, women and children. He also inquired into the circumstances of the failure of British rule in India which had led to the Mutiny. His disgust at the unnecessary hell that his countrymen had made for themselves and for those they had conquered was regarded by some as treasonable weakness, but much of the credit for the policies of clemency and justice which ended the Mutiny belonged to Russell and *The Times*.

He was less successful in covering the American Civil War (1861–65) although he was probably the first to sense the future greatness of Abraham Lincoln. They met and dined several times together in the White House, and of course the newly-installed 16th President was anxious for the paper's support. He acknowledged its importance in a conversation with Russell: '. . . The London *Times* is one of the greatest powers in the world – in fact, I don't know anything which has much more power – except perhaps the Mississippi.' Russell journeyed south, to Charleston, Savannah, Montgomery, Mobile and New Orleans and returned by paddle steamer up the Mississippi. He reported all he saw, including a slave auction, which he loathed, but his main impression of the Confederacy was a land rich in military talent and poor in the wherewithal to fight the punishing war which was about to begin.

He returned to the North in time to report the Battle of Bull Run, the first major clash between the two armies. The Confederate troops were led by first-class generals, including Thomas 'Stonewall' Jackson, and the ill-led and untrained Union troops fled from the battlefield in terror. Once again he coolly reported what he saw:

> The scene on the road now assumed an aspect which has not a parallel in any description I have ever read. Infantry soldiers on mules and draught horses, with the harness clinging to their heels, as much frightened as their riders; negro servants on their masters' chargers; ambulances crowded with unwounded soldiers; waggons swarming with men who threw out the contents in the road to make room, grinding through a shouting, screaming mass of men on foot, who were literally yelling with rage at every halt, and shrieking out, 'Here are the cavalry! Will you get on.'

American reporters had also reported the rout in great and humiliating detail, but the public could not accept what they saw as criticism from a foreigner, especially a Britisher. He became known as Bull-Run Russell, and was ostracized by the government, the military, and the people he knew in Washington. His life was threatened and, worse, he was refused permission to accompany the troops at the front, so he returned to London. Had he stayed, the readers of *The Times* would not have been misled by his replacement, Charles Mackay, who proved to be a fanatical supporter of the South. There can be no doubt that his biased reporting influenced British attitudes and deepened sympathy for the Confederacy.

John Delane was a good judge of journalists, and could recognize star quality in the most unlikely people – Henri Stefan Opper de Blowitz, for example. Of obscure origins, Blowitz was said to look like a bounder and was variously described as brash, egotistical, vain and preposterous. He was appointed Paris correspondent, but was acquainted with statesmen all over Europe. Being a womanizer, he found that their wives were frequently his best sources of information. One wonders what *Times* men of later and stuffier decades would have made of him. He worried Delane at times, but his work was outstanding. His greatest scoop was the 1878 Treaty of Berlin, which redrew the frontiers of the Balkans and ceded Cyprus to Britain. Blowitz's coverage of the Congress was, despite official secrecy, so comprehensive and accurate that Bismarck, the German Chancellor, is said to have lifted the cloth covering the conference table 'to see if Blowitz is underneath'. He finally acquired a copy of the Treaty, and because he was being followed by the Prussian police smuggled it out of the country sewn inside the lining of the coat of another *Times* man.

The tenacity of its reporters did not endear *The Times* to the British government, particularly after its coverage of the Crimean War, and its championing of middle-class opinion offended the Crown, the old Tories and even some Whigs and radicals. Its alleged monopoly was attacked, to which Delane replied that the only monopoly was the quality of its news service. The critics continued their assault, claiming that the stamp tax gave the paper an unfair advantage. The tax, first imposed to stifle and control the press, then reduced in 1836, was repealed in 1855 because *The Times* had become too powerful. It was replaced by postal charges based on weight. The heavier the paper the more it had to pay the post office to deliver copies, and as *The Times* had twice and often three times as many pages as its competitors the new charges were potentially damaging. The paper survived by switching its distribution to W.H. Smith, the newsagents, who kept costs down by taking advantage of the railways' cheaper freight charges.

John Walter III (1818–94), who had succeeded his father as publisher in 1847, was always on the lookout for faster and cheaper production methods. The new and improved Hoe press was imported from the United States in 1858, and output was raised to 20,000 sheets an hour. Walter later invented a press with a new paper feed. Previously newspapers had been printed on separate sheets which had to be fed in by hand, but the Walter press used reels of paper. It was also the first to print on both sides of the paper simultaneously, and output was again raised but with a corresponding drop in costs.

The Times thus maintained its primacy in news coverage and printing, and profits continued to grow, but repeal of the stamp tax led to the popular penny press and the emergence of rivals such as the *Daily Telegraph* in 1855 and the weekly *Manchester Guardian* which became a daily paper in the same year. The *Telegraph* was soon selling more copies than *The Times*, which had pegged its cover price at threepence. This decision had been made because neither Walter nor Delane was prepared to lower editorial standards, and *The Times* now became a high-quality paper read by an educated elite. It was the beginning of the stratification of the British press.

Delane remained the driving force throughout his 36 years as editor. Unlike Barnes, he was not an inspired writer and in fact wrote very little. He participated in the social life of the capital, ate and drank sparingly and kept fit by foxhunting and making his rounds in London on horseback. He had news sense and insatiable curiosity, and almost invariably anticipated events correctly. He was seen everywhere, knew everybody and attended every important function. According to one of his colleagues, he was usually the only commoner at the grand parties he was invited to, although he did not particularly like aristocrats. He accepted their invitation because, in his own words, if you want to get at secrets you must stick close to the centre of them.

Delane was in effect married to the paper. His wife was mentally ill and lived apart under strict medical care. He normally rose at noon and went for a ride in Hyde Park after eating an austere brunch. Then he spent two or three hours at his desk planning the next issue and briefing his editorial writers. Many of his scoops were written as editorials, using the secrets, information and rumours he had picked up the night before. The evening was spent at social functions or dining with a Cabinet Minister, and he returned to Printing House Square after 10 p.m. to take control of every department of the paper. This nightly metamorphosis would horrify modern editors, including those accustomed to working ten or twelve hours a day. Delane was his own political and diplomatic reporter during the day, on easy terms with politicians and ambassadors. When other men were contemplating bed he became night editor, reading, rewriting and sub-editing foreign dispatches and parliamentary reports. He also selected letters for publication from a daily average of about 200. When the last edition was being run off at five in the morning he walked home to his flat in Serjeants Inn. He once remarked that in the course of his career he had seen more sunrises than almost any other man alive.

It was a punishing regime which eventually broke him physically, but it made Delane the most powerful press baron in history. Throughout his career he held fast to the principles referred to in the previous chapter: that the press lives by disclosures, that its first duty is to obtain the earliest and most powerful correct intelligence of the events of the time and instantly to make them the common property of the nation. He refused to accept any limitation on his freedom to report, and if he lived today he would be the subject of innumerable complaints to the Press Council. When Mowbray Morris, the manager of *The Times*, was called before a House of Commons committee in 1857 to substantiate a report that some Members were receiving bribes, he also followed Delane's line and said that the press had the right to do whatever it chose and was not required to explain to anyone. Asked if he was willing to offer any explanation or justification of the charge, he answered, 'I am not.'

Lord John Russell, the Whig statesman, told Queen Victoria that the degree of information possessed by *The Times* with regard to the most secret affairs of state was mortifying, humiliating and incomprehensible. Humiliating or not, the very men who complained provided information in the hope of securing Delane's goodwill. Because so many were eager to cooperate he was in fact independent of any one of them. He wrote to one supplicant: 'I don't care to have confidential papers sent to me at any time because the possession of them prevents me using the information which from one source or another is sure enough to reach me without any such condition of reserve.' The most prominent people sought him out in public, and he was seen one day riding his horse down Whitehall with a duke walking on either side. The Queen complained to Lord Palmerston, the Prime Minister, about his 'atrocious articles', but when Delane criticized her for withdrawing from public life after the death of the Prince Consort she wrote a letter to *The Times* explaining the reasons. The *Saturday Review* said: 'No apology is necessary for assuming that this country is ruled by *The Times*. We all know it, or if we do not know it, we ought to know it. It is high time we began to realize the magnificent spectacle afforded by British freedom – thirty millions of *cives Romani* governed by a newspaper.'

This was power, but Delane was not corrupted; he only wanted news, and had no ambition to run the country. Nor did John Walter III seek favours or preferment. But there was an element of megalomania in their conviction that *The Times* was superior to all other institutions. Henry Reeve, the chief editorial writer, resigned declaring that the paper had reached an extraordinary and dangerous eminence. And indeed it was not to be maintained for much longer. The power, depending as it did on its near-monopoly of official information (despite Delane's denial), began to recede after the repeal of the stamp tax and the removal of the duties on paper some six years later in 1861. That vile tyrant, as *The Times* was once called, was not vanquished, but it was cut down to size by the subsequent competition.

Delane did well by *The Times* and its publisher. The average size of the paper when he took over was eight pages with occasional advertisement supplements, and long before his retirement in 1877 it averaged 20 pages. Both circulation and profits had risen to unprecedented heights. He had created the modern newspaper, and set standards to which most journalists still aspire. He knew that newspapers exist to publish news, that news is the prime source of their power or influence and not the views of publishers or editorial writers. He did not belong to a political party, and his one political ambition was to organize middle-class opinion so that it might become an effective force in government. He won his class war. There was no other public opinion during his time because of the limited franchise, and it was left to the popular press to organize working-class opinion when the franchise was gradually extended, but first Barnes and then Delane were the pioneers. For this they should be remembered.

BENNETT AND GREELEY

James Gordon Bennett I (1795–1872) was a megalomaniac. Of that there can be no doubt. No normal journalist would tell his readers that: 'Shakespeare is the genius of the drama, Scott of the novel, Milton and Byron of the poem – and I mean to be the genius of the newspaper press.' His *New York Herald* became a platform for self-exaltation: 'What is to prevent a daily newspaper from being made the greatest organ of social life? Books have had their day – the theatres have had their day – the temple of religion has had its day.' He went on to proclaim that: 'a newspaper can be made to take the lead of all these in the great movements of human thought and human civilization. A newspaper can send more souls to Heaven, and save more from Hell, than all the churches or chapels in New York.'

Politicians and bankers were judged inferior, as was the legal profession: 'The honesty, the purity, the integrity of legal practice and decisions through-out this country, are more indebted to the American Press, than to the whole tribe of lawyers and judges, who issue their decrees. The Press is the living Jury of the Nation.' His memoirs, supposedly written for him by an anonymous journalist, provide many more examples but few to compare with the announcement of his marriage. Here is the tailpiece of the lengthy article which appeared in the *Herald*:

> In the new and holy condition into which I am about to enter, and to enter with the same reverential feelings as I would Heaven itself, I anticipate some signal changes in my feelings, in my views, in my purposes, in my pursuits. What they may be, I know not – time alone can tell. My ardent desire has been to reach the highest order of human excellence by the shortest possible cut. Association, night and day, in sickness and in health, in war and peace, with a woman of this highest order of excellence, must produce some curious results in my heart and feelings, and these results the future will develop in due time in the columns of the *Herald*.

Little wonder the embarrassed woman fled to Europe as soon as her children were old enough to travel.

This extraordinary man was born in Scotland in 1795. He studied for the priesthood at a Roman Catholic seminary in Aberdeen, but left after two years because: 'the thought of being educated to sacrifice his independence at the dictation of the church was an annoyance to him.' Benjamin Franklin's *Life* impressed him enormously, and acting on an impulse he boarded the first available ship for the Americas, landing in Halifax, Nova Scotia, in 1819.

Bennett was hardly typical of the thousands of young Scotsmen who crossed the Atlantic at that time in search of land or opportunity, and in so doing depopulated the Highlands. Apart from his theological training, he had been well taught in economics, was an omniverous reader and also wrote poetry. On the other hand, Bennett was as much a creature of his time as was the political journalist and essayist William Cobbett back in Britain. Both countries were passing through a period of fundamental change, economic in origin but with far-reaching social and political consequences. In Britain the agrarian and industrial revolutions were transforming the country, and Cobbett reported the misery of landless labourers with high indignation in his *Political Register* weekly that had long been demanding social reform. He also campaigned for the enfranchisement of the new industrial towns. He hated established authority, as did Bennett, and called it The Thing.

The change which confronted Bennett when he arrived in the United States also invited radical journalism; Thomas Jefferson, who had retired from the presidency in 1809, was still alive but his dream of an arcadian commonwealth of yeoman farmers was fast disappearing. The late statesman Alexander Hamilton, one of those who supported an aristocracy of wealth, had been convinced of the wisdom of the property-owning classes and sceptical of the capacity of the masses for self-government. He argued that no society could succeed which did not unite the interest and credit of the rich with those of the state. The Jeffersonians were ill-placed to contest this aspiring aristocracy because it was difficult to organize the western farmers, southern planters and the growing eastern proletariat. The struggle was not decided until Franklin Roosevelt was elected president a century later, but the first battle was won when Andrew Jackson founded the Democratic party from the remnants of Jefferson's Democratic-Republicans. Bennett was won over to the side of General Jackson, the victor of New Orleans and the first president to have been born in a log cabin.

Bennett drifted into journalism, learning his trade in New York and South Carolina, and excelled as a Washington correspondent. In 1830 he was appointed associate editor of the *New York Courier & Enquirer*, which was a Jackson paper until the proprietor was bribed to desert him. Bennett quit in disgust, but his loyalty went unrewarded. The party bosses mistrusted him, and it seems that he was disliked because of his origins. Jackson hated Britain, which was also seen as the ally of American bankers and company promoters. This was the turning point in Bennett's life. He might well have become a great political editor and a force in Democratic politics. Instead, he decided to launch his own newspaper, and at a time when American newspapers were about to be revolutionized.

The nineteenth-century French writer, Alexis de Tocqueville, author of *Democracy in America*, said that the power of the press was second only to that of the people, but in fact the metropolitan papers paid little attention to ordinary people who might have wanted to read a paper. As in Britain, they assumed that only the middle class and the politically interested read newspapers. Home delivery and annual subscriptions were still the rule, and newspapers were expensive. The *New Orleans Picayune* was so named because it cost a picayune or about six cents. The average annual subscription was about $8, the weekly wage of a skilled worker.

The age of popular or penny journalism was slow in dawning in the US although public education was more advanced than in Britain. The majority of immigrants were still British or Irish, and not all of them were illiterate. A large and expanding market was waiting to be exploited by any newspaper proprietor who realized that readers did not live for politics or commerce alone, and that local news and human-interest stories could attract thousands of new readers. That such a market existed was proved by the popularity of the British *Penny Magazine* (launched in 1832 by Charles Knight). It was printed in the United States from plates sent over from London, and had a circulation of 160,000.

There were other lessons to be learned from Britain, where every newspaper, including *The Times*, was sold on the streets. The *London Morning Herald* demonstrated that human-interest stories sold newspapers by publishing colourful or humorous reports of police court cases. Benjamin Day, a New York printer, eventually saw the light and launched the *Sun* in 1833. It was sold on the streets for a cent, and was an instant success. His court reporter, a former compositor, had a lot to learn from his London counterpart but within two years the *Sun* was selling 15,000 copies a day. No other American paper could approach it in circulation. With immigrants arriving at the rate of a quarter of a million a year, and steadily increasing, future expansion seemed limitless, but Day sold out after four profitable years. This was a bad error of judgment on his part, but he had shown the way. On 6 May 1835, when he was 40 years old, and with only $500 to his name, Bennett launched the *New York Herald*.

It is not surprising that the first popular newspapers appeared in New York. The United States was still a pioneering country in the 1830s, and newspapers and journalists such as the London *Times* and Barnes and Delane could not have flourished in such an environment. Washington was a small town of unmade roads and half-completed public buildings. Congress met for only a few months in the year, and nobody dreamed that the White House would become a seat of global power. If it had been otherwise Bennett might have remained in the nation's capital as a political journalist. New York was the largest and most prosperous city in the country, but even the state capital was established upstate in Albany. New York's early newspapers might have developed differently if politics, apart from City Hall, had not been an out-of-town story. Instead, the journalistic talent available was free to report and reflect upon the goings-on of the lively city. New Yorkers also tended to have little respect for authority, an essential ingredient for popular journalism.

The *Herald* began as a small four-page paper, and was printed by a jobbing printer. The office was a Wall Street cellar. Bennett had no money to hire staff and buy furniture, and wrote every word himself on a board laid across two barrels. He also sold the advertising space. An early setback occurred when the printing plant was destroyed in a fire and publication had to be suspended until another printer was found, but the paper prospered. Bennett claimed to subscribe to the concept of *vox populi vox dei* (in effect, 'the voice of the people is the voice of God') and said that the people could only be well informed if newspapers reported the world as it was; the facts must be reported realistically. Important political developments were only briefly mentioned. Despite the hyperbole and his radicalism, the *Herald* became a sensational paper, written only for the day it was published.

The circulation was tripled to 20,000 copies a day within a few months – because he understood his readers. People who could afford only one cent for a paper were unlikely to be interested in politics, and he sensed that his readers either dismissed politicians as crooks or were content to live under any government which left them alone. Their world was New York, a colourful city of contrasts, of ostentatious wealth and terrible poverty. Violence and corruption were endemic. In social terms it could be a dreadful place, but it generated good stories to read after a hard day's work.

Although Bennett introduced financial columns into daily journalism, he decided that crime stories giving all the gory details were what really sold newspapers. The breakthrough came in April 1836 when a prostitute, Dorcas Dorrance alias Helen Jewett, was murdered in a fashionable brothel. The alleged murderer was Richard Robinson, a young man-about-town who was said to have killed her with a hatchet after she had threatened to expose their liaison to the heiress he was about to marry. Murder was not uncommon, but Bennett made the Jewett–Robinson Case a national sensation. He wrote columns of purple prose, and in so doing developed the sob-sister technique of reporting. He described Helen as a church-going girl from rural Maine drawn to the big city where her career was brilliant, but 'baneful to herself and her associates'. Bennett even visited the mortuary and described the corpse 'as white, as full, as polished as the purest Parian marble. The perfect figure, the exquisite lines, the fine face, the full arms, the beautiful bust, all surpassed in every respect the Venus de Medici.'

This was Victorian melodrama guaranteed to attract readers, but Bennett also created some kind of newspaper history by investigating the case himself instead of depending upon police handouts and leaks from the district attorney's office. What was more, his investigation even helped to get the accused acquitted – no mean feat for a man already working 12 hours a day. The *Herald* contained little else during the trial, which was reported verbatim. Other penny papers, including those in Boston and Philadelphia, were forced to compete. The Jewett–Robinson Case was history's first media event, and Bennett emerged triumphant. Thereafter he was always the leader of the pack, and for many years the *Herald* enjoyed the largest circulation in the world.

His next coup was to raise the cover price of the *Herald* to two cents, which increased revenue by about $50,000 a year. It was a large sum in those days, and Bennett boasted that he would make the *Herald* 'the greatest, best and most profitable paper that ever appeared in this country.' To his rivals' consternation sales continued to increase, and the paper was improved because he could afford to hire staff. In 1840 his competitors responded by launching what became known as the 'Moral War' against the paper.

Arguably Bennett was no worse than most of his rivals but only a more inspired sensational journalist. Nevertheless, he had earned some measure of obloquy. His attacks against individuals were often reckless and malicious, and he had been horsewhipped twice. He must have shocked many readers with his studied disrespect of clergymen and religion in general. His rivals published just as many crime stories, but Bennett revelled in sex scandals. His growing megalomania must also have told against him. At first Bennett shrugged off the charges of depravity and unprincipled adventurism and gave as good as he got, but the Moral War was taken up in other cities and even the British press joined in.

In retrospect the 'war' against Bennett was as much political as moral. The *Manchester Guardian* compared the *Herald* to a Chartist newspaper; in other words, not only middle-class morality was offended. Manchester was the birthplace of *laissez-faire*, and as the Peterloo Massacre showed, its mill owners were no more willing than the financial aristocracy in New York to come to terms with the men and women they exploited. Both saw revelations of the dreadful living conditions of the working class which Bennett published as a threat to their expanding wealth and power. Inevitably the *Herald's* circulation began to slip, and Bennett decided to retreat if not submit.

His competitors must have regretted their victory because the *Herald* soon became a very good newspaper. The improvement had begun when the cover price was raised, but Bennett redoubled his efforts after the Moral War. The paper remained 'saucy' and 'spicy' – two of his favourite words – but more space was given to politics, commerce and financial affairs. Foreign news coverage was extended, and correspondents were appointed in the larger American cities. Its reporting of the Mexican War (1846–48) was unrivalled. The *Herald* continued its tradition of always being first with the news. Before the invention of the telegraph its small fleet of boats had sailed out to meet the ships which brought news from Europe, and scored enviable scoops. Bennett now recognized the potential of the telegraph, and used it more extensively than his rivals. The *Herald's* circulation was over 60,000 a day when his son succeeded him in 1868. He died four years later, unloved, and his contributions to journalism largely unrecognized at the time.

Bennett had been the first to introduce financial, sports and social news as regular features, and to that extent he helped to create the modern newspaper. He brought journalism down to earth, and by calling a spade a bloody shovel resisted the Victorian shams imported from Britain. Prudery was also resisted, and in his columns legs were legs and not limbs. He pioneered new printing techniques as did the Walters of the London *Times*, and like that newspaper's Barnes and Delane he established a newspaper independent of government, political party and special interests. This was his greatest contribution to American journalism.

Whether or not he believed that he could make the press 'the pivot of government, society, commerce, finance, religion, and all human civilization', he was not interested in, and never achieved, the kind of power wielded by Barnes and Delane. He was a maverick, and although an immigrant shared the American suspicion of authority. He was against most of its manifestations, and his contempt for politicians increased over the years. He spent vast sums of money covering the Civil War, and was often better-informed than President Lincoln, but was never involved emotionally. He wanted only to cover the news and sell newspapers.

His son, James Gordon Bennett II (1841–1918) is remembered for sending H.M. Stanley to Africa to find Dr Livingstone. There was small reason to believe that the famous missionary was actually lost, but the British adventurer's ten-month trek across the dark continent ended with words that have become immortal – 'Dr Livingstone, I presume.' Stanley covered the British Abyssinian campaign and the Spanish civil war of 1868 for the *Herald*, and afterwards discovered the source of the Congo. The second Bennett was obviously a man of wide interests, but he was also a dissolute spendthrift who preferred to live in France, where he launched the paper's Paris edition. He tried to run the New York paper from his apartment on the Champs Elysées, and the cable costs were so high that he became a partner of the Commercial Cable Company to keep the money in the family. The *Herald* inevitably suffered, but its gradual decline was also due to the continuing success of Horace Greeley's *Tribune*. This former country printer from New Hampshire was very different from the two Bennetts, notably in his longing for power.

Horace Greeley (1811–72) was only 20 when he arrived in New York in 1831, ill-educated and destitute. He looked and sounded like a country bumpkin, but had more than his fair share of Yankee moral superiority. He had no doubts. He believed in progress and the perfectibility of man, and was convinced that the salvation of mankind depended upon the United States. He was no less convinced that his kind, the 'white Anglo-Saxon Protestants' (WASPs) of New England, were the American vanguard, and saw himself as leading the crusade against the enemies of progress and moral purity. He must have been insufferable.

After becoming a partner in a small printing firm, Greeley launched the *New Yorker* in 1834, not the celebrated magazine which still flourishes, but a literary weekly consisting largely of pirated articles and poetry. He also wrote editorials supporting the Whig party, which impressed Thurlow Weed, the political boss who was running William Seward for the governorship of the state of New York. He asked Greeley to edit a campaign paper, the *Jeffersonian*, which did indeed help to elect Seward. Later, again at Weed's request, he edited another campaign paper, the *Log Cabin*, which supported William Harrison's bid for the White House. They proved that Greeley was a superb polemicist.

Weed was a king-maker who ran one of the country's first political machines. Little interested in issues, he was a fixer who loved the rough-and-tumble of electoral politics and was not adverse to lying and bribing his way to victory. His machine controlled the state legislature. Greeley, the moralistic crusader, should have despised this big, florid man who enjoyed his liquor, but money and political ambition won him over. He prostituted himself without a qualm.

In fact, the candidates he was hired to help elect were decent men. Seward was an early opponent of slavery, and subsequently served honourably in the US Senate and as Abraham Lincoln's Secretary of State. Harrison was an old Indian fighter whose father had signed the Declaration of Independence. Greeley was also an ardent supporter of the Whigs, the forerunners of the Republican party, but his work for Weed was utterly cynical. For instance, Harrison was not Weed's first choice. He was primarily concerned in denying the nomination to Henry Clay, and supported Harrison only because his popularity as a frontier hero could win Democratic votes. He was nominated without a platform, the first presidential candidate to be selected on grounds of expediency alone.

Greeley's cynicism was reflected in the title of his first campaign paper – the *Jeffersonian*. It mattered little to him that Jefferson abhorred everything the Whigs stood for, and Greeley afterwards condemned him for 'unscrupulous and licentious personal morals'. The third President was still popular, and the misuse of his name was calculated to win over his admirers. Harrison was duly elected but died a month after moving into the White House. The success of these campaign papers persuaded Greeley that politics could sell newspapers. James Gordon Bennett I had thought otherwise, but Greeley told himself that a Whig newspaper also selling for only a penny could do better than the *Herald* if only because it would be the happy recipient of patronage from the ruling party. The *New York Tribune* was launched on 10 April 1841.

Like the *Herald* it began as a small, four-page paper, but the *Tribune* was dedicated to reform. It claimed to be 'anti-slavery, anti-war, anti-rum, anti-tobacco, anti-seduction and anti-grogshops, brothels, and gambling houses.' And, to quote Glyndon van Deusen, Greeley's biographer: 'running through it like a golden thread of continuity was the purpose that gave it its name, a dedication to the elevation of the masses. The *Tribune* stood first of all for progress and welcomed to its pages all forward-looking men and doctrines.'

It did, indeed. It could be said that Greeley had prostituted himself to Weed because he had his way to make and a wife to keep, and now that he was his own boss he could hope to persuade New Yorkers to aspire to the highest ideal of New England WASPs. Whatever his purpose, the *Tribune* was a success for reasons that should have been obvious to his competitors. Bennett was making a fortune because many New Yorkers loved to read about crime, passion, corruption and other manifestations of the weakness of man – and woman. But other New Yorkers were sober men whose inherent puritanism was offended by the city's easy ways. The anti-slavery movement was already strong, and the temperance tide was seeping down from New England. They were more than ready for crusades against the ungodly and impure.

No less important, they shared Greeley's belief in progress and the perfectibility of man. Many were eager to be educated and informed, and liked being lectured at as their descendants still do today. They believed that the United States was the land of the free and the home of the brave, that it was God's own country created to do His work. The readership was potentially large, but Greeley was not immediately successful. He was a bad businessman and did not know how to run an office. Only after Thomas McElrath became a partner and business manager was he free to devote all his energy to crusading.

He was more than a crusader, of course; he was a newspaperman every bit as good as Bennett. Both of them loved the challenge of bringing out a new paper every night. Both knew what their readers wanted, and both were prepared to spend 12 hours a day and more on the job. Bennett had earlier recognized Greeley's talents and had offered him a partnership, but that would have been disastrous. Bennett was the loner who chose to attack established authority from without. Greeley longed to be part of the Establishment, and to reform it from within. Bennett wanted to cover the news, and Greeley wanted to lead the country towards that wonderful future reserved by God for all good Americans.

Greeley looked to New England for inspiration and found it among the Transcendentalists and at Brook Farm. The former were not disciples of Kant but a group led by the essayist and poet Ralph Waldo Emerson who wanted to create a unique American culture. Brook Farm was one of the many arcadia established by earnest Americans seeking a simple and intellectual or religious life. Brook Farm was better than most, at least it is still remembered, and among its members was Charles Dana, who became managing editor of the

Tribune. Greeley was also attracted by Fourier (1772–1837), the French socialist writer who believed that individualism and competition were essentially immoral. He argued that the full and harmonious development of human potential could only be achieved by cooperative effort. Fourier was also an optimist, believing that happiness and virtue could be attained by the unrestrained indulgence of human passion; that restraints imposed on the gratification of desire led to misery and vice. There was much more to Fourierism, but if some of his ideas were acceptable at Brook Farm they were unlikely to be widely applied in a country increasingly devoted to rugged individualism and Victorian morality.

Some critics concluded that Greeley was not intellectually equipped to understand philosophical concepts, or that only an ignorant country printer could be dazzled by such ideas. Perhaps, but a younger contemporary of Greeley's, Walt Whitman, was also an ill-educated printer before emerging as a great American poet. The reality was that Greeley was editing a newspaper at a time when many Americans, equally ill-educated but intellectually curious, were seeking new directions. They lived in the New World, and their society had yet to be fully moulded. Greeley might have been one of the blind leading the blind, but he developed education as a function of journalism.

Greeley's extensive if untutored reading fed his romantic idealism, but the conclusions he drew and pursued with the enthusiasm of the crusader were not all eccentric. He denounced social injustice, capital punishment, war and flogging in the navy. He advocated tax-supported schools and emphasized the value of vocational training in a pioneering country. He believed that government should actively promote the general welfare; that men had the right to work and the government the responsibility to provide it in hard times. Greeley was not the first to say: 'Go West, young man, go West', but he believed in peaceful territorial expansion and campaigned for a railway to the Pacific.

The lot of the urban working population appalled him, and he exposed the exploitation of the sweatshops and the dreadful living conditions of slum dwellers. He did not question capitalism, but argued that as the rich got richer sufficient wealth should filter down to ordinary folk. But he never pushed his campaigns too far. For all his concern about economic and social justice, he opposed trade unions and only reluctantly accepted the ten-hour working day. Principle was never allowed to get in the way of profits. Van Deusen wrote of him:

> It was perfectly proper in Greeley's eyes to publish accounts of seductions, if proper horror was expressed over the deed. It was legitimate to notice lewd books, if so doing gave the editor an opportunity to denounce rival publishers for putting them out. It was even right to publish in lurid detail the double rape of eighteen-year-old Ann Murphy in the Broadway Cottage, provided sufficient horror was expressed and one could use the affair to

assert that only Democrats ran bawdy houses in New York. The *Tribune*, in such matters, came near to making vice attractive and virtue odious . . .

Hypocritical or not, Greeley made the *Tribune* a great newspaper. He extended its news service and Karl Marx became one of his European correspondents. Marx, who had been expelled from Prussia in 1849, was then living in London in penury, and his income from the *Tribune* helped to keep him going while he was writing *Das Kapital*. Greeley's influence reached far beyond New York because of the *Weekly Tribune*, which eventually had a record-breaking circulation of 200,000. Many of its readers were New Englanders who had joined the wagon trains moving westwards, and Emerson said that Greeley did all the thinking and theorizing of western farmers for $2 a year. Greeley was becoming a power in the land although he was not universally popular among Whigs. His campaign to introduce Prohibition in the state of New York had angered his former employer Thurlow Weed, and not only because he was a Wet (as opponents of Prohibition were known). Greeley had supported all Prohibition candidates regardless of their politics, and this was seen as an inexcusable act of disloyalty at a time when internal dissension was threatening the survival of the party.

Greeley's reputation as a powerful press baron was given the ultimate test before and during the Civil War, and he failed. The tragedy began in January 1854 when a Senate committee 'reported out' a Bill to establish the territories of Kansas and Nebraska. This was the first constitutional step towards statehood and should not have been contentious, but the Bill went much further. It transferred from Congress to the people of the new territories the right to decide whether they should become free or slave states. It also repealed the Missouri Compromise of 1820 which prohibited slavery in territories north of latitude 36° 30′.

The Bill reopened the whole question of slavery, and Greeley damned it as 'an infamous proposition'. He dismissed its author, Senator Stephen Douglas of Illinois, as a 'lying little villain', but recognizing that public opinion was not ready for abolition argued that slavery must be confined to the South. He also knew that the Whigs would not take a stand because of their strong southern wing, and decided to help found a new national party, the Republican party.

This was a great turning point. Without the Republicans, the course of American history would have been very different. It is possible that the United States would have divided permanently between slave and 'free-soil' states (where slavery was prohibited before the Civil War). Greeley was not alone, others had also concluded that the Whig party had to be replaced, but he could do more than most to persuade northern electorates to rally behind the new party. Apart from the daily *Tribune*, the weekly edition was read in many northern states. He was the most powerful press baron in the country, but that

[44]

did not make him infallible. He campaigned for a party dedicated to fighting slavery – and his old enemy, the demon-rum. The fact that many Americans who abhorred slavery liked the occasional drink did not occur to him. The Union was reluctantly facing up to its greatest crisis, and he decided that Wets were not fit to fight for its survival. The following comparison is not wholly apposite, if only because Winston Churchill was a drinking man, but it was as if the wartime prime minister had said that he had 'nothing to offer except blood, toil, tears, sweat and Prohibition'.

The Republican party was in fact founded without a Prohibition plank in its platform. Greeley regretfully accepted the omission as a temporary expediency, but his fertile imagination could not be restrained. Perhaps it was the newspaperman's longing for a new lead story every day; whatever the reason, he claimed that slavery could be peacefully abolished if sufficient freedom-loving Englishmen could be persuaded to emigrate and settle below the Mason–Dixon line (39° 43'N). He confidently expected them to vote for Abolition in state elections. He also warned that the Democrats would retain the presidency in 1860 unless Republicans promised to abolish the army and transform the navy into a mail-steamer service.

These eccentricities help to explain why Greeley did not rise to the greatest challenge of his career, but his political ambition was a damaging distraction. Events such as the Dred Scott Case decision of the Supreme Court, which held that slaveholding in the territories was a constitutional right, and the Abolitionist John Brown's raid on Harpers Ferry in West Virginia (celebrated in the song 'John Brown's Body') brought secession and war closer. Greeley responded well on each occasion, but in between played politics. His editorial line followed his search for public office, zigzagging as he sought the support of one group and then another. He must have thought that he was a second Machiavelli when in 1858 he urged Republicans in Illinois to re-elect Democratic Senator Douglas, the author of the Kansas–Nebraska Bill (which allowed the territories to make their own slavery decisions) whom he had earlier dismissed as a 'lying little villain'.

His argument was that if re-elected Douglas would do great harm to the Democratic party to the eventual benefit of Republicanism, but it only incensed the farmers who subscribed to the *Weekly Tribune*. They wanted to elect their own man, an obscure prairie lawyer who had served one undistinguished term in Congress but was fondly known as Honest Abe. The famous Douglas–Lincoln debates, which were a unique feature of the campaign, demonstrated that Lincoln shared Greeley's views on the great issues. He believed that: 'the legitimate object of government is to do for a community of people whatever they need to have done, but cannot do at all, or cannot do so well for themselves'. He wanted to contain slavery in the South and not try to abolish it immediately, but he also said: 'A house divided against itself cannot stand. I believe that this government cannot endure permanently half slave and half free.'

Greeley was not impressed, and continued to support Douglas until the local papers attacked him for interfering in the state's affairs. The readers of his weekly also became restless, and he retreated before sales suffered. He was hurt by their lack of confidence in his motives, and his subsequent support for Lincoln was at best lukewarm. Perhaps as a consequence the future president did not win a clear victory, and the state legislature decided that the incumbent should retain his seat.

This blundering did not deter Greeley from further meddling if only because the *Tribune*, despite some ups and downs, was doing well. The presidential election was approaching, and he was determined to prevent William Seward from winning the Republican nomination. The reason had nothing to do with Seward's fitness for high office. Greeley just wanted to prove that he was not beholden to Thurlow Weed, who had spent years scheming to get Seward into the White House. Greeley's choice was Edward Bates, a Missouri lawyer and politician who had boasted that like other old Whigs he was 'a respectable gentleman of the old school, who takes his liquor regularly and votes the Democratic ticket occasionally'. He was a decent enough man, but even Greeley had to admit that he was an old fogy. Fortunately for the United States, Lincoln was nominated and elected, and to Greeley's discomfort Seward was appointed as his Secretary of State. Greeley saw this as confirmation that Lincoln was an inferior politician and the tool of other men, although he had belatedly joined the Lincoln bandwagon.

Lincoln's election made secession inevitable, but not for Greeley. His blindness to events was almost inexplicable. He was a talented journalist who travelled widely and knew everybody worth knowing. He was editor of the best paper in the country, with an experienced staff who must have been fully aware of the impending crisis. His lifetime preoccupation with slavery should have given him some understanding of Southern intransigence, but even when South Carolina seceded from the Union he still seemed oblivious of the desperateness of the situation.

His record during the Civil War was inglorious. The self-proclaimed friend and protector of the common man defended the conscription law which allowed the rich to escape military service on payment of $300. He argued that it was a shrewd way of paying for the war, but not surprisingly the New York mob attacked and nearly burned down the offices of the *Tribune*. For a time he pursued a bellicose line, running the slogan 'Forward to Richmond' on the front page every day; but after the terrible slaughter of Union troops in the Battle of the Wilderness he demanded foreign mediation to end the war. He misrepresented Lincoln's position when he, Greeley, met Southern commissioners who claimed that they wanted to negotiate a peace. In any other country Greeley would have been detained and his newspaper closed.

Greeley's treatment of Lincoln was always ambivalent and frequently despicable. The news published in the *Tribune* could be as biased as its editorial opinion. The Gettysburg Address, one of history's most noble speeches, was but briefly mentioned although a verbatim report would not have filled a single column. Lincoln, over-burdened as he was, tried to be conciliatory because he needed the support of the *Tribune*. Greeley promised to cooperate on the understanding that he would receive preferential treatment in the release of official information, but plotted to have Lincoln replaced at the 1864 Republican national convention. When he finally came out in the open against Lincoln's renomination, he wrote that the President had done reasonably well considering his lowly background and inexperience, but was 'not one of those rare, great men who mould their age in the similitude of their own high character, massive abilities and lofty aims.'

Greeley continued to edit the *Tribune* until his death in 1872, but his reputation as a press baron rests mainly upon his work during the Civil War and the years before. In the first instance, it was deeply flawed by his contempt for Lincoln whom he regarded as an ignorant frontiersman who should never have ventured out of Illinois. In his defence, Lincoln was not then acknowledged to be a great president although William Howard Russell of the London *Times* saw the potential for greatness when they met in the White House in 1861. But Lincoln was the freely-elected head of a government fighting a terrible war for a noble purpose, and deserved respect if not unquestioning support.

Despite his Yankee assumption of moral superiority which led him astray from time to time, Greeley was not a megalomaniac like James Gordon Bennett I. He was over-worked and financially insecure because he had sold most of his stock in the company to buy a worthless farm and satisfy the whims of his wife, a difficult woman and a hypochondriac. He undertook long lecture tours to earn more money, and in those early days of railways they must have been exhausting. Nevertheless, almost single-handedly he created a fine newspaper. Without a doubt, he was one of the great press barons in history, and could have been one of the most influential if he had not hungered for political power. This was his undoing.

His biographer van Deusen said that Greeley's views were those of a clever newspaperman rather than those of a statesman, which is how he saw himself. He wanted to be a statesman, and was given the opportunity in 1872, a few months before his death, when the Liberal Republicans (a breakaway party) and the Democrats nominated him as their presidential candidate. He was crushingly defeated by the Republican incumbent, President Ulysses Grant, by 272 to 66 electoral votes.

THE LEVY/BURNHAMS AND W.T. STEAD

The extraordinary expansion and development of the American press in the first half of the nineteenth century was not repeated in Britain, largely because of the stamp tax on newspapers. American newspapers proliferated after Benjamin Day launched the *New York Sun* as a penny paper in 1833, but in Britain the so-called 'tax on knowledge' kept cover prices high and circulation figures low. The number of new titles was correspondingly small. In the United States newspaper printers joined the wagon trains and often set up shop in the new western townships before a sheriff had been elected. In Britain some of the large new industrial cities did not have a daily paper. Apart from the efforts of the Walter family and *The Times*, there was also little advance in printing techniques.

Another reason for the slow development was that while the American press played an essential role in the democratic process, most British proprietors shared the Establishment view that the working classes, which the 1832 Reform Bill had excluded from the extended franchise, were of little interest. At a time when there was a desperate need for crusading journalists, the newspapers addressed themselves to the concerns of their middle- and upper-middle-class readers.

Britain was creating the modern world as we now know it. Internal change was occurring at an unprecedented rate, and *laisssez-faire* ruled almost as shamelessly as it was to do in the United States in the second half of the century. Men such as the statesman and economist Richard Cobden (1804– 65), known as the 'Apostle of Free Trade', opposed the first tentative factory laws in the name of free enterprise, and saw nothing wrong in small children working 13 hours a day under dreadful conditions. In the early years the new industrial cities were administered as if they were still medieval domains. For instance, in the Midlands as late as 1873, the city of Birmingham was one vast slum with open sewers, 20,000 middens, polluted water and 48,000 back-to-back houses.

Visitors to these shores, such as the French writer Alexis de Tocqueville and Friedrich Engels, Karl Marx's collaborator, were appalled by what they saw; but generally speaking the London press did not see. Except for a few radical weeklies, such conditions were only reported if and when they were debated in Parliament.

But for the stamp tax, the complaisance of such newspapers as there were would have been surprising for another reason. Britain was approaching its industrial and imperial zenith. It was becoming the workshop of the world because of the new industrialists and entrepreneurs – the cotton men in Manchester, the metal-bashers in Birmingham and the shipbuilders and engineers on the Clyde and elsewhere. De Tocqueville compared them to Americans; they would try their hand at anything to make money, but the stamp tax made them shy away from newspapers. Only *The Times* made the kind of money that could attract them, and The Thunderer remained unique.

The debilitating effect of the stamp tax was exposed in 1836 when it was reduced to one penny. Within a few years the *News of the World, Lloyd's Weekly News* and *Reynolds News* appeared on the scene and there was little that James Gordon Bennett's *New York Herald*, then one year old, could have taught them. Largely devoted to crime, sex and sports, the *News of the World* was soon selling 100,000 copies and *Lloyd's* became the first paper in the world to achieve a weekly sale of one million. They were a portent of things to come, and when the Stamp Act was finally repealed in 1855, morning papers selling for only one or two pennies sprang up in provincial cities almost overnight. Among them was the *Manchester Guardian*, which had begun as a radical weekly and become progressively more moderate; but the most significant newcomer was the London-based *Daily Telegraph*.

The established daily press had remained largely untouched by these developments. Modelled on *The Times* but without its resources, they continued to be dull, stodgy and relatively expensive. They published political news, long reports of parliamentary debates, foreign dispatches and very little else until the *Telegraph* got into its stride. First sold as the *Daily Telegraph and Courier* in 1855 for twopence, it got into debt and was taken over by its printer, Joseph Moses Levy. He halved the price, and within a few years was selling more copies than all the other London papers combined.

Levy and his son Edward were accused of lowering standards by copying American methods. It is true that they shared with the *New York Herald* the news rights of Stanley's expedition to find Dr Livingstone in deepest, darkest Africa – one of the best stunts in newspaper history – but the Sundays such as the *News of the World* had already demonstrated that British journalists did not have much to learn from their American colleagues. If they needed a model they had only to look back to the London papers of the previous century before the stamp tax and the new morality had smothered the native genius for popular journalism. In any case, apart from introducing larger headlines the *Telegraph* was a very English paper and owned by a family who wanted to join the Establishment.

However, Levy's concept of a newspaper 'for the million' was American in that his penny paper helped to democratize the London press. *The Times* reluctantly reduced its cover price to threepence in 1861, when the paper duties were also repealed. It could have been sold for less, but chose to remain the newspaper for top people. (This fateful decision was to lead to its eventual decline, but one hundred years later it was still boasting that top people read *The Times*.) Fortunately Levy did not make a similar mistake; and when artisans living in parliamentary boroughs were given household suffrage in 1867 the *Telegraph* and other penny papers were available to help them understand what was going on in Parliament and the world generally. This immensely important development had of course begun much earlier in the United States.

Levy's son Edward (1833–1916), later 1st Lord Burnham, became a Christian and assumed the additional surname of Lawson, following his uncle Lionel Lawson's will. He was also determined to educate and entertain as well as inform, employing some colourful writers, and pursuing progressive policies. The paper later swung to the right, but the formula he devised still stands the paper in good stead: competent and comprehensive reports of home and foreign news without embellishment, and due regard and plenty of space for crime and sex stories. He also popularized book, music and dramatic criticism and introduced fashion articles.

By the 1880s the *Telegraph* had one of the highest daily circulations in the world, but remained a serious and readable newspaper. Levy-Lawson could have become a man of considerable power and influence, but the first of the press barons to be ennobled – the Walter family remained commoners despite the prestige of *The Times* – was apparently not interested. Although he may have been content to be a lord, he was probably just a good professional journalist and businessman. His eldest son, Harry Lawson (1862–1933), later the 2nd Lord Burnham, became the sole director of the newspaper on his father's retirement in 1903 and was similarly modest and level-headed. He served in Parliament and on the old London County Council, and was mayor of Stepney, one of its poorer boroughs. He was also chairman or member of numerous committees, and is best remembered for the Burnham scales which decide the salaries of schoolteachers.

Not all the new press barons were so modest. W.T. Stead (1849–1912), the editor of the *Pall Mall Gazette* from 1883 to 1889, probably did not know what the word meant, although he was the son of a Congregationalist minister and deeply religious. One of Britain's greatest popular journalists, he declared that an editor could – and should – exercise as much political power as a Cabinet Minister. James Gordon Bennett had said as much 50 years earlier, but Stead was not, like him, a megalomaniac. By all accounts, he was one of those extraordinary Victorians born with limitless confidence, energy and righteousness. Old photographs show him looking like an Old Testament prophet. Contemporary reports acknowledge that behind the blazing eyes and full beard was a man with immense sexual drive. It certainly influenced his journalism; commenting on the Bulgarian atrocities which incensed Gladstone and other

Liberal leaders, he wrote that: 'the keen sense of female honour is a more potent force to arouse men to generous action than any massacre . . . the honour of Bulgarian virgins is in the custody of the English voter'.

Stead first went to work at the age of 14, as an office boy to a Newcastle merchant, and within two years he had an editorial on the assassination of President Lincoln published in a local paper. He continued to write regularly for the *Darlington Northern Echo* without payment until he was offered the job of editor and £150 a year. He was only 22, and sought the advice of Wemyss Reid, who was then the editor of the *Leeds Mercury*. Reid recalled that Stead did most of the talking and that there were many times – before dawn finally brought the conversation to an end – when he thought the young man was mad:

> I recognized my visitor from the first as a man with remarkable gifts, of
> something that came near to genius. I recognized, too, his honesty
> and sincerity, though I had, even then, forebodings as to what might be the
> consequences of his impetuous ardour and reckless defiance of old
> customs and conventions.

Stead saw the *Echo* as a pulpit, and very quickly his fiery sermons had more to say about national and international issues than local affairs. He also sent copies of his articles to political and religious leaders, and many responded. One of them, the 4th Earl Grey, the statesman and later governor-general of Canada, remarked that this provincial editor of an obscure paper was corresponding with kings and emperors and receiving long letters from statesmen of every nation. An exaggeration, but apparently it was Gladstone, then a newly-elected Member of Parliament, who in 1880 suggested that he should be offered the assistant editorship of the now radical *Pall Mall Gazette*. In 1833, within three years of joining the *PMG*, as it was known, Stead was appointed editor.

In retrospect 1883 was a vintage year for Anglo-American journalism. Joseph Pulitzer returned to New York from St Louis and bought the *New York World*. He was already the successful proprietor of the *St Louis Post-Dispatch* and was about to make the *World* New York's largest-selling newspaper. Stead was still an employee, and the *PMG* was only one of London's many evening newspapers and appealed to a limited audience of cultivated middle-class readers. The two men and their newspapers could not have been more different, but together they were to create 'the New Journalism' and transform the press on both sides of the Atlantic.

The New Journalism, because of the profound effect it had upon the press on both sides of the Atlantic, was easier to recognize than to define. Matthew Arnold, the nineteenth-century poet and essayist, who was probably the first to use the term, correctly connected it with the extension of democracy, but went on to write:

> It has much to recommend it; it is full of ability, novelty, variety, sensation, sympathy, generous instincts; its one great fault is that it is featherbrained. It throws out assertions at a venture because it wishes them to be true, does not correct either them or itself, if they are false; and to get at the state of things as they truly are seems to feel no concern whatever.

That says more about British middle-class arrogance than the New Journalism, and Frank Mott, the American newspaper historian, was naturally less censorious. He saw it as a formula for successful newspapers which included good news coverage and editorials, more pages, illustrations and promotion. As far as it goes that describes what Pulitzer did to the *New York World*, but for Stead it mainly meant journalism with a mission. Raymond Schults, his biographer, wrote that Stead's crusades demonstrated how a newspaper could create and for at least a brief period sustain interest in a cause. In other words, newspapers could dictate the public agenda to some extent, and this explained much of the power wielded by Stead and the press barons who came after.

Stead's first campaign was against the horrors of slum housing. Initially based on Andrew Mearn's pamphlet, *The Bitter Outcry of Outcast London*, Stead wrote with passion of the filth, immorality and brutality of slum life: 'These fever dens are said to be the best-paying property in London, and owners who, if justice were done, would be on the treadmill, are drawing 50 to 60 per cent on investments in tenement property in the slums.' He also attacked the Church and Parliament who, he said, had done little or nothing about the country's greatest problem. Stead kept the campaign going for weeks until a Royal Commission was formed to report on the dwellings of the poor.

The Bitter Outcry campaign was the first of its kind in Britain, and Stead claimed that the establishment of the Royal Commission was a great victory for the *PMG* and the New Journalism. He claimed too much; some worthy people in and out of Parliament had been trying to do something about slums for years, but the campaign did attract wide attention. The public indignation aroused probably prevented the Opposition from defeating the Housing of the Working Classes Act of 1890. Not that Stead was given any credit. Hugh Kingsmill, the novelist and biographer, said that 'his daily paper was, beyond everything else, the means by which he could unremittingly assuage, though never satiate, his passion for creating an emotional situation between himself and the public'.

Stead was accused of adopting what were thought to be detestable American methods when he enlivened the *PMG* with multi-decker headlines, cross-heads, illustrations and signed articles; and his interviews shocked the old guard in Fleet Street for reasons which remain obscure. James Gordon Bennett had published the first-known interview in question-and-answer form many years earlier (a style revived in this century by *US News and World Report*). Other American editors had recognized its merits, as had British foreign correspondents (the reputation of the great Henri de Blowitz of *The Times* had, for example, been enhanced by his interview with Bismarck at the time of the 1878 Treaty of Berlin) but it had never been adopted in Britain. Stead persisted despite the criticism, and his interview with General Charles Gordon changed the course of history. It was a textbook example, although one that has been ignored by many students of journalism, of how the press can shape events even against official opposition.

Peace in Egypt and Sudan was vital to Britain because the two countries straddled its direct line of communication with India. This explained Disraeli's purchase of shares in the Suez Canal Company in 1875. This extraordinary coup – the Prime Minister borrowed £4 million from the Rothschilds without the prior sanction of Parliament to buy 177,000 shares – was regretted by Gladstone, then leader of the Opposition. His fear that it would lead to political and military involvement in the Middle East was soon realized when he was returned to power in 1880. Egypt was in chaos, the Mahdi had launched a religious uprising in Sudan and destroyed an Egyptian army led by a British officer. Gladstone was reluctant to intervene but recognized that Britain had a moral obligation to evacuate the remaining Egyptian garrisons. This was the situation when Stead interviewed Gordon in January 1884.

The two men were similar. Both were deeply religious; in modern terms Gordon was a born-again Christian and had recently spent months in Palestine communing with his evangelical God. Both were self-confident Victorians who believed that they were destined to re-order the world for the greater glory of God and Great Britain. Chinese Gordon, as he was known after long service in China, where he first helped to capture Peking and sack the Winter Palace and then suppressed a rebellion against the imperial government, was larger than life. If Hollywood made a movie about his adventures, critics would dismiss it as romantic nonsense. He was a knight errant, albeit with a drink problem, and although a British regular officer he had roamed the world doing good, as he saw it, in the service of other governments. Apart from China, the Crimea and the Balkans, he had served the Egyptian Khedive (the viceroy of Egypt under Ottoman suzerainty) as Governor-General of Sudan. He had just accepted the invitation of the King of the Belgians to administer the Congo when Stead heard that he was passing through Southampton and seized his opportunity for an interview.

Gordon said that the garrison in Khartoum, the Sudanese capital, could not be evacuated because of the lack of transport. He told Stead: 'You must either surrender absolutely to the Mahdi or defend Khartoum at all hazards.' This would not be difficult, and if the city was held the rebel forces would disintegrate. Gordon also thought that British troops could be withdrawn from Egypt if the Khedive was persuaded to institute reforms. The Egyptians and Sudanese were tired of misrule and corruption. Gordon said he had taught the

Sudanese something about liberty and justice, and it was in Britain's interest to help. He concluded by saying that he did not want to embarrass the government, but if there was anything he could do he would be available.

Stead knew he had a scoop, and hurried back to London and splashed the interview. Commenting that Gordon's views conflicted with those in high quarters, he wrote that Khartoum must be relieved. If Egypt could not do it, and if British troops were not to be sent, the only answer was to send Gordon. This was followed a few days later with a long article entitled 'How to Save the Khartoum Garrison', which analysed the military, political and logistical problems. His readers were assured that 'if General Gordon were in command in the Sudan he would solve the difficulty'.

Stead was on a winner. Gordon was a popular hero, a gallant soldier but also a fervent Christian and a leader of the anti-slavery movement. He appeared to be promising the relief of Khartoum and an early withdrawal of British troops from Egypt once he had transformed the Khedive into an eastern version of the good Mr Gladstone. He therefore appealed to the imperialists and Little Englanders, the Church Militant and the radicals who believed that Britain had a civilizing mission in the world. Stead was not cynical; depending upon his mood he could assume most of these roles, but he planned his campaign carefully and it was taken up by other newspapers. *The Times* also went along, but more cautiously. It was probably better-informed than Sir Evelyn Baring, the British proconsul in Cairo, because it had a special correspondent (later killed in action) sending dispatches from the beleaguered city itself.

The press clamour nevertheless split the Cabinet. The reluctant Gladstone sought the advice of Baring, who was cool to the idea; but the Prime Minister, a regular reader of the *PMG*, felt that he could no longer resist the weight of public opinion aroused by Stead. Gordon was ordered to Khartoum, and a triumphant Stead wrote: 'The whole Egyptian question has been revolutionized in an hour. At yesterday's informal meeting of ministers at the War Office there was taken one of those decisive steps that make or mar the destinies of empires.'

The assumption – indeed, conviction – that one man could save Khartoum, and then once and for all solve the Egyptian Question, was wildly romantic, and in retrospect absurd; and of course it ended in disaster. Gordon had underestimated the strength and fervour of the Mahdi's forces, which besieged Khartoum soon after his arrival. The dispatch of the relief column was delayed in part because of his optimistic reports, and when the troops finally arrived in January 1885 they found that the city had been overrun two days earlier and that Gordon had been killed and decapitated. An epitaph was provided by Slatin Pasha (who had served in Egypt under Gordon), then a prisoner of the Mahdi. When shown Gordon's head, he is reported to have said: 'What of it? A brave soldier who fell at his post. Happy is he to have fallen, his sufferings are over.'

Gordon apparently agreed. He wrote before his death that he was happy and had tried to do his duty.

For Stead, it was a great story and for the first incomplete account he gave a five-decker headline:

TOO LATE!
KHARTOUM CAPTURED BY THE MAHDI
THE FATE OF GENERAL GORDON UNKNOWN
SIR CHARLES WILSON TWO DAYS LATE
THE STEAMERS WRECKED ON THE NILE

He went on in subsequent issues of the *PMG* to demand that Gordon's death be avenged by extinguishing the Mahdi's uprising. Revenge was eventually taken at Omdurman, but as a consequence Britain became deeply involved and as the senior member of the Anglo–Egyptian Condominium ruled the Sudan until its independence in 1953. This was the last thing the British government had wanted before sending Gordon to Khartoum.

To that extent Stead, the former 'provincial editor of an obscure paper', changed the course of British imperial history. He was much resented at the time. The *London Echo*, a radical paper edited by Passmore Edwards, attacked the *PMG* 'which arrogates to itself the right to order ministers about as though they were so many schoolboys'; and sourly added: 'We do not suppose that ministers, weak as they have become, have been throughout the most humble, obedient servants of the *Pall Mall Gazette*; but they certainly on more than one occasion have taken that course, which it demanded they should adopt.'

It was not quite like that, some members of the Cabinet being ardent imperialists, but Stead had no doubt that it was his doing. He afterwards claimed that he ran the Empire from Northumberland Street, where the *PMG* was published. He explained 'my reason for sending Gordon to Khartoum', and claimed that 'I not only said so, but I was obeyed.' An impartial observer, R.H. Gretton, in his *Modern History of the English People,* said that it was: 'probably the first occasion on which a newspaper set itself, by acting as the organizer of opinion on a particular detail of policy, to change a government's mind at high speed'. Baring, who probably knew Gladstone's views on the Middle East better than any man, also blamed the *PMG* for the Gordon expedition.

In terms of causes won, Stead was probably a more potent press baron than the formidable William Randolph Hearst (see Chapter 5). Stead campaigned successfully for a larger navy, although again he had supporters in the government. He advocated an imperial federation but did not live to see the formal establishment of the Commonwealth. He urged the expansion of the Empire and recognition of Britain's responsibilities in South Africa. Alfred Milner, who was Stead's assistant editor for many years, was in 1897 appointed High Commissioner for South Africa. Stead was also willing to help worthy causes, and despite these and other successes is best remembered for his campaign to raise the age of consent for girls from 13 to 16.

There was certainly need for reform. Behind its respectable Victorian façade, London could be an evil place. Young girls were sold by their parents or abducted by procurers to work in brothels frequented by wealthy men and young blades. Others were sold overseas. (Sir) Benjamin Scott, the social reformer, had persuaded the government to introduce preventive legislation; the Criminal Law Amendment Bill was passed by the House of Lords but had been met with apathy and hostility in the Commons. Scott asked Stead to help, and after making inquiries he decided to shame the lower house into taking action.

With his Special Commission of reporters (incidentally Hearst was also to describe his men in Cuba as commissioners) Stead set to work interviewing scores of active and retired procurers, pimps, prostitutes, social workers and former policemen. They provided most of the evidence for the campaign which he headlined as 'The Maiden Tribute of Modern Babylon'. He also bought a young girl from her mother for £5. Eliza Armstrong, who was only 13, had her virginity attested by a midwife. This was standard practice apparently, as was the chloroform provided to make the seduction or rape easier. She was then taken to a brothel bedroom, which Stead briefly visited, and the next morning handed over to the Salvation Army.

The way Stead ran the campaign (in July 1885) still impresses editors of popular newspapers. In an announcement in a Saturday issue, much underlined for emphasis, he said that the *PMG* was to publish the report of a special and secret commission of inquiry into those areas of sexual criminality that the Criminal Law Amendment Bill had been drafted to repress. The intention was to prevent another suppression of the Bill. He added that those who were squeamish, prudish or preferred to live in a fool's paradise: 'of imaginary innocence and purity, selfishly oblivious of the horrible realities which torment those whose lives are passed in the London Inferno, will do well not to read the *Pall Mall Gazette* of Monday and the following days'.

The five instalments had cross-heads such as 'The Violation of Virgins', 'The Confessions of a London Brothel-Keeper', 'How Girls are Bought and Ruined', 'The Forcing of Unwilling Maids', 'I Order Five Virgins' and 'Delivered for Seduction'. Understandably, they were a sensation and the *PMG*'s offices were mobbed every evening by hundreds of people anxious to read the next instalment. Demand outran supply, and old copies were resold at inflated prices. Stead was attacked by rival newspapers which claimed to be outraged, but not by the ecclesiastic press. Church of England, Roman Catholic and Non-Conformist weeklies supported him, and the *Methodist Times* said that Stead had done what 'Jesus Christ Himself would have done in his place'. Lord Shaftesbury, the 7th Earl and great philanthropist, called for the early enactment of the Criminal Law Amendment act designed to protect young girls.

Most Members of Parliament were furious, but anticipating charges of exaggeration and invention Stead had requested the Archbishop of Canterbury, the Roman Catholic Cardinal Archbishop of Westminster, the Lord Mayor of London and other dignitaries to pass judgment on his revelations. Known as the Mansion House Committee because it met in the Lord Mayor's official residence, it reported that they were substantially true. The Bill, which apart from raising the age of consent had other provisions to protect young girls, was enacted in the summer of 1885. Stead had won a famous victory, but a price had to be paid. Mrs Armstrong who had sold her daughter to Stead's agent for £5 applied for the return of her child. Stead and others involved in the campaign were charged and found guilty of abduction. Stead was harangued by the judge, who said that he was a disgrace to journalism, and sentenced to three months' imprisonment.

Stead served his term in the old first division (where well-to-do prisoners were confined), which meant that he wore his own clothes, received friends and colleagues and edited the *PMG* from his cell. He enjoyed his martyrdom and the continuing debate on the 'Maiden Tribute' campaign. Members of Parliament were reluctant to admit that he had made them debate and pass the Bill, but not *The Times*. It concluded that: 'whatever may be thought of his methods, it cannot be denied that his crusade did, in fact, carry the Criminal Law Amendment Act and give impetus to international efforts towards checking the "white-slave trade".'

So much attention may have turned Stead's head because in the following year he expounded his theory of government by journalism in the *Contemporary Review*. Many of his readers must have thought he had become a megalomaniac, like Bennett before him, when he argued that government by the House of Commons was becoming out of date. The telegraph and the printing press had resurrected the days of the Anglo-Saxon Witan, the early style of parliamentary council when the entire community was within hearing and could participate in governmental discussion. The growth of the press indicated the extent to which the nation was taking into its own hands the direct management and control of its own affairs. Once elected, the Member of Parliament left his constituency and plunged into a new and different world, but: 'the editor must live among the people whose opinions he essays to express . . . [his] mandate is renewed day by day, and his electors register their vote by a voluntary payment of the daily pence'.

Stead was not suffering from megalomania; instead, he was arguing that the press had a larger role to play in the life of the nation than politicians were prepared to admit. The journalist was a watchman, and the libel laws should be modified to give newspapers greater liberty to publish the truth. The editor and his assistants should have access to all Cabinet Ministers, and be able to ascertain their views within 24 hours. His representative in the House of Commons should be able to determine the opinions of all Members of Parliament, and his staff should have a close association with people at all levels of society at home and abroad. He admitted that much of this was utopian, but believed that the men and women who served his ideal newspaper would be enrolled in 'the greatest spiritual and educational and governing agency which England has yet seen'.

This theory was not altogether utopian for Stead because he had been an admirer of the Lord Protector of England – Oliver Cromwell – since a boy, and he saw his staff as 'men who put a conscience to their work'. They were his New Model Army. Indeed, some of his ideas were too Cromwellian for nineteenth-century Britain, but his ideal newspaper was a dream because he was an employee who could be dismissed at any time. Henry Thompson, who owned the *PMG*, had given him remarkable editorial freedom and Stead continued to campaign against injustice after his release from prison. But some of the campaigns were not popular, and offended readers and advertisers, and by 1890 the two men had agreed to part. There was no mention in the *PMG* of Stead's departure.

He moved to start his own *Review of Reviews*, and continued to delight and infuriate readers until he was lost in the *Titanic* disaster. Admiral Lord Fisher (quoted by F. Whyte in his *Life of W.T. Stead*) wrote:

> The loss of dear old Stead numbs me. Cromwell and Martin Luther rolled into one. The telegrams here say he was to the forefront with the women and children, putting them in the boats. I can see him, and probably singing 'Hallelujah', encouraging the ship band to play cheerfully. He told me he would die in his boots. So he has. And a fine death.

It was certainly a fittingly sensational departure for one of the greatest and most colourful journalists ever to have worked in Fleet Street or elsewhere. (Sir) George Newnes, who first discovered with his publication of *Tit-Bits* the vast new readership spawned by the 1870 Education Act, once told Stead: 'There is one kind of journalism which directs the affairs of nations. It makes and unmakes cabinets. It upsets governments, builds up navies and does many other great things. It is magnificent. That is your journalism.' It was, indeed.

PULITZER AND HEARST

The Associated Press was founded in 1848 by six New York newspapers which wanted to share the cost of gathering out-of-town news and transmitting it by telegraph. Newspapers all across the country eventually became members, which made the AP the largest and most efficient news-gathering organization in the United States. It was also the first newspaper body to define objectivity. Lawrence Gobright, its Washington correspondent, wrote: 'My business is to communicate facts. My instructions do not allow me to make any comment on the facts. My dispatches are sent to papers of all manner of politics. I therefore confine myself to what I consider legitimate news and try to be truthful and impartial.'

His definition was simplistic. What are facts? What is truth: beauty as Keats had it or a straight report of the words of a dissembling politician? Gobright's approach won the confidence of President Lincoln, whose Gettysburg Address might not have survived but for the AP. The Unitarian clergyman and statesman Edward Everett, a well-known windbag and one-time Minister to Great Britain, was the main speaker at the consecration of the Gettysburg war cemetery in 1863, but the local AP man asked Lincoln for his notes of what were intended to be concluding remarks, and the rest was truly history. Gobright also established standards for brevity and caution which were subsequently adopted by all Western news agencies. On 14 April 1865 he wired: 'The President was shot in a theatre tonight and perhaps mortally wounded.' More than 80 years later when Gandhi was shot, the Reuters correspondent in New Delhi, Doon Campbell, wired: 'Gandhi shot, worst feared.'

The AP was the first to apply modern news-gathering techniques to war. Its numerous correspondents covered every front in the Civil War, but were not always commended by the generals for objective reporting. When General Sherman heard that three of them were missing after the battle of Vicksburg, he said: 'We'll have dispatches from Hell before breakfast.' Nothing is known of what General Custer thought of Mark Kellog, the AP man who also fell while covering the battle of Little Big Horn.

The AP's coverage was so comprehensive that its service was indispensable for any self-respecting newspaper publisher, but it was a cooperative and only member-newspapers had access. AP members understandably tried to prevent rivals from sharing this cornucopia of low-cost news. This situation provided an opening for a Hungarian–Jewish immigrant who was to become one of the great press barons. Joseph Pulitzer, a young and impecunious journalist, bought for a song the St Louis-based *Staats-Zeitung*, a dying German-language paper which was a member of the AP cooperative, and sold it for $20,000 to a publisher who desperately wanted membership.

Joseph Pulitzer (1847–1911) had come to the United States in 1864 after being recruited by Union agents who in the last years of the Civil War roamed Europe looking for likely young men willing to fight in exchange for American citizenship and a bounty. Pulitzer came from a well-to-do family and had always wanted to be a soldier. He had even tried to join the French Foreign Legion, but had been rejected because of poor eyesight. For all his enthusiasm, he was not a good soldier, but fortunately the war came to an end before he could do any harm to himself or his comrades.

He had little money and less English – his regiment was made up of German-Americans – and migrated to St Louis because it had a large German community. He worked on riverboats and as a teamster before joining the Deutsche Gesellschaft. This was a self-help group, typical of the many ethnic organizations formed to take care of immigrants, and the man who ran it was Carl Schurz, his old regimental commander-turned politician and journalist. In 1868 Schurz found him a job on the German-language *Westliche Post* as a reporter. He proved to be a natural journalist and the appreciative proprietor sold him some stock, but Pulitzer was more attracted by politics. He was elected as a Republican member of the state legislature, and achieved some kind of fame by shooting and wounding a prominent lobbyist. He was only fined $105 (causing grievous bodily harm to lobbyists was not apparently a heinous crime in Missouri at the time), and went to work for Horace Greeley at the *New York Tribune* during the 1872 presidential campaign. As previously mentioned, Greeley, as Liberal Republican and Democratic candidate, was defeated by the Republican incumbent, President Ulysses Grant.

At this stage Pulitzer bought and sold the *Staats-Zeitung,* and took time off to read law and improve his English. He also joined the Democratic party, and was a delegate to the Missouri constitutional convention, where he proved to be an excellent public speaker in English and German. Soon afterwards he married a Southern belle, Kate Davis, a distant relative of Jefferson Davis, the former Confederate President; she was somewhat put out when she discovered on the honeymoon that he was Jewish. Still undecided whether he wanted to be a politician or a journalist, in 1878 he bought another worthless paper with AP membership, the *St Louis Dispatch*, for $2500. The proprietor of the *Post* badly wanted to join AP, but this time Pulitzer did not sell. Instead, the two papers were amalgamated and the *Post-Dispatch* became an instant success.

One reason for the paper's popularity was that Pulitzer was still very much a politician, which made him a crusading editor. He cared more about clean streets and chasing riverboat gamblers out of town than national and international news. He assailed political and municipal corruption, and was twice attacked by political enemies or their hirelings. Such assaults were an occupational hazard and many editors boasted about them in their columns as proof of their journalistic and physical virility, but not John Cockerill, the deputy editor of the *Post-Dispatch*. When an outraged lawyer threatened to horsewhip him Cockerill shot him dead. Again there was no arrest, the coroner deciding that it was an affair between gentlemen, but readers took exception and sales dropped alarmingly. Pulitzer, still smarting from his defeat in a congressional election, decided that he had had enough of the Wild West. Leaving the *Post-Dispatch* in Cockerill's capable if trigger-happy hands, he departed to seek his fortune in New York.

Newspaper competition was intense when Pulitzer arrived in 1883, and the only title available was the loss-making *New York World*. It belonged to Jay Gould, one of America's most notorious 'robber barons'. He was a railroad magnate who had made a vast fortune by exploiting the Western farmers' dependency on his railway to move their grain to the ports and cities. He had been found guilty of fraudulent stock trading to the tune of $5 million, but this had not prevented him from taking over the Union Pacific. He controlled 10,000 miles of track when he unloaded the *World* on Pulitzer. The price was $346,000, which was more than Pulitzer could afford or the paper was worth. The circulation was down to 15,000 copies a day, but Pulitzer was eager to begin as soon as possible, and arranged to pay in instalments.

One must assume that Pulitzer resented such daylight robbery, and that it strengthened his natural inclination to expose what he saw as public evil and abuse. Certainly his true colours were quickly nailed to the *World*'s masthead. An announcement said that he was opposed to the 'aristocracy of money' and that the *World* would be the organ of the true aristocracy – 'the aristocracy of labour'. It would fight for the man who supported his family in respectability by honest, earnest toil; the man who fought his way through life courageously, maintaining his good name through privation and temptation, and won his children's respect and love. A ten-point programme was next announced: the government should tax luxuries, inheritances, large incomes, monopolies and privileged corporations; impose a tariff for revenue (graduated income tax), reform the civil service, and punish corrupt officers, vote-buying and employers who coerced their employees in elections.

His populist programme was well received, and for reasons which should have been obvious to other crusading editors. During the post-Civil War period of immense economic growth, the American social and political system was based on industrial property rights to a degree greater than was ever the case in Europe. The new proletariat of Britain's Industrial Revolution was grossly exploited, but the government was not run exclusively for the benefit of industrialists. *Noblesse oblige* had not disappeared entirely. No such tradition existed in the United States; instead, industrial freeholding was the foundation of the social system. The industrialists and other robber barons – the title was apposite – also took advantage of Constitutional loopholes with the approval of the US Supreme Court. For judges and lawyers the Fifth and Fourteenth Amendments were significantly different from Magna Carta. The latter secured the rights of all free men; the Amendments the rights of all persons, and the Court accepted that in law persons could be real or fictitious, an unemployed labourer or a gigantic corporation.

This reading of the Constitution created legal immunities for corporations, and established a basic inequality between individuals and corporate persons of wealth, economic power and political influence. It thus caused great misery for millions of ordinary Americans and as Charles Beard, the historian and educator, wrote on 'Corporations and Natural Rights' in the *Virginia Quarterly Review* (1936):

> If corporations cannot provide employment for the millions of the American proletariat – for such we have, in spite of the claptrap to the contrary – can corporate persons expect to protect themselves forever, through constitutional and judicial processes, against the distresses and distempers of natural persons twisting and turning in their search for the rights of life, liberty and property declared in the American creed?

These were Pulitzer's sentiments, but before embarking on a crusade he first had to win readers and advertisers in order to pay the instalments to Gould. His approach became the model for most future publishers and editors who took over ailing newspapers. He fired most of the editorial staff, hired his rivals' best journalists, brought in his own men – including Cockerill from St Louis – and sensationalized the news. He also created news by running campaigns and organizing stunts. The people of France had commissioned Auguste Bartholdi to carve the Statue of Liberty, but it languished in boxes at a French port until the *World* ran a campaign to raise the $100,000 needed to build the pedestal on Bedloe's Island in New York harbour. His star reporter, Nellie Bly, sailed from New York in 1889 to beat the record of Phineas Fogg, the hero of Jules Verne's *Around the World in Eighty Days* (published some 16 years earlier). On the final lap from San Francisco the *World* brought her back in a special train. Her time was 72 days, 6 hours, 11 minutes and 14 seconds.

The *World* also pioneered newspaper illustration, first with single-column woodcuts and eventually with half-tone blocks. Political cartoons became a daily feature and the Sunday edition was given a comics section. All this was sugar on the pill to help his readers swallow the medicine he thought the nation required. This included investigative reporting of the New York Central Railroad, the Standard Oil Company, the Bell Telephone monopoly, the white slave traffic, and contractors who built dangerous tenement buildings.

Pulitzer was prepared to spend money on news-gathering at home and abroad, and the *World* became well informed and internationally-minded. The editorial page was recognized as a platform for liberal America. To that extent the paper ceased to be the organ of the working classes, but it continued to take care of their interests. A staff of 35 doctors also ran a free medical service, and coal and turkeys were given to the poor at Christmas. It was loyal to Democratic principles; Grover Cleveland said that he would not have been elected president without its support, but the paper was not beholden to the party. Pulitzer was determined to raise the standards of public life, and his paper became the scourge of Tammany Hall bosses and other such corrupt politicians. Named after a Red Indian chief, Tammany Hall was the head-quarters of the Democratic party in New York City. It helped immigrants by providing jobs and helping them when they got into trouble but in return the immigrants were expected to vote for the party. Guaranteed this enormous bloc vote, the bosses ran the city and inevitably became corrupt. They survived long after Pulitzer because presidential candidates needed their support. No other paper spoke out more vigorously against government by and for the privileged and the 'money power'. Prohibition was opposed in the name of individual liberty, and a lonely battle was fought against the annexation of the Philippines, Hawaii and the Virgin Islands.

Pulitzer's commercial success was phenomenal. The circulation of the *World* steadily increased until by 1898, at the time of the war with Spain, it was almost 1,500,000 copies a day – a hundredfold increase in 15 years. The evening and Sunday editions also sold well as did the *Post-Dispatch*. Pulitzer became a multi-millionaire, the first of the press barons to do so, and he lived like one. He had three very large residences in the United States and another in the South of France. His ocean-going yacht was probably the largest afloat.

The press had come a long way since the first penny papers were launched 50 years earlier, in part because of technical progress: cheap and improved newsprint, the Hoe web-fed quadruple press which was capable of printing 24,000 sixteen-page papers an hour, Ottmar Mergenthaler's Linotype machine and photo-engraving. Urban growth had created the ideal market for mass-circulation newspapers, and was revolutionizing their style and content. Immigration provided an ever-increasing flood of new readers – 17,729,563 immigrants arrived in the three decades of Pulitzer's control of the *World* – and newspaper language was further simplified for their benefit.

To attract customers who bought their papers at news stands, the first page became the front page as we know it today. Large headlines clamoured for attention, and more white space helped display. Pictures also relieved the grey columns of text, first woodcuts and then half-tone blocks. Reading in crowded streetcars and the 'El' (the elevated railway cars that used to run at rooftop level through the streets) demanded shorter and livelier stories with the main news condensed in the first paragraph. More space was given to sport and entertainment, and as ever crime was extensively covered. More important, reporting in most newspapers became more objective for fear that blatant partisanship would offend potential readers. It also reflected a subtle but fundamental change.

The days when men such as James Gordon Bennett and Horace Greeley could indulge their megalomania or pursue personal political objectives were by no means over as William Randolph Hearst was to prove; but as newspapers expanded from four to 16 pages the average reader gave less attention to editorials. The news columns became politically more influential because expanded staffs could report what was said and done in Washington, Albany, City Hall and Tammany. This development was not clearly understood by many newspaper proprietors; and even today, especially in Britain, politicians still attach greater importance to newspaper editorials than to the news columns. But Theodore Roosevelt was quick to grasp the significance when he succeeded to the presidency in 1901 after the assassination of William McKinley. He had hardly moved his family into the White House when he called in the chief Washington correspondents of the Associated Press and other agencies, and said that he would keep them informed and would always be available. Regular presidential press conferences were not held until after Woodrow Wilson's Inauguration in 1913, but Roosevelt ensured that White House stories flowed into the country's newspaper offices every day. To that extent the power of their proprietors was undermined.

The dominance of news over opinion also led to a dichotomy of editorial control. In Britain the editor remained responsible for the entire contents of the paper, and generally devoted a great deal of time to the editorials; in the United States the *managing* editor became responsible for news and the *editorial-page* editor, the junior partner, for opinion.

Demographic and technical change did not altogether explain the outstanding success of the *World*. Other newspapers enjoyed their benefits and tried to exploit them, but the genius of Pulitzer made it a great and innovating newspaper. The *Dictionary of American Biography* says: 'Its courage was boundless, especially in its complete freedom from advertising domination. Indeed, it would be impossible to measure the great influence of the *World* upon the political life and the press of the country after it abandoned its career of sensationalism and vulgarity.'

There have been very few press barons so highly praised and respected during and after their lifetime. The young Alfred Harmsworth (later Lord Northcliffe) came from London to learn from the master, and was allowed to bring out a special edition of the *World*. His methods were studied and copied, but Pulitzer was unique; and despite the 50 years which separated the launch of Bennett's *Herald* and Pulitzer's *World* a comparison of the two men is illuminating.

Bennett and Pulitzer had much in common. Both were immigrants, although this was to prove not unusual among press barons. (Beaverbrook, Thomson and Murdoch were immigrants to Britain, if from Commonwealth countries; Northcliffe was born in Ireland.) Both were well-educated by the standards of the time, and interested in the arts. Both were born journalists and radical liberals. Whether or not one explains the other, they were probably better journalists because of their radicalism. Both were completely devoted to their newspapers. Even when Pulitzer went blind and was suffering from nervous exhaustion, he still ran the *World* with the enthusiasm of a cub reporter. He had a team of secretaries, most of them English, who were his eyes and ears. He could be brutal to his staff if their work did not come up to his exacting standards, but perhaps it was the only way a blind man could maintain control.

Unlike Greeley, both were content to be journalists. Pulitzer had been attracted to politics, and in his early days might well have become a politician. He ran twice for Congress, the second time successfully (in 1885), but his heart was not in it. He spent more time in the Washington office of the *World* than in the House of Representatives, and resigned within the year.

The two men differed in that while Bennett became pathologically suspicious of established authority and persuaded himself that the country could best be run by newspapers, Pulitzer had a clear and sober understanding of the relationship between government and the press. He believed with Bennett that the press was no less indispensable, but acccepted that it had separate functions and responsibilities. Unlike John Delane of the London *Times*, he did not seek the company of those who ran the country. He neither wanted to share the confidences of politicians nor help to formulate policies. He did not aspire to the role of *éminence grise*.

Pulitzer's personal aloofness and professional impartiality both strengthened and narrowed the influence of the *World*. Its influence stemmed from impartial reporting of events and developments that politicians and others were reluctant to make public, and by reflecting public opinion. Even in its campaigns against the trusts, or monopolies, Pulitzer insisted that both sides should be heard. The *World* was more influential than its rivals because Pulitzer understood the functions of a free press.

His concern for professional standards eventually led him to establish the Pulitzer Prizes for various categories of newspaper work in the fields of fiction, drama, history, biography, poetry and music. He also endowed the school of journalism at Columbia University, where he defined the higher functions of a newspaper: 'Above knowledge, above news, above intelligence, the heart and soul of a paper lies in its moral sense, in its courage, its integrity, its humanity, its sympathy for the oppressed, its independence, its devotion to the public welfare, its anxiety to render public service.'

Pulitzer tried to live up to these ideals, but never forgot that he had to sell

[65]

newspapers; hence the lively stories to attract customers who rode trolleys and the 'El' to work. In this way he was the creator of modern popular journalism, or the New Journalism as it was called. He also believed in making profits, and when his handsome returns from the *World* were threatened by a newcomer he did not hesitate to stoop to conquer. The struggle which followed was hardly ethical, but it made newspaper history.

The newcomer, William Randolph Hearst (1863–1951), was destined to give press barons a bad name. He was an enigma, a split personality; in the words of his biographer, W.A. Swanberg, a Prospero and a Caliban. Swanberg illustrated this by writing two obituaries to describe the two selves, and they have not been bettered. He said that one would have to be decidedly unflattering:

Spoiled as a child, he never reached emotional maturity in eighty-eight years. He spent his life trying to gratify his overwhelming passions for wealth, power and position. Truth and principle seldom bothered him. His venomous attacks on those in office reflected his own envy and frustration. While he spoke piously of ideals in journalism, he left no gutter unexplored. He pushed the United States into war with Spain, sought to do the same in Mexico, but howled against wars that did not have his authorization. An immoralist, he assailed immorality in others. Aloof, driving, ruthless, he terrorized his own executives. In the depression, when Americans were starving, he squandered millions in self-indulgence and had the nerve to complain of taxes. When crossed, he could wallow in a blind rage. Selfish, arrogant, distrustful of others, he thought himself so indispensable that he clung to the reins of his empire until death stiffened his fingers.

But the other obituary would show a different man:
Heir to millions, he had the character to choose work over idle luxury. He had many of the winning traits of a child. Shy, excessively courteous, he was so sentimentally soft-hearted as to be almost womanly. The kindnesses he performed for friends and employees were innumerable. He could show the same concern for humanity in the abstract. His sympathies were so aroused by the plight of the Cubans that he insisted on saving them. He was so indignant at the exploitation of the common people that he became their defender against privilege. He never sat on the fence. He proved his patriotism by taking strong stands on issues which could not benefit him personally and in some cases lost him money and popularity. In one love he was true and devoted for more than thirty years. Wonderfully optimistic, he was also superlative in his sense of humour. He loved to do things for others, and many who received his bounty at his castles, on his yachts or on his group excursions to Europe and Mexico, still cherish his memory. He was tolerant of all religions. No miser, he believed in spending his money, keeping it in circulation, paying good salaries. He stood stoutly behind his

editors and reporters, and if his executives feared him, they nevertheless venerated him. Gentleness and consideration were a part of his indefinable charm. Two of his warmest admirers were his valet of a quarter-century, George Thompson, and his horticulturist for thirty years, Nigel Keep. During the minute of silence when the presses stopped, thousands of Hearst employees knew that a titan had passed whose like would never be seen again.

Hearst was the pampered son of a Californian prospector who had struck it rich. He was expelled from Harvard for playing an obscene joke against members of the faculty, but not before serving as the business manager of the university's satirical magazine, *Lampoon*. This gave him a taste for journalism, and he studied newspapers in Boston and New York before persuading his father to give him the *San Francisco Examiner* in 1887. His father had acquired it for political purposes – he had been a US senator – which probably explained its failure to attract readers and make a profit. The younger Hearst changed all that. He took Pulitzer's *World* as his model and that paper's Sam Chamberlain as his managing editor – but the new paper's ethics were all his own. News was invented or distorted with a panache which surprised and delighted the citizens of what was still a frontier city, and within two years the paper was paying for itself.

San Francisco may be every American's favourite second city, but it was too small for Hearst. With a gift of $7,500,000 from his widowed mother, and with the knowledge that more was to come eventually, he paid off the prostitute he had been living with and headed for New York. His ambition was to own a newspaper which would more than rival the *World*, and he bought the loss-making *Morning Journal* which had once been owned by Pulitzer's younger brother, Albert. There can be no doubt that he had a talent for sensational journalism, but more important at that time he had a lot of money and was willing to spend it on the paper. He hired the brightest journalists he could find and at whatever price they demanded, including Stephen Crane, author of the classic *The Red Badge of Courage* (1895), and other *World* writers. He bought the entire staff of its Sunday edition, which with its coloured comics section was very profitable. Pulitzer got them back briefly by offering them more but Hearst raised his bids and the *World* lost them for ever.

Pulitzer discovered a good replacement for his Sunday editor in Arthur Brisbane and paid him $200 a week, but he, too, was hijacked by Hearst, who eventually raised his salary to $260,000 a year. This was the equivalent of a declaration of war, and at first Pulitzer was ill-placed to defend himself. He had cut the cover price of his morning paper from two cents to one in order to compete with the *Journal*, had lost advertisers when advertisement rates were raised, and was barely covering costs. Hearst was a formidable opponent. His lurid journalism was capturing the lower end of the market, and he was prepared to lose millions of dollars to defeat Pulitzer.

Hearst sent Mark Twain to London to cover Queen Victoria's Diamond Jubilee, and organized two expeditions to the Klondike when gold was discovered. He also emerged, to Pulitzer's surprise, as a crusader. He even championed strikers, which was unusual in those days; and supported the populist leader known as 'The Commoner', William Jennings Bryan, for the Democratic presidential nomination. Much of this was good for circulation, but it was generally conceded that his sympathy for the underdog was sincere and that he was devoted to the Democratic party. Winston Churchill remembered him as a Liberal.

Hearst also loved newspapers, and like Pulitzer, Greeley and Bennett spent more time in the office than most employers. He often returned to the *Journal* building after midnight, in evening dress and with an actress on each arm, and remade the front page just as the paper was due to be put to bed. Despite his enthusiasm, which was catching, his editors began to realize that there was an element in his character of the poor rich kid who wanted to be amused. He had to be the centre of attention and was prepared to manufacture news if necessary. He was undisciplined, and lacked any sense of news standards and priorities. He even planned to send a squad of reporters to Devil's Island to release Dreyfus, the Jewish French army officer wrongly imprisoned for betraying his country, but was distracted by an unusually bloody murder case. His reporters investigated the case, detected the murderers and triumphantly handed them over to the police.

Such swashbuckling operations and lavish salaries and expenses attracted to the paper young adventurers who normally would not have gone into journalism. Some of them were graduates, recently down from an Ivy League college and anxious to see the world on an expense account before settling down in their fathers' businesses. They were not required to know anything about journalism, or politics and economics for that matter. It was sufficient that they were prepared to do anything and go anywhere, and they were ideal recruits for Hearst's personal war with Spain.

Cuba was then a restive Spanish colony, and the nationalists who had fled to the United States had won some sympathy for their cause. Hearst had genuinely supported them in the *San Francisco Examiner*, but the incipient insurrection (of 1895) had dragged on too long to be a good story. Moreover, Hearst was preoccupied with the murder case that had made him forget poor Dreyfus, and there were other more immediate stories. For example, there was the row with his well-to-do neighbours who objected to the tramps and other derelicts who hung about in the street waiting for his soup kitchen to open. Another began when the police raided a fashionable restaurant and surprised some leading citizens watching 'indecently exposed' belly dancers.

Theodore Roosevelt was reported to have been invited, although this was hotly denied. These stories all made splendid copy, and Hearst was enjoying himself when Sylvester Scovel, the *World*'s special correspondent in Havana, was arrested by the Spanish authorities. Pulitzer ran a 'Free Scovel' campaign which brought Cuba back into the news and sold newspapers. Hearst was incensed, and began what was to be the most infamous campaign of his long career.

He had long been determined to have a circulation war with Pulitzer, and Cuba was seen to be the best battleground whatever the cost. Frederick Remington, who was famous for his paintings of the Wild West, was dispatched to Cuba with Richard Harding Davis as an illustrator-and-writer team. They were given the grandiose title of 'commissioners' and paid $3000 a month each. A young Yale graduate was hired to run arms to the insurgents and present their leader with a gold sword. Reinforcements were sent to Key West in Florida to hire a fleet of fast boats to ferry arms and medical supplies to the island. Sam Chamberlain was appointed generalissimo, and Hearst held a 'War Cabinet' every day.

The expense was enormous, but his men in Cuba could not find the insurrection. They stayed in Havana's best hotel and interviewed Cubans who claimed to have witnessed clashes between the insurgents and Spanish troops. Washington had proclaimed a policy of neutrality and non-intervention and American gunboats prevented the *Journal*'s fleet from leaving Key West. They could not prevent their crews from fabricating stories about hostilities. Their fiction filled the *Journal* but there was nothing for Remington to draw. It was at this stage when the following exchange of telegrams was said to have taken place:

HEARST JOURNAL NEW YORK
EVERYTHING IS QUIET THERE IS NO TROUBLE HERE THERE WILL BE NO WAR WISH TO RETURN REMINGTON

REMINGTON HAVANA
PLEASE REMAIN YOU FURNISH THE PICTURES AND I'LL FURNISH THE WAR HEARST

Hearst did his best by publishing more fabricated reports of Spanish atrocities. He also organized a worldwide appeal for the release of an imprisoned daughter of a rebel leader, and at least 200,000 signatures were obtained in Britain alone. The appeal was a great success in that it increased circulation, but perhaps afraid that Spain would submit and grant clemency, Hearst decided that the lady should be rescued. One of his best reporters, Karl Decker, bribed prison guards to look the other way while he conducted Señorita Cisneros from her quarters, but his story was much more dramatic.

The headlines shouted:

EVANGELINA CISNEROS RESCUED BY THE JOURNAL
An American Newspaper Accomplishes at a Single Stroke What the Best Efforts of Diplomacy Failed Utterly to Bring About in Many Months.

The greatest journalistic coup of the age, the story said, was a feat equalled only by the rescue of Mary, Queen of Scots.

Despite Hearst's efforts, Frank Mott suggests in his book *American Journalism* that there would have been no Spanish–American war if Hearst had not challenged Pulitzer to a circulation war at the same time. Certainly Pulitzer, whose memories of the Civil War inclined him towards pacifism, joined in the campaign because he was losing circulation. He withdrew his best correspondent from Cuba because his reports were objective, and published unsubstantiated stories such as 'Spanish soldiers habitually cut off the ears of the Cuba dead and retain them as trophies.' The *World* also announced that Nellie Bly, the reporter who had gone round the world in 72 days, was to recruit and lead a regiment of Amazons to fight for Cuban independence.

The two press barons continued their campaigns against Spain and each other until an unexplained explosion aboard the USS *Maine* sank the warship in Havana harbour in 1898, which in the heated atmosphere generated by them made war inevitable. Hearst was overjoyed, and went off to cover the Spanish–American War. He proved to be a good war correspondent, but the best account of his activities was given by James Creelman, one of his correspondents, who was wounded in the fighting near El Caney:

> Some one knelt in the grass beside me and put his hand on my fevered head. Opening my eyes, I saw Mr Hearst, the proprietor of the *New York Journal*, a straw hat with a bright ribbon on his head, a revolver in his belt, and a pencil and note-book in his hand. The man who had provoked the war had come to see the result with his own eyes and, finding one of his own correspondents prostrate, was doing the work himself. Slowly he took down my story of the fight. Again and again the tinging of Mauser bullets interrupted. But he seemed unmoved. The battle had to be reported somehow. 'I'm sorry you're hurt, but' – and his face was radiant with enthusiasm – 'wasn't it a splendid fight? We must beat every paper in the world.'

Much of the mythology about the power of press barons stemmed from the campaigns of Hearst and Pulitzer to involve the United States in the Cuban insurrection. Hearst is remembered as the guilty man, but arguably Pulitzer's behaviour was more despicable. Hearst was very young – 35 when the *Maine* was sunk – and according to his editors intellectually immature. There is no real evidence that the telegrams between him and Remington were actually exchanged. They could have been inventions like so much of the copy written by his correspondents. Pulitzer was the older man, experienced, a pacifist and an editor who espoused responsible journalism. While Hearst believed passionately in Cuban independence, Pulitzer's only motive was to defend the circulation of his newspapers.

Their campaigns were infamous because they invented rather than reported news, but how much they were responsible for American intervention is another matter. The combined circulation of their newspapers was nearly three million at the height of the campaigns – each producing several editions every day – and their stories were carried by the AP and reprinted in papers across the country. There can be no doubt that they helped to generate a national mood which made the prospect of war acceptable to most Americans, but there was already widespread support for Cuban independence. Theodore Roosevelt questioned President McKinley's manhood because he was reluctant to involve the country, and when war came led his Rough Riders into battle at San Juan Hill (a vain-glorious little episode that did not hurt him when he became president).

No less important, the Monroe Doctrine (opposing the interference of foreign powers in the American continent) had conditioned American thinking for generations, and anti-colonialism was an article of faith especially when United States interests were involved. After the Cuban intervention Richard Olney, the Secretary of State, said: 'The United States is practically sovereign on this continent, and its fiat is law upon those subjects to which it confines its interposition.' The Platt Amendment, a rider to the 1901 Army Appropriations Bill, provided for intervention in Cuban affairs and practically made the island an American protectorate. That rider was still the official American attitude to Cuba when President Kennedy supported the invasion of the island in 1961.

When he ran for public office, Hearst discovered that he did not wield great political power. He served two terms in the House of Representatives (1903–07), but was an inactive member and succeeded only in offending powerful Democratic Congressmen. He was nevertheless determined to become president, and the extension of his chain of newspapers was in part dictated by this ambition. He ran a bad second at the Democratic National Convention in 1904, losing to a lacklustre candidate; and was also defeated when he ran for mayor of New York and governor of the state. He supported the presidential candidates of the Independence party in 1908, and they did so badly that they won fewer popular votes than Eugene Debs, the Socialist candidate. His final bid for public office, again for mayor of New York in the following year, was equally disastrous.

Hearst must have been mystified by these defeats. Nearly everybody agreed that he was a personable candidate, better looking than most and a good public speaker once he had conquered his shyness. He was no less sincere in his electoral campaigns against the monopolies and his concern for the condition of the working classes than he was in his support for Cuban independence. He campaigned against Tammany in the New York mayoralty elections, and wrote the platform for the Independence party. Its planks included federal control of the monopolies, an eight-hour working day, nationalization of railways, the creation of a federal Department of Labour, the election of US Senators and a big navy. His publication during that campaign of letters proving that Standard Oil had many federal and state politicians on its payroll drew praise from President Theodore Roosevelt and led to legislation requiring publication of campaign contributions.

The policies he espoused commanded wide public support and with the help of his newspapers he should have done very much better in politics than he did. His biographer Swanberg concluded that the electorate had little or no respect for his integrity. He was also too impatient and could not cooperate with others: 'Of these qualities the great egotist had almost nothing. In any organization or movement he was connected with, he had to rule – absolutely.'

Many Americans were also shocked by the violence of his opinions, and may well have believed that he was responsible for the assassination of President McKinley. He was not; the demented assassin, Leon Czolgosz, confessed that he had been inspired – if that is the word – by a lecture given by Emma Goldman, the anarchist. However, when assailing McKinley as the tool of the trusts the *Journal* had editorialized that: 'if bad institutions and bad men can be got rid of only by killing, then the killing must be done'. And when William Goebel, an obscure Kentucky politician, was killed in an election brawl, the following quatrain was published:

The bullet that pierced Goebel's breast
Cannot be found in all the West;
Good reason, it is speeding here
To stretch McKinley on his bier.

To be fair, at the turn of the century the United States was still a frontier country although the physical Western frontier was assumed to have been occupied and pacified by the 1880s. The robber barons – oil, railroad, meat-packing and other tycoons striving to establish monopolies come what may – were still behaving like so many medieval barons in Britain before the Tudors imposed some kind of centralized and accountable control. The early trade unionists, the Chartist refugees from Britain and the socialists from eastern Europe were outside the law and were killed or beaten up by company police as well as by official law-enforcement officers. The Supreme Court's *Plessy* v. *Ferguson* decision had established the doctrine of 'separate but equal' which in effect condemned blacks to peonage (servitude) and second-class citizenship without recourse to the law. New York, Chicago, Memphis, St

Louis and Los Angeles were in many ways more lawless than the so-called Wild West. Almost anything went as long as the robber barons, major and minor, could corrupt and use politicians and the law as freely and recklessly as the Western gun-slingers had used their Colts and Winchesters a few years before. Compared with the Astors, Vanderbilts, Goulds, Morgans and other barons, Hearst had some kind of social conscience and patriotism. He fought the monopolies, or trusts, even when his Boston newspaper was almost ruined by their withdrawal of advertising and their refusal to carry copies on the railroad.

That said, Hearst was the creature of his age, and his wealth and absolute control of his publishing empire fed his egomania. At the height of his power he owned 43 daily and Sunday newspapers representing about 15 per cent of national circulation. King Features Syndicate gave him access to most other American papers, and he owned 13 major magazines, eight radio stations, three news services and two film companies. No other man before or since has controlled so many such enterprises. Presidents and politicians treated him with respect, even when they hated his guts. His editors treated him as an oracle, and did his bidding unquestioningly although it became increasingly erratic and eccentric.

He was pro-German during the First World War, and employed a Berlin correspondent who was in the pay of the Germans. In 1918 he urged the immediate recognition of the Soviet Union, 'the most democratic government in Europe.' In 1932 he helped to elect Franklin Roosevelt, who anxious for his support had promised through an intermediary to legislate much of the platform Hearst had written for the defunct Independence party. Their honeymoon did not last long; Hearst accused the President of being a wild-eyed radical and virtual dictator before the end of his first term, and turned to Europe where he saw much to admire in Mussolini, the Italian dictator who was ridding himself of political opposition with 'rubber truncheons and castor oil'. He interviewed Hitler in Berlin, and convinced himself that he had persuaded the Nazi leader to stop persecuting Jews. But on his return to New York, he said: 'Thank Heaven for one thing. The nation which has shown the greatest return towards prosperity is England. And England is very definitely a democracy.'

Finally convinced that he did not have a political future and perhaps bored with running his newspapers, which he had been doing for more decades than he cared to remember, Hearst gave increasing attention to his art treasures and real estate. Among other holdings, he had inherited more than 250,000 acres (over 390 square miles) mid way between Los Angeles and San Francisco. It included 50 miles of shoreline with one of the few safe anchorages between the two cities, and a hill on which Hearst built a castle looking like a northern Spanish cathedral and which he called San Simeon. This extraordinary pile, surrounded by lesser but still magnificent buildings, terraces and a classical pool which any Roman emperor would have envied, was designed to house one of the world's largest personal art collections. Marion Davies, a former Ziegfeld Follies showgirl, was installed as the chatelaine of San Simeon.

By this time Hearst was going rapidly downhill. Even his enormous fortune could not sustain his regal style of living and the endless buying of antiques and art during the Depression, and in 1937 control of his chief holding company was assigned to a trustee. Part of his collection of antique furniture, paintings and tapestries was sold in department stores, but he recovered financially during the Second World War. The film *Citizen Kane,* made by Orson Welles in 1940, gave a not unsympathetic if exaggerated version of his decline – the aging titan left with nothing but his millions, his castle, and the once-vivacious showgirl doing jigsaw puzzles and sipping gin to pass the time.

Hearst died in 1951 leaving a personal estate of $59,500,000. He is best remembered as the creator of yellow journalism, so-called because during the circulation war between the *Journal* and the *World* both papers carried coloured cartoons with a yellow dog as their hero. Said one of Hearst's men:

> Your true yellow journalist can work himself into quite as fiery a fever of enthusiasm over a Christmas fund or a squalid murder, as over a war or a presidential campaign. He sees everything through magnifying glasses and can make a first-page sensation out of a story a more sober paper would dismiss with a paragraph inside.

According to his biographer Swanberg:

> . . . in the strict sense, the Hearst papers were not newspapers at all. They were printed entertainment and excitement – the equivalent in newsprint of bombs exploding, bands blaring, firecrackers popping, victims screaming, flags waving, cannons roaring, houris dancing, and smoke rising from the singed flesh of executed criminals.

That description of yellow journalism is itself a fine example of the writing demanded by Hearst, and it will be recognized as such by readers of today's popular press. It has won peerages and knighthoods for its British proprietors and editors, and with some reason. Behind the screaming headlines and the cheesecake most of them publish as much hard news as is given on extended television news programmes, and some can boast of their crusading and investigative journalism. To that extent they defend the interests of their working-class readers.

Similarly with Hearst as well as Pulitzer. Much of the latter's ten-point programme and the Independence party's platform, which contained most of Hearst's editorial objectives, subsequently became law. They might not have been wholly responsible, but their crusading was almost certainly a major influence. Although Hearst never achieved the political power he craved, by the end of their lives, he and Pulitzer could boast that they had achieved more than most politicians.

NORTHCLIFFE AND ROTHERMERE

There was never any question as to the choice of a career for Alfred Charles Harmsworth (1865–1922), the 1st and only Viscount Northcliffe, the creator of Britain's modern popular journalism. To use a German prefix – as in Goethe's *Urmensch* (archetypal man) – because there is no other way of describing him, Northcliffe was an Ur-journalist, an original destined for Fleet Street long before he was old enough to make an objective choice. He was given a toy printing set when a small boy, and launched a school magazine at the age of 13. He had a compulsion to acquire, and pass on, information. He loved news-papers as other men love women (although he loved them too) and was steeped in the history of journalism. He lived to control the largest-ever concentration of newspapers and magazines.

Lord Salisbury, the Prime Minister and Foreign Secretary, sneered that his newspapers were written by office boys for office boys. Winston Churchill wrote of him that:

> He wielded power without official responsibility, enjoyed secret knowledge without the general view and disturbed the fortunes of national leaders without being willing to bear their burdens. Thus a swaying force, uncertain, capricious, essentially personal, potent alike for good and evil, claiming to make or mar public men, to sustain or discipline commanders, to shape policies and to fashion or overthrow governments, introduced itself in the absence of all parliamentary correctives into the conduct of the [First World] war.

More of Churchill's so-called parliamentary correctives are mentioned later on, but apart from Salisbury's aristocratic snobbery Northcliffe (who was not ennobled until 1917) emerges from most contemporary judgments, including that of Churchill, as the archetypal press baron – one of the baddies. Geoffrey Dawson (editor of *The Times* from 1912 to 1919 and 1923 to 1941) who knew him well thought differently and did not regard him as much of a political force either for good or evil.

Dawson said that Northcliffe's real claim to fame was that he was a consummate journalist who changed the whole course of British journalism. He was endowed to a pre-eminent degree with two of the journalist's essential qualities: an intense interest in everything that was happening around him and an uncanny prescience of what was likely to attract the public. That was the true secret of his success, although he did enter journalism at a peculiarly favourable moment. He owed something of his style to American newspapers, which he studied incessantly, and particularly to the methods of Joseph Pulitzer; but his impact on British journalism was due mainly to his own qualities. He woke it up and made it come alive.

That may sound unfair to W.T. Stead, but the *Pall Mall Gazette* never sold more than 12,250 copies a day, even when running the 'Maiden Tribute' campaign against prostitution, whereas Northcliffe's papers sold in millions. As Francis Williams wrote, the *PMG* and other journals of its kind, so elegant and influential, were only: 'the bloom of a hot-house plant. The tragedy of that time – if tragedy indeed it was – lies not in the Northcliffe revolution but in the *trahison des clercs* that allowed it so easy and so complete a victory.' In other words 'betrayal by the intellectuals' – those alert and cultivated nineteenth-century London editors made no attempt to communicate with the masses.

Dawson who had small reason to be grateful to him, also said that Northcliffe had made British journalism prosperous. The great fortune he accumulated for himself was reflected throughout the newspaper world. The prizes of journalism were multiplied a hundredfold. Salaries and wages were raised to scales which were unknown in Fleet Street before his arrival. For the first time journalism took rank with the recognized professions in the range of opportunities it offered to young men. The best and most enduring monument of Northcliffe's life's work was the final demolition of Grub Street.

But there was another side to the picture, Dawson added, in the vast amalgamations of newspaper interests and the dictatorial habits of their proprietors, for which the Chief – as Northcliffe demanded to be known – set the example. It was a new experience for the working journalist that some legitimate difference of opinion with his employers might mean his permanent exclusion from a whole series of allied publications. Nor was it to the national advantage that a number of independent provincial newspapers, each with its individual point of view, should be crushed out in the process of expanding publishing empires. But these developments, which began with Northcliffe, reached their climax after his death.

This extraordinary man, born near Dublin, was the first of ten surviving children of an impecunious schoolmaster, Alfred Harmsworth Sr, who soon afterwards moved to London to read for the Bar. He died when the future Lord Northcliffe was still in his teens, which meant that the youngster became the family breadwinner. He reported for the *Hampstead & Highgate Express*, a North London weekly (whose editor had earlier given him that toy printing set), wrote cricket articles for the *Telegraph* and other national dailies, and edited a cycling magazine. Within a few years he was writing editorials, long ones for two guineas (£2 and ten pence) and half-price for shorts. He afterwards said: 'I could turn my hand to anything as every capable journalist should be able to do.' In 1888, at the age of 23, he launched a weekly magazine entitled *Answers to Correspondents on Every Subject under the Sun*, which was soon reduced to *Answers*. Its success explained a great deal about Northcliffe and his early times.

Answers was not the first magazine of its kind; indeed, Northcliffe for all his greatness was not an innovative journalist. He modelled it on *Tit-Bits*, the brainchild of Sir George Newnes (1851–1910) which had been founded some seven years earlier. It was Newnes who told Stead of the *Pall Mall Gazette* that his – Stead's – kind of journalism directed the affairs of nations, made and unmade Cabinets etc. but, Newnes had added:

> . . . There is another kind of journalism which has no great ambitions. It is content to plod on, year after year, giving wholesome and harmless entertainment to crowds of hard-working people craving for a little fun and amusement. It is quite humble and unpretentious. That is my journalism.

It was also Northcliffe's.

Tit-Bits contained 16 pages and sold for a penny, and its contents were well described by its earlier title, *Tit-Bits from all the Most Interesting Books, Periodicals and Newspapers of the World*. It was a ragbag of bits of information which earned its proprietor a fortune. Northcliffe's *Answers* was similar; apart from answering readers' questions, it provided nuggets of information on subjects as varied as strange medical practices and the building of railways, and jokes and short profiles of famous people appeared regularly. But Northcliffe differed fundamentally from Newnes. The latter was a shrewd businessman who happened to stumble upon a good thing and made the most of it – he was earlier a representative of a fancy-goods firm – but Northcliffe indulged his craving for information; any kind of information, from Queen Victoria's height (4 foot 10 inches) to the colour of Mr Gladstone's socks (red).

Their success could not be entirely explained by the 1870 Education Act, which in making elementary education compulsory created a vast potential readership. It was essential to the success of the *Daily Mail* (1896) and other halfpenny newspapers which came afterwards, but the large circulations of Sunday newspapers such as the *News of the World* launched much earlier – in 1843 – indicated that the conventional press had long ignored literate men and women who were not very interested in the affairs of government. The Sundays were of course sensational newspapers, and *Answers* and *Tit-Bits* were family magazines. Their popularity was not to be despised.

Northcliffe and Newnes were contemporaries of H.G. Wells, and the readership they served was lovingly described in his novels of lower middle-class life such as *Kipps*, published in 1905. That young man and many more like him grew up in a world without radio, films or television; most of them were oblivious of politics despite the extension of the franchise. Politics was for toffs, or had they known it for earnest artisans who read *The Times* and the *Telegraph* as well as radical weeklies in working-class clubs. They came from homes without books except perhaps for the Bible. They knew or felt that they were living in a changing world, their own condition and modest aspirations were evidence of that, and in an age of invention. Many were eager to read a paper, if it was cheap enough, which could satisfy their curiosity of what was happening beyond their street, corner shop or office. Both *Answers* and *Tit-Bits* did just that; or to put it another way, Northcliffe and Newnes did for the emerging lower middle-class what Barnes and Delane had earlier done for the new middle class.

Northcliffe did it better because he instinctively understood his readers. Not that his mother, Geraldine Harmsworth, saw her brood as lower middle-class. A strong-minded Ulsterwoman, well-read and a talented musician, she had middle-class standards and boundless ambition for her children. Nevertheless, the family had been brought up in genteel poverty, the father had been a failure professionally and would have died happier in Dublin's publand, and the children were sent to cheap private schools. Wells, who taught in one of them, said that these schools failed to give their pupils a coherent outlook and dispatched them as 'irresponsible adventurers into an uncharted scramble for life'. Perhaps, but one of Northcliffe's biographers, A.P. Ryan, said that he remained true to his cheerful suburban background, and what interested him most was what interested people with the same lower-middle-class background.

Northcliffe prospered but was desperately over-worked, and his mother insisted that his brother Harold (the future 1st Lord Rothermere) leave his Civil Service job to help him. Harold Harmsworth (1868–1940) was not a born journalist but a good businessman who became a financial genius. Together, in 1890, they launched a string of magazines such as *Comic Cuts* and *Home Chat*, and then some four years later bought the moribund *Evening News* for £23,000. Northcliffe made it London's largest-selling evening paper within a year.

Northcliffe was now rich, and splurged some of his wealth on large cars and the first of many fine houses for his wife, but he was already thinking of launching a daily newspaper the like of which Britain had never seen. He was convinced that a cheap daily, not a penny but a halfpenny paper, would sell if it could be a kind of *Answers* plus news. Although still apolitical, he believed that the prime function of a newspaper was to provide comprehensive news coverage; but knew that his lower-middle-class readers would have to be amused and instructed. His reading of the American press and his own experience also told him that all its news stories would have to be short and written in plain English.

Whether or not he realized the potential political influence of a mass-circulation newspaper, Northcliffe's reading of newspaper history had persuaded him that politicians must be regarded as adversaries if its independence was to be preserved. This he never forgot, and remained a non-party man to the end. He was no less dedicated to planning; market surveys were unknown in those days, and apart from his sixth sense he had little to go on. The new paper was therefore given 60 dummy runs – that is 60 issues were written and made-up before the first copies hit the street.

Launched on 4 May 1896, the *Daily Mail* was an instant success. Nearly 400,000 copies were sold on the first day, and four years later after he had built a second printing plant in Manchester, the circulation almost reached one million. It was now Northcliffe's turn to claim the world's largest net sale, an achievement all the more remarkable because the *Mail* was not a 'yellow' sheet. He was not another Hearst. Perhaps because of his mother, that formidable lady with whom he kept in touch one way or another every day of his life, and certainly because he understood his lower-middle-class readers, the *Mail* was not a sensational newspaper. It carried its fair share of crime stories, but no sex stories. He used cross-heads and illustrations as did his American mentors, but the front page carried advertisements instead of screaming headlines. It was a respectable-looking newspaper which his aspiring readers could peruse without embarrassment in trains and buses; and the short, snappy features, the women's page and serial story – Northcliffe was rightly convinced that a good serial would make readers want to read the next instalment – and his serials were always suitable reading for the family in the evening.

The success of the *Mail* reflected social change in Britain, and it was the portent of a newspaper revolution which was to have significant social and political consequences. These can best be established by comparing the British and American press then and now. In the United States, the press generally developed a universal readership – that is, most newspapers appealed to and were read by men and women of all social classes and income groups. In Britain, the press divided into two broad groups, the 'quality' and the 'popular' papers, with further subdivisions for the more specific class and political differences.

Apart from Northcliffe, there were numerous reasons for this. The United States was and remains a relatively classless society. Americans moving up the social ladder invariably discover class and snobbish traps, all the nastier because they are not apparent to the unwary, but broadly speaking the country is a socially-relaxed democracy. As for the American press, after a slow start it developed very quickly. In the first half of the nineteenth century the socially prominent in New York were reluctant to admit that they read James Gordon Bennett's *Herald*, but times and the *New York Herald* changed. By the time Northcliffe's *Mail* first appeared most American newspapers enjoyed, or hoped to enjoy, a universal readership. Thereafter because of mergers and takeovers readers had little choice. At the time of writing, New Yorkers can either read their *Times* or the *News* or *Post*. Most cities now have only one newspaper, and there is no national press. Even the *New York Times* is a regional newspaper. This is slowly changing as the *Wall Street Journal* and the *New York Times* take advantage of facsimile printing, but the vast majority of American newspapers must have a universal appeal – they have to run comic strips as well as syndicated columnists and the Associated Press information if they are to prosper.

In Britain, as we have seen, newspaper development was retarded by the stamp tax, and although the *Telegraph* began as a kind of universal newspaper, an English penny was worth more than an American cent and it gradually moved up-market. Little or no attempt was made to cater for the majority of Britons until the *Mail* was launched. It greatly extended newspaper readership, but by aiming at the lower middle-class Northcliffe began the social division or stratification of the British press. It might have been difficult to avoid in any event because of the class structure, but Northcliffe made it inevitable.

The process of stratification was encouraged and made possible because, compared to sub-continental America, Britain is a tight little island. If London and Glasgow were as far distant from each other as New York and Los Angeles, the national press with its sharp divisions would be impossible. Fortunately or otherwise, Northcliffe, who as editor of *Answers* had published more than one story on how railways were run, realized that newspaper trains could deliver a national newspaper printed in London to Glasgow and the smallest village in the kingdom, and before breakfast. This permitted him and subsequent proprietors and editors to aim at specific social, income and political groups: *The Times* at its alleged top people, the *Manchester Guardian* at the left-of-centre and the 'socially aware', and the *Sun* despite its Tory populism largely at the apolitical who want something to read and cheesecake to look at when travelling to work.

The stratification of the press in Britain has been regretted, but after many years of reading American provincial papers I am not so sure it is a bad thing. Apart from about half a dozen metropolitan dailies, I cannot remember reading an American paper which kept me informed or strove for high intellectual standards. Their very universality condemned them to mediocrity. British readers at least have a choice of ten national newspapers. The quality papers, including the Sundays, are very good, and the tabloids should not be disparaged as they so often are. For instance, the *Daily Mirror* carries shrewd and honest editorials, a couple of the best columnists in the business, and more essential news than the extended television news programmes of the British Broadcasting Corporation and Independent Television. They also sell regularly to the types of people who in the United States rarely read a newspaper, a fact quickly proved by comparing the audited circulation figures of the two countries.

Northcliffe was not very interested in politics when he launched the *Mail*, but his revolution also led to the British press becoming more overtly political. Historians can argue with good reason that this development only revived a very old tradition, but the Left complains that the British press is largely controlled by the Right. At first sight there is a lack of balance – and to a degree – of choice but readers do not have to buy the *Telegraph* or the *Sun* instead of the *Guardian* or the *Mirror*. There is nothing to prevent them from reading the *Morning Star*, the communist paper, or *Labour Weekly*. That very few of them do suggests that the British majority are either conservative or do not take their newspapers seriously. There can be no other explanation, apart from the dreary earnestness and ideological shrillness of most left-wing journals. As Stead of the *Pall Mall Gazette* remarked, an editor's mandate is renewed day by day when 'his electors register their vote by a voluntary payment of the daily pence'.

Northcliffe also began the commercialization of the British press. To quote the 1949 Royal Commission on the Press, before he arrived in Fleet Street newspapers were private or family properties valued 'for the prestige and the political and social influence their possession conferred rather than as a source of dividends.' Northcliffe was not then particularly interested in prestige, political and social influence or dividends, he just loved newspapers. The *Mail*, however, was the first paper to become a public company (in 1905) offering shares as a commercial proposition. Perhaps commercialism would have occurred in Britain without Northcliffe (although it was not as sweeping in France and Germany), but growing literacy, the Hoe rotary press and the Linotype machine (America's greatest contribution to popular journalism), and consumer advertising made newspapers an attractive investment for the first time in Britain. It was a growth industry, and being first in the field Northcliffe was able to expand to an extent that would not now be permitted in Britain or the United States under the anti-monopoly and anti-trust laws.

Within a few years, the brothers Northcliffe and Rothermere owned – apart from the *Mail* and the *Evening News* – *The Times*, the *Observer*, the *Daily Mirror*, the *Weekly Dispatch*, the *Continental Daily Mail* (published in Paris) and some provincial newspapers. This list of titles may not sound impressive when compared with subsequent newspaper chains, but most of them were national newspapers. They were bought or read by about half of the population. Their newly-formed company, Amalgamated Press Limited, also published a host of magazines aimed at all classes and giving good value for money. Some of the best writers, including H. G. Wells, Joseph Conrad, Arthur Conan Doyle, O. Henry and Stephen Leacock, were regularly published; as were leading politicians such as Winston Churchill and the Lords Birkenhead and Fisher. Largely on the initiative of Rothermere, the brothers also acquired a tract of land in Newfoundland larger than the state of Massachusetts, and created a vast pulp and newsprint business. As Francis Williams said: 'There has never been a newspaper empire like it; never in the history of journalism a career quite like his.'

Northcliffe was said to have been hungry for power from the beginning; the evidence being that as a young man he tried on Napoleon's hat at Fontainebleau and, as he expected, found that it fitted him. It seems flimsy evidence, and the memoirs of friends and colleagues recalled that at first he was relatively unaffected by his accruing wealth and potential power. He was remembered as a handsome and engaging young man, who enjoyed life and affluence but with little of the ostentatiousness of the newly rich. He was well-liked, and women loved him. He was said to have had a Bohemian love of ease and a natural simplicity; that he had something of Prince Hal's fondness for the society of his inferiors; and that he remained a schoolboy well into adult life, poking fun at the pompous and old-fashioned. But for all his love of life, he was first and foremost a newspaperman.

Northcliffe was capable of expending enormous energy on his newspapers. For instance, after launching the *Mail* he went home and slept for 22 hours before being awakened by an alarmed servant. His mental and physical exhaustion were such that he would have slept longer. Equally demanding was the launch of the *Mirror* in 1903, his first and only flop despite the £100,000 spent on advance publicity. It was conceived as a paper written by women for women, a very modern idea, but the lady journalists were a refined lot with little or no newspaper experience. Within a year the circulation dropped from 400,000 to 40,000 and he reluctantly got rid of the women and re-launched the paper as a halfpenny for working-class readers. Words of one syllable were used wherever possible, but the *Mirror* was only saved when he made it a picture paper. One of his editors had been using the new half-tone blocks on a flat-bed press, and suggested that they could be developed for rotary presses. Northcliffe gave him a rotary to play with, and after many expensive experiments the first daily picture tabloid was published. It was a huge success and a spectacular money-maker.

Northcliffe soon became rich beyond the dreams of most men, but he did not follow Pulitzer's example and buy an ocean-going yacht. Nor did he build a fantasy castle, as did Hearst. Instead, he continued to work harder than any of his editors, and the constant toil and bouts of frenetic activity gradually wore down this once-likable man. And as his empire grew larger he could not hope to edit or supervise closely all his newspapers. Overwork and frustration – even his best editors could not hope to match his genius for journalism – led to ill health, deteriorating eyesight and growing irrationality. It might have been different if he had learned to relax, or if there had been enough competition to keep him on his toes, but he was the undisputed Napoleon of Fleet Street. He was the Chief, and could not be crossed.

He asserted his authority by terrorizing his executives, appointing two men to do the same job and phoning them at all hours of the day and night. He employed company spies, awarded generous bonuses and issued unreasonable dismissal notices without cause. Fleet Street buzzed with such stories, actions calculated to strip men of their dignity and make them utterly dependent upon him. They knew that if offended, Northcliffe could also strip them of their handsome salaries and perks.

It was this total and corrupting power which gradually affected his political judgment and the view he had of himself and his place in the world; but even before he began to show great interest in politics the politicians had become more circumspect. If a few were stupid enough to sneer at his halfpenny newspapers, the majority recognized that he was a new and potent force in British politics. The Lord Salisburys would take a long time to disappear; but new men, such as the Chamberlains (Joseph and his sons Austen and Neville) from Birmingham and Lloyd George from Wales, understood that his mass-circulation papers were part of the extraordinary changes which were trans-forming Britain at the turn of the century. It was another example of the inter-action between newspapers and the development of democracy.

The 1867 Reform Act had doubled the electorate, and it was not surprising that the political parties decided to woo the newly enfranchised urban voters. In so doing, they ceased to be political factions and gradually became the modern parties as we know them today – decades after Andrew Jackson had created the Democratic party in the United States. The Conservatives, for instance, founded the National Union of Conservative and Unionist Associa-tions, and as the sociologist R.T. McKenzie noted in his *British Political Parties*, the directness and urgency of its approach to the working classes was the most striking feature of the early work of the National Union:

> The Conservative leaders of the day were vividly aware, as Lord Derby [who was then Foreign Secretary] put it in an address to a meeting of Conservative working men in 1875, that 'the (working man) is master of the situation. His class can, if it chooses, outvote all other classes put together.' The inspiration for the campaign to woo the working classes came, of course, from Disraeli himself. In a magnificent phrase written on the second anniversary of Disraeli's death, *The Times* recalled that: 'In the inarticulate mass of the English populace which they held at arm's length (Disraeli) discerned the Conservative working man as the sculptor perceives the angel prisoned in a block of marble.'

The working man, whose support Disraeli and the more intelligent Tories sought, largely belonged to the lower middle-class who read papers such as the

Mail and *Dispatch*. The real working class such as factory workers and labourers had to wait to be enfranchised; but the extra votes created by the 1867 Reform Act gave the new mass-circulation papers a political significance previously reserved almost exclusively for *The Times*. They were the only medium of mass communication between the parties and the electorate, and the man seen to stand between them and about half of the voters was Northcliffe. Hence the change of attitude on the part of the politicians.

Geoffrey Dawson of *The Times* described Northcliffe's uncanny prescience of what was likely to attract the public as meaning in political terms that he understood their aspirations and modest expectations of their elected representatives. To that extent Northcliffe admirably performed one of the basic functions of journalism, but he also misused this prescient talent and eventually saw it as a source of personal political power.

The first spectacular and iniquitous misuse of his political power was the hounding of Lord Haldane, the Scottish lawyer who had reorganized the British army when he was Secretary of State for War from 1905 to 1912. Haldane was also responsible for the creation of the imperial general staff, which made cooperation possible between the imperial armies, and for the agreement with France for military cooperation and planning. But for Haldane, Britain would have been less prepared than it was to fight Germany in 1914. He was Lord Chancellor (1912–15) and when war was declared the generals had wanted him to return to the War Office, but he was a German scholar and admirer of German philosophers. He had also visited Germany twice as agent of the Cabinet seeking an understanding that might have prevented war. It was rumoured that he was pro-German, and opposition to his return to the War Office grew.

The choice, as Lord (Hugh) Cudlipp wrote in *The Prerogative of the Harlot: Press Barons and Power*:

> . . .was between an able, proven minister who knew German weaknesses
> as well as strengths, and [Lord Kitchener] a brave, unsmiling, inflexible,
> celebrated warrior who had served his country overseas for 40 years but
> knew naught of Cabinet work and regarded civilian ministers with contempt.

There was no choice for Northcliffe. He knew that most of his readers shared his own hatred of Germany, and so he pursued his victim relentlessly in *The Times* (of which he had acquired control in 1908) and the *Mail*. The rest of Fleet Street joined in the witch-hunt. To quote Cudlipp again:

> The bachelor was said to have a German wife. The son of a pious Scottish
> family was alleged to be the illegitimate brother of the Kaiser. He had
> corresponded secretly with the German government and concealed from his
> Cabinet colleagues his knowledge that the Germans intended war. He had

delayed the mobilization and dispatch to the Continent of the British Expeditionary Force.

All this was obviously untrue but Northcliffe's venom overwhelmed the Cabinet, and not a single minister spoke out in Haldane's defence. Lloyd George (who was Chancellor of the Exchequer at the time, and later Prime Minister) wrote in his *War Memoirs* that: 'his abandonment by men who were his devoted friends – at least by men to whom he was devoted – at the instigation of the fussy and noisy patriots that always danced around the flag as if they owned it, was one of the meanest betrayals in British history.' It was also a measure of ministerial circumspection, in some cases bordering on intimidation, and it could be said that their weakness was another source of Northcliffe's growing strength.

Not that he always wielded it for personal or discreditable purposes. He was still very much a newspaperman. In the spring of 1915, in a heavily censored message from the front, *The Times* reported that the shortage of shells and other munitions was slowing down the offensive and losing British lives. It was well known in Westminster and Whitehall that Kitchener's inadequacy was responsible for the shortage, and Northcliffe decided that the man he had helped to put in the government had to go. He wrote the *Mail* editorial himself, and all over Britain placards blazoned his message: 'Kitchener's Tragic Blunder'.

This was not the work of a newspaper proprietor interested only in circulation and profits or self-glorification. His staff had warned him of the possible consequences, including imprisonment, and he was reported to have said: 'I don't give tuppence for the consequences. That man is losing the war.' Sales of the *Mail* slumped, and copies of the *Mail* and *The Times* were burned on the floor of the London Stock Exchange. Police had to be called in to defend Carmelite House, Northcliffe's main office in London, against the mob. Churchill (then 1st Lord of the Admiralty) even demanded that *The Times* be taken over by the government – a ploy he tried again in the General Strike of 1926.

Northcliffe's campaign, though eventually abandoned in the face of massive circulation slumps, nevertheless hastened the fall of H.H. Asquith's Liberal government, and Lloyd George was appointed Minister for Munitions. While Kitchener remained at the War Office until he was lost at sea on his way to Russia, many of his responsibilities were transferred to the Chief of the Imperial General Staff. Moreover, conscription, for which Northcliffe had long pressed, was introduced. It may well have been his finest hour, but this demonstration of the power of the press gave him an appetite for more. It also seems to have convinced him that he could order things better than the politicians.

The war was still going badly, but Northcliffe insisted that the generals should fight the war largely free from civilian control. This brought him into conflict with Lloyd George, who had formed the second coalition government in 1916. The new Prime Minister was similar in background to Northcliffe, and was typical of the aspiring lower middle-class that Northcliffe had wanted to educate when he launched the *Mail*. At that time Lloyd George was vulnerable in that he had been deserted by most members of his Liberal party, but he understood the importance of the press and its developing role in society. He therefore sought to work with Northcliffe. No other press baron in Britain or the United States has ever been courted so assiduously by a head of government, but their relations soured because Lloyd George questioned the generals' 'war of attrition'. The rift was so serious that Northcliffe even refused to take the Prime Minister's telephone calls.

The attrition strategy was terrifyingly simple, based as it was on the assumption that if each side killed about the same number of men the Allies would eventually win because they had more of them. Recalling in his memoirs the horrors of the Somme and Verdun, Lloyd George wrote that it was the story of: 'two or three [generals] who would rather the million perish than that they as leaders should own – even to themselves – that they were blunderers.' He added that he would have stopped the carnage but for considerations such as Northcliffe.

This sounds like special pleading. It might well have been impossible to change the strategy at that stage. The Dardanelles was such an attempt, and it was a miserable and costly failure. But the country was war weary, the 'flower of its manhood' decimated, and neither Northcliffe nor anybody else outside Parliament could have prevented him from trying to change course. Lloyd George might now be remembered with more affection and respect if he had tried.

There is in fact no evidence that Northcliffe succeeded in making Lloyd George do something he did not want to do. He could only make life difficult for the Prime Minister, who tried to buy him off by offering him a seat in the Cabinet. Northcliffe refused because his freedom of expression would have been lost; but Lloyd George persisted and eventually he agreed to lead the British War Mission in the United States and later directed propaganda against the enemy. He did both jobs well, but they were not nearly as important as some of his biographers claimed. Probably the main reason he was offered these two jobs was that he could do little mischief while engaged on official business.

The final trial of strength between the two men came when Lloyd George refused to make him an official delegate to the Versailles Peace Conference in 1919. Northcliffe had published his own peace terms, and they were both warlike and vindictive. He tried to organize a backbench revolt in the House of

Commons and failed, in part because French Intelligence revealed his machinations to the Prime Minister. In order to quell the revolt, Lloyd George left the Peace Conference briefly, and in a parliamentary debate said that the war had been won without Northcliffe and 'diseased vanity' would not be allowed to sow dissension between the allies. No names were mentioned, but it must have been a painful rebuff for Northcliffe.

President Woodrow Wilson included press representatives in the American delegation, inviting an aspiring young journalist, Walter Lippmann (who had been Assistant to the US Secretary of War in 1917) and even an Englishman, Wilmot Lewis (who was to become the London *Times* correspondent in Washington) because of his superb command of French. But Lloyd George obviously could not have accepted Northcliffe on the British delegation. He afterwards wrote that: 'had I done so I should have been his man in possession at Downing Street, and he would have wanted to make clear to his readers that I was his nominee. That position was incompatible with the independence and dignity of the high office I held. I elected to break with him.'

This rebuff may well have affected Northcliffe's sanity. There is no way of proving it; his 'diseased vanity' immunized him from reality, there had long been signs of mental illness and this final frustration could have pushed him over the top. He had after all developed what Hamilton Fyfe (one-time editor of the *Daily Herald*) described as a 'mystical belief that he was the man appointed to clear up the chaos into which the world had fallen.'

After the war he embarked on a lengthy world cruise during which the symptoms became obvious. While crossing the Atlantic aboard the *Aquitania* he ordered the *Mail* to print the menus of all its dining rooms every day. He informed King George V from New York that he had embraced Roman Catholicism. From China he ordered *The Times* to campaign against the Anglo–Japanese Treaty, which it dutifully did, and the Treaty was abrogated but mainly because of American pressures. Back in London he appointed one of the commissionaires at Carmelite House to approve all display advertisements before publication in the *Mail*. He remained convinced that the Germans were determined to kill him, and one day he was found in a hotel bedroom scantily dressed and clutching a loaded pistol. Life was becoming unbearable for the poor man. He could not stand noise – Pulitzer was similarly afflicted during his last years – and Victor Cavendish, the 9th Duke of Devonshire let Northcliffe build a wooden chalet on the roof of his London house in the quiet of Carlton Gardens. He died there on 14 August 1922 at the age of 57.

It was a tragic end to a brilliant career. His mental illness was attributed officially to bacterial endocarditis, but Hugh Cudlipp reported that Stanley Morison, the historian of *The Times*, and Cecil King, a third nephew, believed that he died of general paralysis of the insane, the only cause of which is syphilis. Cudlipp added that the Harmsworth descendants who through family pride or personal loyalty sought to establish that Northcliffe was sane to the end did no service to his memory. Insanity, in the clouded years, was his alibi.

Whether Northcliffe ever realized that his influence on events was minimal – apart that is, from the collection and publication of news – is impossible to say; but he must have known that he was finally defeated by the editorial staff of *The Times*, the men he called the Black Friars, Monks, or the Brethren. It was an extraordinary victory for a small group of journalists who put their livelihood at risk throughout the years of Northcliffe's control.

He had wanted to do his best by *The Times*. He knew its history better than any member of the staff, and Barnes and Delane were his heroes. He wanted to be a worthy successor to John Walter II, who led the struggle for a free press, and John Walter III, who had made *The Times* the most technologically advanced newspaper in the world before the Americans invented the Hoe printing press and the Linotype machine. As the paper's official *History* says, he saw his task as getting the old 'barnacle-covered whale off the rocks and safely into deep water.' This he did, and the staff were grateful. They knew that only Northcliffe could transform the early Victorian relic into a contemporary newspaper with a prospect of a commercial future not less impressive than its past.

Northcliffe could count humility among his virtues when he bought *The Times* in 1908, but within a few years he expected his orders to be obeyed unquestioningly. He wanted to be the Chief, as he was at Carmelite House. He could not learn the lesson that on *The Times*, personal power whether of the proprietor or the editor, must be limited; that the quality that gave the paper its distinction was not conferred by one man but was the collective contribution of the staff. Nor did he understand, to quote the official *History* again, that the paper's long history, and the first principles out of which it grew, gave independence and strength to men whom he expected to be easily manageable. Instead, and despite their gratitude, some of the best men saw in his whims something that in their loyalty to the standards of *The Times* they had to resist.

Northcliffe would of course have defeated them if he had lived, for already he had driven one of the Black Friars to an early grave and suborned others; but he died before he could do any more damage. His dying request, so typical of a great journalist, was for 'a full page [obituary] and a leader by the best available writer on the *night*'. Wickham Steed (editor of *The Times* from 1919 to 1922) who had borne most of the anxiety in the final years, did his best but failed to explain this extraordinary man. All he could do was to commemorate his genius as a newspaperman before the clouded years of insanity.

McCORMICK-PATTERSON AXIS, SCRIPPS-HOWARD EMPIRE AND THE U. P.

Americans tell visiting Europeans that New York is not the United States and this is certainly true. The differences are not only those of a great city and the provinces. They have developed because of environment, climate, ethnic mix and history. President Gerald Ford was loath to bail out New York City when it could not pay its bills in the 1970s, and not only because he was a Republican appalled by the profligate spending of the Democratic mayor. The folklore of the Middle West had kept alive memories of how the railroads and banks based on New York exploited prairie farmers by charging high freight and interest rates. Those memories were the main fount of distrust and suspicion of New York and the East Coast, and physical isolation – a prairie farm was a lonely place before the coming of the automobile – fostered political isolationism and xenophobia. They also helped to explain the attitudes of Middle Western newspaper proprietors, the most outstanding example of this breed being Colonel Robert R. McCormick (1880–1955) of the *Chicago Tribune*.

Not that McCormick was the son of a poor prairie farmer. His father was a diplomat, and belonged to the family which developed the combine harvester and made a vast fortune. His mother was the daughter of Joseph Medill, who bought the paper in 1855 when it was eight years old. McCormick attended a British preparatory school when his father was attached to the American legation in London, and went on to Groton in Massachusetts, where Franklin Roosevelt was a contemporary. Then came Yale and Northwestern law school, and service in the US army as a combat and staff officer in the First World War. Known in the family as Bertie, he lived on a vast estate outside Chicago and flew round the world in his own aircraft. He looked every inch the English gentleman with his Savile Row suits and moustache, but he hated both Britain and America's East Coast from early childhood. On the occasion of the *Tribune*'s 100th anniversary in 1947, *Time* magazine wrote that the paper:

> . . . still sees silk-hatted Wall Street bankers lurking around every State Street corner, and redcoats behind every red oak tree. In 1943, he [McCormick] solemnly told a Detroit audience that after World War I he had helped the US General Staff work out plans to repel an invasion from Canada by 300,000 British regulars.

McCormick inherited his hatreds from his grandfather, who never had any use for easterners and Englishmen. Of Scots–Irish stock, Medill was one of the founders of the Republican party and once told Abraham Lincoln to 'Dammit, Abe, git yore feet off my desk'. McCormick also inherited his grandfather's ultra-conservatism. Senator Joseph McCarthy was not the first American to see a red under every bed and behind most desks in the State Department. Fears of a communist conspiracy after the First World War led to police raids and the mass deportation of aliens, but for Medill and McCormick the struggle against the red threat began much earlier. A strike at the McCormick works in 1886, during which several workers were killed by the police, led to one of the most famous incidents in the history of Chicago. Strikers, alleged to be anarchists, held a protest meeting in Haymarket Square, a bomb was thrown and many policemen were killed or wounded. The perpetrator was never discovered, but seven strikers were condemned to death for advocating violence. Medill exploited the story at the time, and McCormick though a small child retained vivid memories of the day when four of the strikers were hanged. Later on McCormick was always accompanied by an armed bodyguard.

Strangely enough, Medill's and McCormick's prejudices were generally impersonal. Britain was vilified in the *Tribune* but the managing editor, who made it one of the country's best-selling newspapers in the early 1900s, was James Keeley, an Englishman. Keeley also supported the Progressive party, which in splitting the Republicans enabled Woodrow Wilson (much to McCormick's disgust) to win the presidential election in 1912. McCormick was also the first Middle Western newspaper proprietor to subscribe to Reuters, the British news agency. He ranted against the Democrats, but lived in harmony with the Democratic machine which ran Chicago. But his prejudices were not always impersonal. I once sat next to the Colonel aboard an airliner flying from Bangkok to New Delhi – his private aircraft had developed engine trouble in Thailand – and we amiably discussed Asian affairs until he realized that I was an Englishman. Thereafter we flew through the night in silence.

McCormick also inherited his grandfather's journalistic flair, but the *Tribune* only indirectly. The company was left to a family trust, and his uncle, R.W. Patterson, edited the paper. Not that McCormick objected; he then saw himself as a future member of the US Supreme Court, although he did work part-time on the business side of the paper. During that period he got to know his cousin, Joseph Patterson (1879–1946), and after Patterson Sr died in 1914 the two of them took over joint control of the paper. As McCormick said: 'There was no one else to take over the paper, so we "elected" us to the newspaper business.'

The results were superficially bizarre. Each took it in turn monthly to edit the paper, and while McCormick was already an ultra-conservative, his cousin, despite his wealth and Ivy League education, was a radical who believed that socialism was the elixir for all the world's economic and social ills. Cousin Joe was an interesting man. While still at Yale he had gone to China to act as a legman for the *Tribune* correspondent covering the Boxer Rebellion in 1900. He had then worked as a reporter for $15 a week, and probably got closer to the working class than most sociologists who came after him. He was a genuine American democrat-cum-populist, a breed Europeans have yet to understand. He was also a very good journalist prepared to do his own legwork by travelling in commuter trains and buses, and drinking in working-class taverns in order to understand the first- and second-generation Americans who comprised much of the paper's readership. This may have been the reason why he promoted the comic strips and other non-serious features of the paper first introduced by the Englishman, Keeley. McCormick had other interests no less important for the development of the company, such as leasing vast Canadian forests and building papermills.

If the Patterson-McCormick cooperation was bizarre, it was only superficially so because whoever was editing the paper and writing the editorials – McCormick the conservative or Patterson the socialite socialist – the circulation continued to rise. It appeared not to matter what the editorials said, the very mixed ethnic population of the five-state circulation area bought more and more copies of the *Tribune*. The partnership was nevertheless odd, and towards the end of the First World War Colonel McCormick and Captain Patterson – the former had enlisted as a major and the latter as a private soldier – met somewhere behind the lines in France and amicably decided to go their separate ways. Patterson, who had taken advice from Lord Northcliffe, decided in 1919 to launch an illustrated tabloid in New York, and his *Daily News* became the best-selling tabloid in the United States. McCormick took over control of the *Tribune*, which became the best-selling standard-size paper.

The success of the *Tribune* under McCormick's guidance afterwards bothered journalists on the East Coast when they became rather pompous about the role of the press in a democracy, but perhaps they did not give due consideration to the background. Chicago during McCormick's lifetime became the heart of the country's industrial and agricultural development. The hub of the trans-continental railroad system – New Yorkers travelling to the West Coast had to change trains in Chicago – the business and corporate centre of the industrial northeast, and the slaughterhouse for vast herds of cattle driven from as far afield as Texas, Chicago was no mean city. The raw energy of the heartland of American wealth pulsated through its banks and commodity exchanges.

Its very newness was both invigorating and frightening; in comparison New York was an ancient city. Chicago was a tiny village when it became the seat of justice for Cook County in 1831. After a period of phenomenal growth it was almost completely destroyed by fire in 1871, nine years before McCormick was born – which may explain why he apparently did not know that of the $1 million contributed from abroad in what may well have been history's first 'foreign aid' programme, Britain provided at least half. In a few years Chicago became a great city. Only two years after the fire, its banks were among the few to survive the financial panic of 1873.

Chicago was different from New York in other ways which helps to explain the *Tribune*'s rabid jingoism, and the Stars and Stripes and Stephen Decatur's famous toast of 1816 'My Country Right or Wrong' on the masthead. Many of its early inhabitants were prairie populists and therefore xenophobes. Chicago also grew up much more quickly, and the ethnic groups were less assimilated. As recently as 1960, more than 40 languages were spoken in the city, and many neighbourhoods were to all intents and purposes foreign quarters. The newcomers from eastern and southern Europe must have felt terribly isolated – not only by populist resentment but also by the city's environs, which with Lake Michigan on one side and the prairie on the other are flat and featureless. Only immigrants who went directly from the boat to company towns like Gary, Indiana, could have felt less American and had a harder time becoming one.

Ethnic tensions were strong even before the blacks arrived in large numbers from the South, and the *Tribune*'s frequently expressed hatred of 'aliens' did not help. At least not at first, but ethnic groups learned that the easiest way to be accepted was to be more patriotic than the patriots; and the *Tribune* became one of the main vehicles for this assimilation process. The results were often ugly for those who cringe away from jingoism, but it was one way of bringing the various groups together. It was also good for circulation.

The kind of journalism practised by McCormick was known by its critics as Know-Nothing journalism, which was a misnomer. The 'Know-Nothings', a nativist anti-Catholic and anti-Irish party (whose official name was the Native American party) flourished briefly before the Civil War and disappeared when the Republicans became the dominant WASP (White Anglo-Saxon Protestant) party. The *Tribune* was anything but anti-Catholic and anti-Irish, but the anti-intellectualism of the Know-Nothings survived in political and other forms and was one of the driving forces of most Chicago papers of the period. It was what gave them great gusto and a rough-and-tough approach which came to be recognized as the Chicago school of journalism. Arguably no other would have flourished in what was a very tough town, and not only because of Al Capone and other gangsters. Upton Sinclair's novel *The Jungle* (1906) was a realistic study of social conditions among immigrant workers in the stockyards. It led to the introduction of pure food laws, but the immigrants' conditions did not improve for many years. Corruption was rife and municipal government rotten. This environment demanded a special kind of journalism breeding muckrakers and encouraging ruthless competition, of the kind celebrated in Ben Hecht's play *The Front Page* (1928), later adapted as a movie.

The *Tribune* did it better than any of its rivals. McCormick's right-wing Republicanism should have made it unpopular in a city run by an entrenched Democratic machine, but about three in four of his readers were Democrats. His isolationism and hatred of President (Franklin) Roosevelt remained undiminished during the Second World War. He was even condemned for giving comfort and aid to the enemy by being an exponent of the Nazi propaganda line. The *Tribune*'s report of the Battle of Midway in 1942 revealed that the United States had broken the Japanese naval code. It was utterly irresponsible, and should have angered Chicago's super-patriots, but circulation and advertising revenue did not suffer.

The paper's continuing success baffled its critics. For a start, Chicago dramatically changed in character as well as population during McCormick's lifetime. It became the country's second city in every way. The stockyards disappeared, and while many of the slums remained a handsome and elegant new city grew up in the vicinity of Michigan Avenue and along the Lake Shore. McCormick built the Tribune Tower, a 36-storey gothic pile and perhaps the most impressive newspaper office in the world. In comparison, the *New York Times* office looks like a garment factory. Music and the arts flourished, and the University of Chicago became a great centre of learning with an international reputation as a centre of research. Enrico Fermi, the late Italian physicist, did much of the early work on the atomic bomb there, and the university press is no less famous. The Democratic machine long continued as a quasi-tribal and feudal organization, with Mayor Richard Daley as the last of the big city bosses, but a society emerged no less cultivated, liberal and internationally-minded than that of New York or any great capital city.

This transformation was reflected by the city's press. The foreign-language press – Czech, German, Greek, Italian, Polish, Swedish and Yiddish – still outnumbered the English papers in titles if not circulation, but the *Daily News* developed a fine foreign news service. Marshall Field III, angered by McCormick's isolationism and war against Roosevelt, launched the liberal and interventionist *Sun* in 1941, but to no avail. The *Tribune* remained unchanged and unbeatable. To quote *Time* again:

> . . . after shattering his lances on the *Trib*'s tough hide for 5½ years, White Knight Marshall Field, at a cost of about $10,000,000, has proved one thing, if nothing else: that it takes more than good intentions, an unlimited bankroll and an Associated Press franchise to make good in the newspaper business. What it takes, the Colonel has got.

The big reason for the *Tribune*'s success, the magazine added, was that McCormick had simply made it indispensable. No paper could match its overwhelming coverage of the news. When a big story broke, the *Trib* could throw a score of men on it to out-report and out-write the opposition. In sports, in comics, women's pages, signed columns and display ads it offered all things to all people. It was the housewife's guide, the politician's breakfast food, a bible to hundreds of small-town editorial writers. A classless paper, it was read on the commuter trains from swank Lake Forest, and on the dirty 'El' cars taking blue-collars to the factories. A further reason perhaps was its cocky self-confidence. When another newspaper publisher commented that its strength lay in its animal vigour and not in its comic strips, the *Tribune* crowed: 'Comes the dawn. It ain't Orphan Annie. It's the hair on our chest.'

McCormick could be compared with Lord Beaverbrook (see Chapter 8). They were both superb journalists who loved newspapers. The Colonel had ink in his veins, and was fond of recalling his grandfather's last words, 'What is the news this morning?' Beaverbrook came new and relatively late to Fleet Street, but had a similar flair. Both created and sold very readable newspapers. They could both be seen as eccentrics rich enough to indulge in personal hatreds that were irrational and occasionally despicable, but the comparison could not be taken too far. Beaverbrook was much more involved in politics, and was influential before becoming a newspaper proprietor, whereas McCormick for the most part tilted at windmills.

The British Empire was the obvious example. His youthful suspicions were of course widely-shared throughout the United States, and to that extent he merely reflected public opinion. Prior to the Second World War the US army had only two war plans, one for hostilities against Japan and the other against Britain. But McCormick continued to contest the supposed threat long after the British Empire had ceased to exist. It was ridiculous, all the more so because he dressed like an Englishman and the retention of the military title was also very English. He could behave like an imperious feudal lord. His staff were the best-paid in the business, but were expected to be as servile as medieval villeins. His cousin Joe Patterson said: 'Bertie certainly likes to crack the whip and watch the serfs march by'.

He was of course born into the local establishment, and at a time when the rich did not pretend to be classless. He could have become a national figure in Republican politics, perhaps even president of the United States. He was shrewd, wealthy and well-connected, and there was not much competition at the time – Harding, Coolidge and Hoover all made it to the White House between 1921 and 1933. Instead, like James Gordon Bennett I (who launched the *New York Herald* in 1835) he chose to be a maverick. Their circumstances were different of course; Bennett was a poor immigrant on the make who was frozen out of Democratic politics while McCormick was a Middle Westerner and a proud citizen of Chicago. Unlike his Patterson cousins, Joe and Cissy, he could not have deserted Chicago, although their success with the *New York Daily News* and the *Washington Times-Herald* suggests that he would have done as well in either city. He was a first-class newspaperman.

His decision to remain was understandable, however. He was proud of Chicago and refused to accept the cultural, financial and social hegemony of New York and the East Coast. For him, Chicagoland, as he called the Tribune's five-state circulation area, was also the heartland of the United States. It still produced much of the wealth of the country, was 'untainted' by European influences, and he therefore believed that Chicago was destined to become the first city.

This was one reason why he claimed that the *Tribune* was the 'World's Greatest Newspaper'. The greatest city in the world obviously had to have its greatest newspaper. It was nothing of the sort, but its record was not all bad. Chicago produced some of the best journalists in the country, and by paying his staff the highest salaries in the country, and giving them generous fringe benefits, he attracted the best. Those I knew were fond of him, and did not regard themselves as professional prostitutes because they paid no attention to the editorials. And not all of his campaigns were dishonourable or irrational. If McCormick is remembered as a union-basher he was also enraged by the excesses of his fellow capitalists. He had a gut belief in the untrammelled freedom of the press, even if it did mean freedom to rewrite the news.

This does not excuse his excesses, but they were perhaps less heinous than was thought at the time because they had little or no effect upon public opinion. I am once again reminded of Beaverbrook. For all his journalistic flair and the success of the *Tribune*, McCormick wielded little or no power. He helped to deepen and prolong the period of isolationism which hamstrung American foreign policy at a crucial point in world history and when a strong American voice might have persuaded America into the war, but his influence could only have been marginal. He had little or no influence on national politics. For all his campaigns against Roosevelt, Chicago and the state of Illinois voted for F.D.R. in 1932, 1936, 1940 and 1944. The final frustration came in 1948 when Harry Truman was elected president, and gleefully displayed the front page of the *Tribune*, which claimed victory for the Republican candidate, Thomas Dewey.

Cousins Joe and Cissy were also very good journalists, but they suffered the same frustrations when they set up shop in cities politically more powerful than Chicago. Joseph Patterson's *New York Daily News* became the best tabloid in the country. Some of its scoops, notably a photograph of Ruth Snyder dying in the electric chair at Sing-Sing, created public indignation, but it covered the news and generally pursued liberal policies in its editorial columns. Patterson also supported Roosevelt's New Deal, but with the approach of war his Middle-Western isolationism emerged. The *News* became one of Roosevelt's most hostile critics, some attacks being so outrageous that the President presented one of its Washington correspondents with a German Iron Cross.

Cissy – Eleanor Medill Patterson (1884–1948) was a wealthy woman who went to Washington to forget a disastrous marriage. A celebrated society hostess before persuading Hearst to appoint her editor of the loss-making *Washington Herald* in 1930, within a few years she out-reported her rival, the *Washington Post* (which Eugene Meyer had bought in 1933) and was as radical as her brother. She even reprinted some of his pro-New Deal editorials knowing that her boss hated Roosevelt and all his policies. Eventually she bought the *Herald* and the local *Times*, and in amalgamating them (in 1939) and injecting the family flair made the *Times-Herald* the national capital's best-selling newspaper. But like her brother, she could not stomach Roosevelt's interventionism, and the three papers became known as the McCormick–Patterson Axis. They ranted and roared, made a great deal of money, but failed to influence public opinion.

The failure of the McCormick–Patterson Axis was instructive. The three newspapers, the largest in their respective circulation areas, did not try to persuade their readers to do something they did not want to do. The vast majority of the American people did not want to become involved in the European struggle. A minority, mainly of German origin, actively supported Hitler, and Irish–Americans, a larger and more vociferous group, hated Britain. To that extent, McCormick and the Pattersons reflected public opinion when they opposed what they saw as Roosevelt's efforts to become involved. Nor were they alone. Most newspaper proprietors were isolationists in varying degree, but they could not prevent the President from helping Britain during those vital months before Japan attacked Pearl Harbor and Germany declared war on the United States. It was a classic example of the powerlessness of the press.

McCormick was the best-known press baron in the Middle West, but he was only one of many. Melville Stone, who launched the *Chicago Daily News* in 1875, was an outstanding journalist who ran a fine newspaper. William Nelson founded the *Kansas City Evening Star* five years later when the townsfolk had nothing to boast about except the outlaws Frank and Jesse James. Typical of most newspapers in the region, the *Star* was mainly concerned with local news; but Nelson was an active and reforming editor, and his campaigns helped to transform a dreary river town with mud streets into a thriving and well-governed city. Farther West, F.G. Bonfils, a West Point graduate and an organizer of crooked lotteries, together with H.H. Tammen, a bartender, bought the *Denver Post* a few years after it was founded (1892) and made it one of the most sensational and profitable newspapers in the country. The most successful press baron, however, was Edward Wyllis Scripps. He was not the first to own more than one newspaper, but he was the first to develop a chain as a coherent organization with its own news agency, the United Press (founded in 1907), to provide his many newspapers with national and international news. For this reason his contribution to American journalism was greater than McCormick's.

E.W. Scripps (1854–1926) was born on an Illinois farm, thirteenth and youngest child of an English immigrant, and he came from a newspaper family. His grandfather was a journalist and a relative was the editor of the *True Briton*, one of the many London morning newspapers which failed in the 1850s because of competition from *The Times*. In the United States, a cousin was one of the early editors of the *Chicago Tribune* (which Joseph Medill had bought in 1855), and various cousins and uncles were journalists. His half-brother, James, launched the *Detroit Evening News* (1873), the first cheap evening tabloid. Edward went to work for him when still in his teens, and after a trip to Europe borrowed $10,000 from the family and launched the *Cleveland Penny Press* in 1878. He also bought newspapers in St Louis and Cincinnati before he was 30.

Scripps was an extraordinary man, a farm boy who made a fortune of $50 million but not a Horatio Alger hero rising from rags to riches by hard work and clean living. He was lazy, and a drunk who preferred to play poker when he was not chasing women. He was said to drink a gallon of whisky a day, and was half blind and had the shakes when he reached middle age. He also smoked 40 cigars a day. Then he pulled himself together, and lived to a quarrelsome old age. He fell out with most members of his family, and boasted of having few friends and no admirers. With little formal education himself, he regarded university education as a grave disadvantage for a newspaperman. Unlike McCormick, he was an Anglophile who campaigned for American entry in the First World War, and believed that the English-speaking countries should police the world. His favourite tune was 'Onward Christian Soldiers'.

Scripps was obviously influenced by his first European trip. In Rome, he recalled Gibbon, who his half-sister, Ellen, had persuaded him to read, and after spending several night hours at the Colosseum resolved to pursue power and not glory. He afterwards wrote that:

> I decided that I would establish a little kingdom such as Rome was in its prehistoric beginning. I decided that I would extend this kingdom of mine, which would consist of my first newspaper, to another and then another newspaper, and I determined so long as I lived to go on extending my kingdom into perhaps an empire of journalism.

London brought out another side of his character. Strolling along a West End street one evening, he stopped to watch men and women in evening dress entering a great town house where a ball was in progress. He became aware of the wretchedly-poor people who were also watching, and decided that while he would become rich he would always help the poor. Perhaps the contrast of silks and rags stirred his inherited English radicalism; whatever the reason, he thereafter championed the interests of ordinary working folk. He told his editors: 'The first of my principles is that I have constituted myself the

[97]

advocate of that large majority of people who are not so rich in worldly goods and native intelligence as to make them equal, man for man, in the struggle with the wealthier and more intellectual class.'

In a letter to his son, Robert, he wrote:

> I would prefer that you should succeed in being in all things a gentleman, according to the real meaning of the word, than that you should vastly increase the money value of my estate. Being a gentleman, you cannot fail to devote your whole mind and energy to the service of the plain people who constitute the vast majority of the people of the United States . . . You are, and can be, continually, entirely free from any temptation to cater to any of your fellow citizens for profit. You have not had nor should you at any time ever have any ambition to secure political or social eminence.

The exhortation to become a gentleman must have sounded strange from an old reprobate who had broken most of the Ten Commandments, wore working-men's clothes, and had earlier told journalist Lincoln Steffens that he did not think like a rich man: 'I think more like a left labour galoot, like those dynamiters.' This was a reference to the McNamara brothers whom he defended when they were charged with trying to dynamite the offices of the *Los Angeles Times* in 1910. He did not defend the crime, but supported the 'belligerent rights' of working men to defend themselves against the ruthless capitalism of the time. His newspapers devoted more space than most to social injustice, and his editors were required to 'serve the interest of the poor and the working classes'.

They needed all the help they could get. Trade unions were slow to develop, in part because of the continuing flood of immigrants. Nearly three million arrived in the 1870s, and more than five million in the 1880s. The peak was reached in the first decade of the twentieth century, when 8,795,000 (more than 10 per cent of the existing population) were admitted. Desperate for work and largely unaware of their rights, they represented a constantly-refilled pool of cheap labour to be exploited by unscrupulous employers.

Hopes for improvement were rarely realized because industrialists who had built up vast economic empires were determined to defend *laissez-faire*. They were possibly more ruthless than British industrialists; certainly they were more successful in delaying reforms. They bribed and bought politicians, and the US courts remained a strong ally long after the 1871 Trade Union Act and other legislation had improved the worker's legal status in Britain. According to Justice Oliver Wendell Holmes, the US Supreme Court seemed to believe that the English philosopher Herbert Spencer's *Social Statics* (1851), with its strongly expressed ethical and social views supporting economic and social *laissez-faire*, was part of the Constitution. Certainly most of the industrialists agreed that the functions of government should be limited to national defence and the maintenance of law and order, and that they did not include labour regulations, and factory and welfare legislation.

The birth of American trade unions was marked by violence and counter-violence. Strikes were ruthlessly broken by company police or state forces, and in the anthracite coalfields of Pennsylvania a secret miners' union known as the Molly Maguires terrorized pit owners and managers throughout the 1860s. When the railway workers struck in 1873 there were pitched battles between strikers and the militia in Pittsburgh and Chicago, and federal troops were called in to restore order. The first of the big unions, the Order of the Knights of Labour, became strong enough to lobby Congress against the importing of contract labour, but collapsed after the Chicago Haymarket riot in 1886. An English immigrant, Samuel Gompers, eventually organized the American Federation of Labour that same year but violence continued well into the next century.

Scripps, unlike Patterson, did not toy with socialism. He was more in the tradition of William Cobbett and some of the other early radical journalists, but had no political ambition. To reverse W.C. Fields's quip, he just wanted to give the suckers an even break. An admirable attitude, but it is difficult to assess the influence of his newspapers. Although numerous (he owned 52 at one time), they did not have large circulations and were not read by lawmakers but they were probably a comfort, perhaps a promise of better times to come, for his blue-collar readers. They must have felt very vulnerable before the unions were eventually established.

It is doubtful whether Scripps expected to achieve much more. He once commented that: 'It is easier for a rich man to enter the Kingdom of Heaven than it is for a successful newspaper publisher to give democracy a square deal.' But he did his best. His newspapers reported strikes objectively, if sympathetically, and crusaded against local political bosses and rapacious utility and public-transport companies. They were liberal in their politics, and supported Theodore Roosevelt's reform campaigns. Roosevelt recognized that human rights were as important as property rights, and was the first president to act as representative of the people in industrial disputes. His sympathy for working people was not shared by many newspaper proprietors, but Scripps was one of his staunchest allies.

Scripps was not a do-gooder. He remained true to the task he set himself that night in Rome, but he never forgot the majority of Americans who could not defend themselves in those harsh times. He protected his readers from fraudulent advertising, despite the loss of revenue. Long before the advertising industry set its own house in order, he appointed a senior editor to scrutinize all advertising copy before it was accepted for publication.

Scripps built up his empire mainly by launching newspapers in small but expanding industrial towns which did not have a cheap afternoon paper for factory hands to read. It was run on a shoestring, old buildings were rented, used presses and Linotype machines bought, and the capital provided was rarely more than $25,000. Bright young men were appointed to run the new ventures, and given their head and a salary of $25 a week. They were also given a large block of stock if they were successful, and many became millionaires. Scripps retained 51 per cent of the stock, or absorbed the loss if the paper failed. One-third of the profits was ploughed back into the parent company. It was a simple but effective way of running a growing empire which spanned the Middle West with outposts on both coasts.

The editors were not completely independent. Daily reports had to be sent to Scripps, who dictated overall policy from Miramar, his Californian ranch. He rarely moved out of it after suffering a stroke, but the world came to him. Men who had something to say were welcome, and they were rumoured to include scientists, artists and senior military officers. The editors were required to attend from time to time, and were often treated curtly if not roughly because Scripps, on his own admission, could be harsh and dictatorial.

Most of the Scripps papers were too small to run an adequate news-gathering operation outside their circulation areas, and until 1900 the Associated Press (AP) news agency was available only to members of the cooperative. But one advantage of a large chain is that it can centralize a number of a newspaper's requirements, and in 1897 the Scripps–McRae Press Association and the Scripps News Service were established; the former to serve the Middle West papers and the latter to take care of the outlets elsewhere. Milton McRae was Scripps's business manager until they quarrelled and parted. The service was extended by exchanging news with the Publishers' Press Association, which Scripps eventually bought in 1907. The three were merged to form the United Press.

The UP, as it quickly became known, sold its service to other newspapers, and within a few years had more than 500 subscribers. It was managed by Roy Howard, who was only 25 years old when appointed, and bureaux were opened in all the major news centres at home and abroad. The UP reflected the personality of Scripps. It also was run on a shoestring, with rented or leased, rather than bought, office space and communications equipment. Its foreign correspondents for decades looked hungrier than AP men, presumably because they were expected to beat the opposition despite smaller staffs and fewer facilities. They knew what the milkman in Kansas City wanted to read – that mythical figure personified the readership Scripps wanted to reach – and their reporting tended to be lively and colourful. Scripps also launched general feature and science services which helped to improve the quality of many small newspapers, but of all his contributions to journalism the UP was arguably his greatest achievement. It was so successful in breaking the AP monopoly of national and international news that William Randolph Hearst followed its lead and in 1909 set up the International News Service (INS) which was eventually sold to the UP.

In its early years the UP had a rather raffish reputation. Even its foreign correspondents behaved as if they were alumni of Chicago's school of hard-boiled journalism, and were said to be more interested in scoops than in considered and objective reporting. They were certainly fast workers, making their competitors sit up and take notice, but the generally unwarranted slur can probably be traced to Roy Howard after he had become the agency's president. He visited France in the closing weeks of the First World War and scored a world scoop when he reported the Armistice. His dispatch was as follows:

UNIPRESS NEWYORK
PARIS URGENT ARMISTICE ALLIES GERMANY SIGNED ELEVEN SMORNING HOSTILITIES CEASED TWO SAFTERNOON SEDAN TAKEN SMORNING BY AMERICANS

It was a model of condensation, even for an agency man, but keeping down cable costs was fundamental in Scripps's shoestring empire. It caused a sensation, and there was dancing in the streets in all the Allied capitals. Alas, it was sent on 7 November 1918, four days before the Armistice was actually signed. Critics condemned it as a dreadful example of irresponsible journalism – newspapermen called it jumping the gun – but Howard's source was Admiral Henry Wilson, the American naval commander in Europe. You could say that Howard should have sought confirmation even though the source was impecc-able, but agency work is frequently a case of instant reporting. The competition has to be beaten regularly to attract new clients and satisfy existing subscri-bers. In any case, the German forces were retreating, and the end of the war was imminent. Howard also thought that he had the scoop of the century.

He subsequently tried to check out the admiral's source, and discovered that he had been informed by the American naval attaché in Paris, who in turn was told by a French Foreign Office official. At least, the attaché thought that his informant was a diplomat because they had conversed over a secure telephone circuit; but Howard concluded that the original informant was a German secret agent who had tapped the so-called secure wire. If true, it was probably history's first case of wire-tapping, and Howard convinced himself, if not the competition, that the desperate Germans had hoped that the Allies would have to accept an immediate Armistice once their peoples believed that the terrible war was over.

Howard survived and flourished, and because the irascible Scripps quarrelled with his relatives, Howard eventually became president of the empire which was renamed Scripps–Howard in 1922. He was more conservative than the old man and at first opposed the Newspaper Guild, the journalists' trade union, but the UP also flourished. By 1940 it had as many subscribers as the AP, but much fewer in the United States, and inevitably dropped back into second place. Nevertheless, its competition revolutionized news-agency journalism everywhere. Not only the AP but Reuters and other European agencies had to extend their services to survive, and in so doing they became indispensable to newspapers and eventually radio and television. Great newspapers such as the London *Times* and the *New York Times* came to depend upon them to some degree despite their own large editorial staffs, although until the 1950s the London *Times* thought that it had somehow failed when it had to publish an agency report. In the United States, the entire national and international news coverage of the vast majority of papers is provided by the agencies.

If what power the press wields depends largely upon the provision of news, as I believe it does, the agencies should be more powerful than any great newspaper or large television network. They dictate the news schedules, which means they decide much of the news published. They broaden the horizons of their subscribers and counterbalance the reporting of staff correspondents. No newspaper can fabricate or misreport a story when an agency man is also filing it.

Communist and Third World member-states of UNESCO (United Nations Educational, Scientific, and Cultural Organization) want to limit agency operations largely because their objective reporting exposes aspects of their regimes they would prefer to go unreported, but the agencies are not as powerful as their near-monopolies would suggest. They service subscribers of all political and ideological complexions, and their reporting must necessarily be free of all bias if they are to retain their subscribers. Their very objectivity can diminish the impact of the news, and to that extent they cannot normally compete with good staff correspondents. They are the workhorses rather than the masters. They would have to be invented if they did not exist, because the area of interest of the average newspaper reader has become too big for any single newspaper to cover. Some of the credit for the development of news agencies and for the speed and quality of their reporting worldwide must go to Scripps, who launched the UP in the first instance to gather news for his chain of little newspapers.

One year before Scripps died in 1926, the journalist and satirist H.L. Mencken said that he was 'probably the most successful newspaper-owner America has ever known.' He was certainly one of the best because he loved newspapers, unlike some others who ran their papers for profit or political influence. At least one, Frank Munsey (1854–1925), made an enormous fortune by actually closing them down. He became known as 'the butcher of American newspapers'.

Munsey also began his working life on a farm, but unlike Scripps his rise from rags to riches was achieved without a bottle of whisky and 40 cigars a day. By all accounts he was an insufferable person, as most Horatio Alger heroes must have been, and he had illusions of grandeur. He claimed that a Munsey fought with William the Conqueror at Hastings, and that his mother's family had 12 ancestors on the *Mayflower*. If true, he would have outranked all the Boston Brahmins, but his first job was with Western Union in Augusta, Maine. He migrated to New York in 1882, and after a couple of false starts launched *Munsey's Weekly* in 1889. It was the beginning of the golden age of American magazine publishing, and by cutting the cover price to ten cents he made a fortune. He invested in one of the first grocery chains and in real estate, and with millions at his disposal entered the daily newspaper field.

Munsey was a prolific writer and had some good ideas about popular journalism, but again success did not come easily. He withdrew to consider the future, and decided that the days of small-scale production had passed forever. There were too many metropolitan newspapers competing with each other, and he concluded that they had to amalgamate to produce the kind of profits he wanted. Altogether he bought 16 newspapers, and killed or merged 14 of them. The *New York Sun*, the first of the successful penny papers, was merged with the *Herald*, which in turn was sold to the Reid family and merged with the *Tribune* in 1924. Thus the two newspapers which pioneered the penny-paper revolution disappeared. Munsey was not the only proprietor to merge or kill newspapers. Scripps-Howard afterwards bought Pulitzer's once-great newspaper the *New York World* and merged it with the *Telegram*, but it could not survive the competition of the reinvigorated *Herald-Tribune* and the up-and-coming *Times*. With rising newsprint and labour costs the time for consolidation would seem to have arrived, but the columnist Robert Duffus spoke for most American newspapermen when he passed judgment in the *American Mercury* in 1924:

> Munsey has acquired no following in daily journalism; he has created nothing. Indeed, he is not so much a force as a portent of journalism. He has demonstrated that newspapers are not institutions, like schools and churches, but commodities, like motor cars. He has legitimatized journalistic murder. He has invented a new and effective method of doing away with free speech.

The butcher died in the following year while trying to buy the *Chicago Daily News*. Duffus was right in thinking that he was a portent of the shape of things to come.

ROTHERMERE AND BEAVERBROOK

Alfred Harmsworth, Viscount Northcliffe's legacy to Fleet Street, as Geoffrey Dawson wrote in the *Dictionary of National Biography*, was not wholly benign. He woke it up and made it come alive, but he also commercialized it. Newspapers became big business capable of earning large profits, which led rich men to believe that they could become richer and politically powerful if they owned a newspaper. It was only half true, as Harold Harmsworth (1868–1940), the 1st Viscount Rothermere, discovered after his brother's death when he gained control of the *Daily Mail* and most of his other newspapers (but not *The Times* which Major J.J. Astor bought). Rothermere made a lot of money, much more than Northcliffe, but apart from being offered the crown of Hungary his political machinations came to nothing.

By all accounts, Rothermere was an unpleasant man with none of his brother's charm and none of his genius for journalism. He was sexually promiscuous – he once said that old masters were cheaper than old mistresses – and his main ambition was to become the richest man in the land. He was probably the third richest man in Britain, and although this was due in some part to his successful speculations in North America, it does give some indication of the money then to be made in Fleet Street.

His nephew, Cecil King, wrote in *Strictly Personal* that Rothermere lacked integrity and was an incredibly inept politician. His attacks on Stanley Baldwin were so foolishly conducted that they probably saved the Prime Minister and Conservative leader at a time when the party on its own initiative would very properly have thrown Baldwin out. He seemed to regard politics as similar in kind to stock exchange speculation. You could switch your support to Hungary or to France, to Sir Oswald Mosley, the fascist leader, or against him, without any consistent purpose. His support for Hungary was said to be due to an attachment to a princess, who was widely believed to be a German spy. His enthusiasm for Hitler was deplorable.

King, presumably trying to be charitable to an uncle who had given his mother a nest-egg of £100,000, added that Rothermere was a most forceful and able man, disgusted by the ineffectiveness of British governments between the wars; hence his contempt for Baldwin and his admiration for Mussolini and Hitler whom some people felt at the time at least got things done. There is no way of knowing if he regretted his support for the two dictators when the Second World War started because he destroyed all his private papers.

Writing of 'Myself and the King Question' in the *Daily Mail*, Rothermere claimed not to have known the why and the wherefore of the extraordinary offer. Hungary was on the 'wrong' side during the First World War and lost more than two-thirds of its territory. The economy was devastated when Rothermere and his entourage arrived in Budapest in the spring of 1927. Allegedly encouraged by the Princess Hohenlohe-Waldenburg, he wrote, or had written, an editorial in the *Mail* entitled 'Hungary's Place in the Sun'. It was the first of many, and Hungarian leaders must have been gratified by so much attention from a British press baron. Nobody else was interested in their plight. The prospect of the cancellation or re-scheduling of their debts persuaded the monarchists – Hungary was a regency at the time – to offer him the Crown of St Stephen.

It must have been tempting for a man who had begun his career as a 12-shilling-a-week clerk in the Board of Trade; especially because he was assured, or so he wrote, that: 'in the prevailing enthusiastic mood of the Hungarian people, a plebiscite in my favour would be practically unanimous'. But presumably he still aspired to be the richest man in Britain, and the offer was reluctantly refused.

Perhaps it would have been better for all concerned if he had accepted. His financial expertise might have worked wonders for Hungary, and that crown would surely have satisfied his yearning for power. It would certainly have been better for the British press because without a doubt he was mainly responsible for giving it a very bad name. The press, especially the British press, has always had a bad name. Politicians talk about its essential role in democracy, proper obeisances are always made on appropriate occasions; but when a paper steps out of line, when it reveals something embarrassing, or potentially embarrassing, they invariably respond with mixed broadsides of threats and shock-horror laments of irresponsible journalism. The basic fact that good journalists faithful to their calling must be irresponsible – that is, they cannot be responsible to any politician, party or cause – is beyond them. Only yes-men are good guys. This is the cross most journalists are willing to bear; but Rothermere delivered them over to the enemy. Here was a man, not mad as was his elder brother in his last months, but possessed by his own ambitions, greed, prejudices and fears; and with no one to resist him as Northcliffe was resisted by the 'Black Friars' at *The Times*. He added nothing to the reputation of Fleet Street.

Rothermere, like so many of the rich at the time, had been frightened by the Russian Revolution, and the General Strike of 1926. He saw the working class as a threat and was determined to curb their escalating power. He wanted to cut government spending on labour exchanges, unemployment pay and the primitive national health service introduced by Lloyd George. In 1924 he saw the Labour party's first electoral victory as the spectre of revolution, although

Ramsay MacDonald's minority government was dependent upon Liberal support, which was why the notorious Zinoviev Letter was published in the *Mail* just before the second general election that year.

It is still not known if the letter was a forgery. Allegedly signed by Grigori Zinoviev, the president of the presidium of the Third Communist International, it instructed British communists to prepare for armed insurrection. If it was genuine, Zinoviev must have lived in a fantasy world (which was not impossible), because the CPUK had only 3500 members, and Labour supporters were loyal to King and country. Suspicion should have been aroused if only because copies found their way to the Conservative party and the *Mail* as well as the Foreign Office. MacDonald had drafted a protest to the Soviet government while waiting for authentication when the *Mail* published its contents under the headline 'Moscow Orders to Our Reds'. It commented that:

> The letter is addressed by the Bolsheviks in Moscow to the Soviet
> government's servants in Great Britain, the Communist party, who in turn
> are the masters of Mr Ramsay MacDonald's government, which has signed
> a treaty with Moscow whereby the Soviet is to be guaranteed a 'loan' of
> millions of British money.

Baldwin was returned to power for another four years, but there is no reason to believe that the letter was the decisive factor. Labour actually increased its vote, and Baldwin's decision to drop economic protectionism from the Conservative party's programme may well have won the election. Free trade was still an article of faith for Liberals, and many of them switched their votes because their party was in a state of disarray.

Baldwin handled the General Strike with a firmness surprising for those who thought him too lethargic to do anything but smoke his pipe, but Rothermere was not reassured. He appeared determined to prove that he was an incredibly inept politician. In the run up to the 1929 election, he threatened to support the Labour party if the Tory leader did not show an interest in Hungary. Labour won without the help of Rothermere, and Baldwin remained unmoved and unmoveable. His silence said a great deal about the man who was Prime Minister three times and served without distinction. Rothermere's newspapers were probably read by about eight million people, certainly commanding a larger audience than any other newspaper proprietor. Moreover, the *Mail* had become the only popular daily largely read by middle-class and upper-middle-class men and women. In theory at least, Baldwin should have sought its proprietor's cooperation. Expressions of sympathy for Hungary or his other pet projects would have been a small price to pay, but Rothermere discovered to his chagrin that he had no more influence than the editor of a local paper – he could bring no pressure to bear on Baldwin. His subsequent behaviour was not so much inept as utterly irrational.

First, the *Mail* nominated Lord Beaverbrook for the Tory leadership. Beaverbrook was a rival press baron, a political intriguer and equally determined to get rid of Baldwin. Secondly, the paper launched the United Empire party. It was to contest half of the parliamentary seats at the next election, and presumably eventually replace the Conservatives as the party of the right. Thirdly, Rothermere wrote a letter stating that he would not support Baldwin:

> . . . unless I know exactly what his policy is going to be, unless I have complete guarantees that such policy will be carried out if his party achieves office, and unless I am acquainted with the names of at least eight, or ten, of his most prominent colleagues in the next ministry.

His brother, Lord Northcliffe, had made similar outrageous demands of Lloyd George but had not been vain or stupid enough to put them in writing. Baldwin, speaking at a political meeting which the *Mail* had predicted would be his swansong, read out the contents of the letter and added: 'A more preposterous and insolent demand was never made on the leader of any political party. I repudiate it with contempt.' He was loudly cheered in the hall and later at the House of Commons. For all his supposed power, Rothermere had only succeeded in making a triumph out of a swansong.

Any other man in Rothermere's position would have taken a long vacation and waited until public derision had evaporated, but instead Rothermere turned his attention to continental Europe. Within a few weeks he was in Munich, where he met Hitler and wrote, or had written, a 3000-word dispatch:

> Under Herr Hitler's control the youth of Germany is effectively organized against the corruption of communism. It was with some such purpose that I founded the United Empire party in England, for it is clear that no strong anti-socialist policy can be expected from a Conservative party whose leaders are themselves tainted with semi-socialist doctrines.

The article went on to say that the British people should 'give full appreciation to the service which the National Socialist party has rendered to western Europe', and the tenor of the *Mail*'s coverage of Germany did not change after Hitler became Chancellor in 1933 and established an absolute dictatorship. Very few reports of Nazi atrocities were published; instead, Hitler was defended, and reports published elsewhere dismissed as 'pure moonshine'. Rothermere met Hitler again in Berlin in 1934, and described him as 'simple and unaffected and obviously sincere.' There was no man living whose promise he would sooner take. His enthusiasm embarrassed even Hitler; after he had advocated the return of Germany's former African colonies, he was asked to desist because Hitler looked forward to close collaboration with Britain.

The persecution of the Jews was defended in the *Mail* because, it was claimed, Germany had fallen under the control of alien elements:

In the last days of the pre-Hitler regime there were twenty times as many Jewish government officials in Germany as had existed before the war. Israelites of international attachments were insinuating themselves into key positions in the German administrative machine. Three German ministers only had direct relations with the Press, but in each case the official responsible for conveying news and interpreting policy to the public was a Jew. It is from such abuses that Hitler has freed Germany.

Among the Jewish refugees who arrived in Britain was Professor Albert Einstein, who spoke at a protest meeting in London. He was well supported by political and ecclesiastical dignitaries, but the *Evening News* wrote:

> The lecture is a piece of alien agitation on British soil; its promoters ask nothing better than that it shall make bad blood between this country and Germany . . . Intelligent and patriotic people will stay carefully away . . . not because they necessarily approve of everything done under the Hitler regime but because 'fair play' as they see it means allowing the Germans to run their own country in their own way exactly as we demand the right to run our country in our own way.

Rothermere was not the only anti-Semite in Britain, and many people, including some of those he had misinformed, admired Hitler for building the autobahns and Mussolini for making Italian trains run on time. The years of economic depression, made all the more hopeless by the failure of democratic governments in western Europe and north America to do anything about it, encouraged some to follow false prophets. A few years earlier the then *Manchester Guardian* had taken a tolerant view of the excesses of Stalin until Malcolm Muggeridge reported the horrors of man-made famine in the Soviet Union. Left-wing intellectuals were just as blind or perverse as the Colonel Blimps and Unity Mitfords. George Orwell said of them that they chipped away at English morale and tried to spread an outlook that was sometimes squashily pacifist, sometimes violently pro-Russian, but always anti-British.

It was a bad time, but that hardly excused Rothermere who apparently believed he was destined to play an influential role on the world stage. Such was the effect, to quote Baldwin again, 'of an enormous fortune rapidly made and the control of newspapers of your own.' Busy as he was, ordering the affairs of states and increasing his own fortune, Rothermere did not forget the Hungarians: 'one of the most distinguished and most gallant peoples in Europe'. They were urged to ally themselves with Germany, and Princess Hohenlohe was sent to Budapest to persuade the Regent to restore the Hapsburgs to the throne. He was more eager than ever for Britain to become part of the New Order, and after his earlier failure to persuade Lloyd George to work towards 'a modified political dictatorship' – he appeared not to know that the former

Prime Minister was a spent force – turned to Sir Oswald Mosley.

Mosley, the 6th Baronet was wealthy, then married to a daughter of the statesman Lord Curzon and a renowned womanizer. He was said to be intelligent, and was a Member of Parliament who had changed sides twice: first serving as a Conservative, then as an Independent and finally on the Labour benches. He tried to launch a Socialist party in 1931, and when that failed founded the British Union of Fascists in the following year. He attracted about 20,000 thugs and anti-Semites whose marches through London provoked the violence most of them longed for, and Rothermere decided to give them a helping hand. The *Mail* ran a recruiting campaign for them, and the *Mirror* assured its readers that as 'a purely British organization, the blackshirts will respect those principles of tolerance which are traditional in British politics. They have no prejudice either of class or race.'

The latter was obviously untrue, and their black shirts and military formations were hardly traditionally British. Other newspapers fully reported the terrors of Nazism in Germany, and the trickle of Jewish refugees became a steady stream. Rothermere was not deterred at first, his papers continuing to report Hitler and Mussolini in almost reverential terms until advertisers became uneasy. Some withdrew their advertising, and the threat of a boycott was enough to make Rothermere change his mind. Mosley recalled in his autobiography, *My Life*, that:

> Lord Rothermere explained that he was in trouble with certain advertisers, who had not liked his support of the blackshirts . . . I said, 'Do you know what Northcliffe would have done? He would have said, one more word from you and the *Daily Mail* placards tomorrow will carry the words JEWS THREATEN BRITISH PRESS. You will have no further trouble.' The long struggle fluctuated, but I lost. He felt that I was asking him to risk too much.

In other words, he was not prepared to risk his profit margins for what presumably he saw as his principles. This was despicable by any standard, although a moralist could argue that in this case greed, despite being one of the deadly sins, had a virtuous effect. What is beyond doubt is that Rothermere betrayed all the principles of journalism.

Rothermere misled his readers, and misused whatever power his news-papers gave him; but there is no evidence that he had his own way outside his own organization. Baldwin, his main opponent, survived his attacks although as Prime Minister he failed to rise to the challenge of unemployment at home and the fascist threat abroad. The *Mail* was, and remains, a Tory paper, but Baldwin refused to change or adjust his policies to win its editorial support. Instead, he publicly expressed his contempt for its proprietor on numerous occasions. The influence Rothermere had on his readers is harder to assess. He no doubt encouraged the admiration many of the well-to-do had for Hitler in the early years, but failed to popularize the British Union of Fascists. He also failed to persuade them to vote against Baldwin. The question remains whether Rothermere would have been politically powerful if he had not been such an incredibly inept politician. It can perhaps best be answered by comparing him with Beaverbrook.

William Maxwell Aitken, the 1st Baron Beaverbrook (1879–1964), was the son of a Presbyterian minister in Maple, Ontario. His financial dealings made him a millionaire by the age of 30, when he retired from business and entered British politics. He became a protégé of Andrew Bonar Law (later Prime Minister, 1922–23) who was also born in Canada, and within a year he was elected to Parliament and knighted. He was anything but inept politically, and is credited with helping to make both Lloyd George and Bonar Law Prime Minister. High Tories dismissed him as the 'little Canadian adventurer', but he was the friend and ally of men such as Winston Churchill and the Labour politician Aneurin Bevan. The intimacy of the friendships may have been exaggerated – he spent a great deal of time and money ensuring that his role in politics would not be overlooked by historians – but they did exist. He was a member of the Cabinet in both World Wars; in charge of Information in the first and of Aircraft Production in the second. In the second job he made a great contribution to the war effort. He bought the *Daily Express* in 1916, founded the *Sunday Express* two years later and acquired the *Evening Standard* in 1923. With little previous experience, he proved to be a brilliant if wayward journalist.

These two self-made men were very different. Rothermere was mainly interested in making money. Beaverbrook made a fortune in order to enter British politics, and having made his mark bought newspapers to carry on politics by other means. Rothermere was an unpleasant man; Beaverbrook could be just as nasty, but most of the journalists he employed were captivated by him. For Michael Foot, who afterwards became the leader of the Labour party, it was something more. He was hired to work on the *Standard*, and afterwards wrote in his *Debts of Honour*:

> For the next 25 years of my life I knew Beaverbrook until the day of his
> death as well, I believe, as almost any man did (not attempting for the
> moment to compete with the women), and for all that time, with
> occasional spasms of fury or hatred and one of four years of something
> worse, I loved him.

Foot had previously written for the left-wing weeklies *New Statesman* and *Tribune*, and other friends found the friendship inexplicable, discreditable, and even evil. They saw Beaverbrook as a Dracula, Svengali, Iago and Mephistopheles rolled into one. Anyone who worked for him jeopardized his immortal soul. Foot's partial explanation was that the devotion Beaverbrook could excite

[110]

in the most unlikely quarters derived from the nature and scale of his emotional radicalism. He was a rampaging individualist who favoured the rumbustious, marauding private enterprise system which had enabled him to become 'a multi- or, as he would call it, a Maxi-millionaire'. But he had inherited from his Covenanting Scottish ancestors and the traditions of American populism a detestation of the stuffiness, stupidities and snobberies of the English Establishment. He was an instinctive radical, in the true meaning of the word, with the urge to get to the roots of the question and the will to wrench them up with both hands.

Foot's appreciation is perhaps too glowing, for he has always been loyal to his friends, but Beaverbrook was a remarkable man and it showed in his newspapers. They reflected his belief in money, capitalism, Britain and the superiority of the English-speaking peoples. He was also a hyperactive editor-in-chief, and made sure that his personality, radicalism and mischievousness were evident in the pages of his papers. He told the first Royal Commission on the Press in 1949: 'I run the paper purely for the purpose of propaganda, and with no other motive.' Nevertheless, he was an inspired journalist, and knew that readers had to be entertained as well as informed. The pill had to be sugared if they were to be receptive to his propaganda. He hired the best reporters and writers available; first-rate foreign correspondents and political and labour reporters as well as the trendiest gossip columnists. They brought the glamour and excitement of the rich and powerful into the homes of ordinary people. His papers always exuded optimism. 'The *Daily Express*', Beaverbrook said, 'stands for more life – more hope – more money – more work – more happiness.'

The formula worked. The circulation of the daily rose from about 250,000 to more than four million, and a printing plant had to be built in Glasgow (in addition to the Manchester one) to handle the massive print order. It worked because the *Express* was a wonderful read, especially in its heyday after the Second World War, and because most people prefer to look on the bright side. Another reason was the social changes which Beaverbrook was the first press baron of his generation to recognize although Orwell had written about them many years before. Other left-wing writers saw life in terms of the class struggle, they still do, but Orwell saw that one of the most important developments in Britain since the First World War was the upward and downward extension of the middle class which made the old classification of society into capitalists, proletarians and small property-owners almost obsolete.

Property and financial power were concentrated in very few hands, as Marx had anticipated. Few people owned anything except clothes, furniture and possibly a house. The peasantry had long since disappeared, the independent shopkeeper and the small businessman were diminishing in numbers. Modern industry, however, was so complicated that it could not get along without great numbers of highly-paid managers, salesmen, engineers, chemists and technicians of all kinds, who in turn called into being a larger professional class of doctors, lawyers, teachers, artists, etc. In other words, the tendency of advanced capitalism was to enlarge the middle class and not to wipe it out.

Much more important, Orwell continued, was the spread of middle-class ideas and habits among the working class, who were better off in almost all ways than they were before the First World War. This was partly due to the trade unions, but mainly to the mere advance of physical science. However unjustly society was organized, certain technical advances were bound to benefit the whole community because certain kinds of goods were necessarily held in common. Nearly all citizens of civilized countries enjoyed the use of good roads, germ-free water, police protection, free libraries and free education of a kind. The rich and the poor could read the same books, see the same films and listen to the same radio programmes. (Later on, and more importantly, they would share the same television programmes.)

Differences had also been diminished by the mass production of cheap clothes and improvements in housing. The clothes of the rich and poor differed less. The modern council house, with its bathroom and electric light, was smaller than the stockbroker's villa, but it was recognizably the same kind of house. The effect of all this was a general softening of manners. In tastes, habits, manners and outlook, the working and middle classes were drawing together. The unjust distinctions remained, but the real differences were diminished. The old-style proletarians – collarless, unshaven and with muscles warped by heavy labour – were decreasing in numbers, and after 1918 there began to appear something that had never existed in Britain before: people of indeterminate social class.

These social changes were not much in evidence until the 1930s, but the success of the *Express* was assured once Beaverbrook had identified his market. Unemployment was still rife in this decade, but the economic upturn began earlier in Britain than in the United States and the new lifestyle of Orwell's indeterminate social class became increasingly evident. New suburbs, often large tracts of identical semi-detached houses, sprang up round the bigger cities. Montague Burton, 'The Tailor of Taste', dressed clerks and skilled workers in three-piece suits for 37 shillings and sixpence (£1.87½ – although this sum today bears no comparison with the original value). The £100 car became available, although most of the new suburbanites commuted to work by train or bus. And millions of them bought the *Express* because Beaverbrook, the Canadian born outside the British class system, understood their interests and aspirations. Critics sneered at him for taking sophistication to the suburbs, but few sneers were heard on the early-morning commuter trains to London. They loved it.

The *Express* should have been a superb medium for Beaverbrook's propaganda. Most of its readers belonged to the new indeterminate class; they lived in a changing world and welcomed guidance. The paper also had a universal readership of sorts because of its brightness and verve. It was read by politicians and duchesses as well as clerks and skilled workers. But the pill was so well sugared that few people noticed the medicine. Most of his campaigns came to nothing; indeed, they went unnoticed outside the columns of his newspapers. Tom Driberg (later Lord Bradwell), another Labour politician who worked for Beaverbrook and was not much less sympathetic than Michael Foot, wrote in his *Beaverbrook*:

> He has the money, he has the brains: where is the power? It has escaped
> him. He has achieved high office, but not the highest. Most men have their
> price, but not every man. He has failed signally to influence public opinion,
> among those high in the state or among ordinary citizens. The former
> mostly regard him as a menace; the latter buy his newspapers in millions for
> their entertainment value, consistently disregard their editorial advice, and
> think of him politically, not without the bantering affection proper to a
> national institution, as a comic 'character' . . . To the public he is 'The
> Beaver' – a zoological symbol of tireless industry.

Randolph Churchill, who also worked for Beaverbrook but invariably bit the hand that fed him, said that he 'never espoused any cause which was both honourable and successful'. Perhaps Churchill had in mind the hate campaigns against the British Council and Lord Mountbatten which were animated by the spirit of vendetta, but some of Beaverbrook's campaigns were honourable if not successful. He liked to be known among his staff as 'The Lord', but was against hereditary titles and privilege. He was opposed to Winston Churchill's intervention in the Soviet Union at the end of the First World War, and afterwards his return to the Gold Standard. He wanted an Irish settlement, and appealed to his readers to give the first Labour government 'a fair chance'. He reversed himself in 1945 and ran one of the dirtiest press campaigns in recent electoral history, but it was not as dirty as Churchill's. Sir Stafford Cripps, the Chancellor of the Exchequer, rightly complained of 'guttersnipe politics'. Beaverbrook was an appeaser, but did not echo Rothermere's adulation for the dictators. He supported Munich and the dismemberment of Czechoslovakia, but reflected rather than led public opinion. He insisted to the end and against all the evidence that there would be no war in 1939. He went on to oppose wartime food rationing, and in 1942 demanded a Second Front to relieve the German pressure on the Soviet Union.

It was a very mixed bag. Some of the campaigns were nasty or mischievous, others were wrong-headed and a few above reproach. Opinions vary about their content, but the undeniable fact is that they failed. Apart from his early years as a politician when his wheeling and dealing was effective, power, as Driberg wrote, escaped him. His greatest disappointment was the failure of his campaign for imperial economic unity.

The Empire Free Trade Crusade, as Beaverbrook preferred to call it, was launched after the 1929 general election and was continued on and off until his death in 1964. It was always a non-starter; neither the British nor the other Commonwealth governments wanted an arrangement that was the reverse of free trade in that its tariff walls would have damaged trade with the rest of the world. It was thus rejected at the 1930 Imperial Conference, but Beaverbrook was obdurate and continued to champion his cause, taking the United States as his example. Despite the Depression, which had its beginnings in the United States, free and unimpeded trade between the states had undoubtedly contributed to its economic success; but Beaverbrook ignored the fact that it was a sub-continental union, and that in trade and tariffs the US Constitution vested an authority in the federal government which Westminster could not exert over Ottawa, Canberra and other Commonwealth capitals. It revealed his lack of understanding of how Britain was governed, of its relations with the rest of the world and of British life in general. His campaign for Splendid Isolation from continental Europe, which would have won votes in Chicago, was another example of a lost and misguided cause. He remained a North American until the end.

The vendetta which Rothermere and Beaverbrook waged against Baldwin has already been mentioned, but their defeat was particularly painful for the Canadian. They were old adversaries. Beaverbrook had helped the former ironmaster from Worcestershire up the political ladder in 1916 when he suggested to Bonar Law that Baldwin would be a good parliamentary private secretary because he was 'rich, reticent and neutral in character'. No doubt it was intended as a joke, but Baldwin's political career prospered and he confessed later that the two of them had fought for Law's soul. Beaverbrook probably resented his subsequent advancement, and certainly the rift between them widened when Baldwin became Chancellor of the Exchequer and failed to consult him. Beaverbrook then decided that Churchill was the man to oust Baldwin from the Tory leadership. It was a ridiculous idea because Churchill was not then popular in the party, but his victim struck back with a ferocity that caused a political sensation. He attacked the two press barons in an interview published by the *People*: 'I care not what they say or think. They are both men that I would not have in my house. I do not respect them. Who are they?'

This should have warned them that they were dealing with a man who could take care of himself and was confident of his position in the country if not within the party. But perhaps because he was Canadian-born, Beaverbrook did not realize that his adversary's Englishness, the pipe-smoking and lazy pragmatism, appealed to the public. The vendetta was continued with and without the cooperation of Rothermere. They were always unsuccessful, but Baldwin was finally sufficiently angered by their machinations to deliver what was intended as a *coup de grâce* at a by-election meeting in 1931:

> The newspapers attacking me are not newspapers in the ordinary sense. They are engines of propaganda for the constantly changing policies, desires, personal wishes, personal likes and dislikes of the two men.
>
> What are their methods? Their methods are direct falsehood, misrepresentation, half-truths, the alteration of the speaker's meaning by publishing a sentence apart from the context, such as you see in these leaflets handed out outside the doors of this hall; suppression and editorial criticism of speeches which are not reported in the paper. These are methods hated alike by the public and by the whole of the rest of the press . . .
>
> What the proprietorship of these papers is aiming at is power, and power without responsibility – the prerogative of the harlot throughout the ages.

That famous last phrase was originally coined by Baldwin's cousin, Rudyard Kipling, in conversation with Beaverbrook (then Max Aitken) with whom he had been friendly until they split over Ireland. Its use here by Baldwin secured his political career until he chose to retire. It also damaged the reputation of the British popular press, perhaps irreparably. Certainly its critics, including those who hate the idea of a free press immaculate or otherwise, still use it with effect. Of course it did not stop Beaverbrook or Rothermere.

Beaverbrook's last duel with the Prime Minister was in 1936 over the Abdication crisis, which was brought about by the determination of Edward VIII – not yet crowned – to marry Wallis Simpson, an American who had just divorced her second husband. It was a crisis which shook the Establishments of Britain and the Commonwealth countries to their foundations. The King sought Beaverbrook's advice, and according to Hugh Cudlipp in his *The Prerogative of the Harlot*: 'Edward's happiness, the threat to the standing of the Monarchy, and the developing constitutional predicament were of less concern to Beaverbrook than the opportunity to challenge his adversary yet again in an unexpected and august arena.'

This is not altogether fair. Again, being an outsider, Beaverbrook had no instinct for the curious, almost semi-mystical bonds between the British Crown, Parliament and People. He was indifferent to the constitutional dangers posed by a King who tended to speak and act independently of his ministers. More surprisingly, he did not seem to understand that the monarchy was the linchpin of the Commonwealth. For him, it was merely a useful institution. He had not known the King before the crisis but warmed towards him because he also loved the Empire. He was not shocked by the liaison with Mrs Simpson, perhaps because his own sex life was, to say the least, unconventional. That said, Beaverbrook's motives were mixed and, according to Edward: 'an additional impulse was furnished by his long-standing enmity for Mr Baldwin'.

Beaverbrook was in it from the beginning. He persuaded the other press barons to report Mrs Simpson's second divorce without reference to the King, and for many weeks the British press maintained a silence although the world press was full of stories on the royal liaison. The silence was not imposed by official censorship – neither the King nor Parliament had that power – but by what was known as a gentlemen's agreement. Given that breathing space, Beaverbrook's strategy was to delay events in the belief that a morganatic marriage – which would have made Mrs Simpson a wife but not a Queen – would eventually become acceptable to Westminster and the Commonwealth parliaments. The gaff was blown by the then Bishop of Bradford, whose sermon criticizing the King was reported by the *Yorkshire Post*, whereupon all the national dailies rushed to break the story. Baldwin, however, realizing that the supremacy of Parliament over the monarchy was being challenged, had already acted. He had established that a morganatic marriage was unacceptable to Commonwealth premiers, and had then presented the King with two stark alternatives: break the liaison and remain on the throne, or marry and abdicate. It was a masterly performance.

Beaverbrook lost, as usual; but to be fair, Edward, befuddled by passion, had been less than honest with him. Nevertheless, it must have been a bitter defeat. Apart from Churchill, who was shouted down during the debate in the House of Commons, and the Beaverbrook and Rothermere papers, Baldwin had won the support of Parliament and the rest of the press as well as the Commonwealth governments. Moreover, the one journalist who played a decisive role in resolving the crisis was not Beaverbrook but Geoffrey Dawson of *The Times*. The old Thunderer and not the *Express* was the one voice to be heeded in Downing Street.

Beaverbrook's rancour was revealed many years later when he reviewed the fourth volume of *The History of The Times*, which gave a full account of Dawson's activities during the crisis. Apart from the Prime Minister, he said, Dawson was the most important factor in compelling the King to abdicate, and he did it by methods which many would condemn, pursuing his quest with a vigour that seemed more like venom. This was a travesty of the truth. The King certainly felt that Dawson was an important factor – after the story broke he ordered Baldwin to find out, and if necessary stop, what was going to appear in *The Times*. Also Dawson certainly had greater access to the Prime Minister than most Cabinet Ministers, but the notes he made after their meetings suggest that he acted as a reporter and not as an adviser. He passed on the opinions of readers as expressed in letters to the paper, for rightly or wrongly he had decided not to publish correspondence on the crisis until it was resolved; but he did not compromise his editorial independence and integrity.

For instance, when an embarrassed Baldwin, at the King's behest, asked to see an editorial before publication, Dawson sent him a proof just before midnight – when the first edition was already being printed.

This fourth volume of *The History of The Times* deals with contemporary criticisms of the press in general and *The Times* in particular. It said that there was no official or unofficial censorship of the press, that the nearest approach to interference was the customary request from Buckingham Palace to respect the King's privacy during his annual holiday. There was no general collusion except in regard to reporting Mrs Simpson's second divorce. Moreover, the King's marriage was a very serious question, involving constitutional issues of great importance, and was not seen as an issue to be debated in the press until the King's intentions were indisputably established.

So much for the position of the British press in general. By modern standards, the proprietors and editors were over-cautious, if not diffident, but the First World War and the Roaring Twenties had not much diminished the national respect for the monarchy. Edward was also very popular, and was seen by many to represent the new generation who would eventually rejuvenate the nation. The attitude of the press was understandable, if nothing more.

The case of *The Times* and its editor was somewhat different. Its staff regarded the paper as unique and rightly deserving the respect of all right-minded men, and Dawson was the embodiment of this view. Educated at Eton and Magdalen College, Oxford, he was elected a fellow of All Souls before going to South Africa at the turn of the century as private secretary to the High Commissioner, Lord Milner. He became a journalist almost by accident, when Milner persuaded the owners of the *Johannesburg Star* to appoint him editor. He also wrote for *The Times*, and Northcliffe appointed him editor in 1912. Northcliffe's determination to use *The Times* as Beaverbrook used the *Express* led to Dawson's resignation in 1919. He returned to the editorial chair in 1923 on the condition that Astor (later Lord Astor of Hever), the new proprietor, confirmed the independence that all editors of *The Times* had enjoyed before Northcliffe. His control over the editorial content of the paper was absolute, and was the envy of editors on both sides of the Atlantic.

Dawson, however, saw himself as 'the secretary-general of the Establishment', which would have horrified Barnes and Delane who had made *The Times* the greatest newspaper in the world. He was an elitist who believed that affairs of state were best left to men of his own kind. He knew what was at stake better than most, if only because his class had flourished under the kind of monarchy which had evolved before Edward became King. He also had access; Baldwin was an old friend, and they belonged to the same club. According to his own lights, he behaved impeccably. For instance, the *History* records that Dawson knew that *The Times* was expected to give a lead,

[117]

but he did not go out of his way to influence other editors when they sought his advice. The charge that Baldwin used the paper for his own purposes was dismissed. Dawson did not receive instructions from the Prime Minister or in turn try to influence government decisions to an improper degree. Baldwin was glad to discuss with him questions of procedure and constitutional correctness, but there was no evidence that Baldwin ever tried to inspire anything printed in the paper. Arguably he did not have to – Dawson and Baldwin belonged to the same class. Rightly or wrongly, under Dawson *The Times* was the Top People's paper.

There can be no doubt, however, that Dawson played an important role in resolving the crisis. To that extent Beaverbrook was right. When Rothermere's *Mail* threatened to break the agreed press silence on 23 November 1936, with a leading article panegyric on the King's virtues entitled 'The King Edward Touch', Dawson felt that it was time to respond, however subtly. On 25 November *The Times* contained a mischievous editorial, ostensibly about the choice of a governor-general for South Africa: 'It is the position – the position of the King's deputy no less than that of the King himself – that ought to be kept high above public reproach or ridicule, and that is incomparably more important than the individual who fills it . . .'. Once the sermon of the Bishop of Bradford had opened the sluice gates, his editorials set the direction and tone of the national debate. This was power, legitimate power in that *The Times* reflected the opinion of the informed majority and transformed it into a political weapon which destroyed a King who believed that he had a divine right to marry an unacceptable woman regardless of the constitutional and political consequences. The paper helped to demolish the so-called King's party, a group including Churchill, Beaverbrook, Rothermere and a mixed bag of right-wing Tories and left-wing intellectuals who had their own reasons for advocating a morganatic marriage. When the *Express* announced that the Abdication crisis was over, *The Times* said that such a marriage would have only served to acknowledge the fact that the woman the King wanted to marry was not fit to be Queen.

The Act of Abdication was signed and announced on 10 December 1936. Determined to destroy any idea of the retiring King as a romantic figure, who might retain the sympathy of some of his subjects and perhaps inspire a party bent on his restoration, Dawson wrote an editorial (11 December) entitled 'King Edward's Choice'. It is worthy of extensive quotes. After expressing regrets over the King's decision and repeating that the initiative had come from him, he went on:

> Above all let us have no talk of 'romance' about what is indeed a drama, but a drama of the deepest tragedy. King Edward had most of the qualities that would have made him a great Constitutional Monarch. He had shown himself

brave, completely free from pompousness, chivalrous where his affections were engaged, conscientious in his everyday public duties, attractive to a crowd, genuinely interested in the condition of the poor as he went about among them. He was unfortunate, no doubt, in some of his intimates; but he also had advisors who served him with courage and prudence, and it would have been well if he could have brought himself to prefer them to the others . . .

They profoundly misunderstood the earlier signs of division in this country who represented it as an issue between 'the people's King' and a hide-bound set of aristocrats and ecclesiastics. It would be far more accurate to say that His Majesty's circle was too largely composed of men and women, some of them of high birth and all of them remote from 'the people', who cared far less for his welfare than for their own amusement. The real clash was between the thoughtlessness of an exotic society and the hard core of a British tradition of conduct which is common to all classes in this country; but it must also be said in fairness that none of us can realize how hard is the path of a King in choosing good friends.

That, amid all his great qualities, there was also something lacking in himself is sufficiently shown by the unprecedented decision recorded this morning; for it is proof of obstinacy rather than of strength that it must have been reached in the face of a very human reluctance to abandon a position which afforded him so many proofs of success. For those of us who are more humbly and happily placed there is assuredly nothing but relief in being able to avoid the burdens of a Crown. What seems almost incredible is that any man who was born and trained to such high responsibilities, who had clearly the capacity to undertake them, and who had in fact begun to exercise them with the complete good will of the nation, should sacrifice it all to a personal preference for another way of life. *Omnium consensu capax Imperii nisi imperasset* – the well-worn quotation from Tacitus is irresistible. It can hardly have been a better verdict upon the Emperor Galba than it is upon King Edward that all men would have judged him worthy of the Throne if he had never ascended it.

They don't write editorials like that any more, and not only because few readers even of the posh papers would recognize the Latin tag. It was the greatest moment in the post-Northcliffe history of *The Times*. Never again would it play such a role in the life of the nation, in part because of Dawson. Indeed, even before he wrote that editorial he had begun to ignore the principles of Barnes and Delane, and, no doubt unwittingly, was walking in the footsteps of Northcliffe, Rothermere and Beaverbrook. He ignored the noble traditions of *The Times*; that while the editor had complete control over the paper's contents, personal power must be limited; that the quality that gave the paper its distinction was not conferred by one man, but was the collective contribution of the editorial staff. In other words, he was prone to use the paper as an instrument for his own propaganda.

The History of The Times put it differently in trying to explain why Dawson articulated, if he did not actually conceive, the policy of appeasement of Hitler and Mussolini. Dawson had no personal experience of continental Europe, and spoke none of its languages; he was an imperialist who viewed European realities in the light of Empire issues. He came to look upon the Continent with the detachment of a Commonwealth journalist. The 1937 Imperial Conference laid emphasis upon peace between nations and the adjustment of national needs by cooperation, joint inquiry and conciliation. These were clichés which an experienced journalist should have questioned, but Dawson found them a perfect expression of his own conception of foreign affairs.

Moreover, he was not convinced that Germany was determined to dominate Europe. He was not alone in this. Few Britons were prepared to face up to reality, but if the editor of *The Times* was traditionally expected to reflect informed opinion, he was also required to seek out truth; in the words of the famous *Times* editorial of 1852 (quoted in Chapter 1): '. . . to present to his readers not such things as statecraft would wish them to know but the truth as near as he can attain it.'

This Dawson failed to do. In pursuit of his political ends he did not hesitate to censor the dispatches of his foreign correspondents when they disclosed facts which, in his view, could turn public opinion against the policy he espoused. Instead of being *primus inter pares* (first among equals), he centralized his authority over the paper and for long periods acted as his own foreign editor and military correspondent. In the end he was no better than Beaverbrook, conceivably worse. At least the readers of the *Express* ignored Beaverbrook's propaganda; the readers of *The Times*, or many of them, put their faith in the paper – and were betrayed.

ADOLPH OCHS AND THE SULZBERGERS

The respect a newspaper commands around the world depends largely upon the country in which it is published. A perfect paper would go largely unrecognized if it was published in Luxembourg or Monaco. During the heyday of the British Empire, when vast areas of the world were administered from London and the remainder was affected in one way or another by British policy, the London *Times* was required reading in all capital cities. The paper was not the official voice of the government, but the editor and his senior writers had easy access to the seats of power in Whitehall and Westminster. It also reflected the attitudes and concerns of the Establishment. Foreign ministers knew that in most instances *The Times* was better informed than their embassies in London, and its foreign correspondents were often treated as if they had ambassadorial rank. The old story of the butler announcing the arrival of 'the press and the gentleman from *The Times*' may not have been true, but it was an indication of the respect the paper enjoyed.

This changed when London ceased to be the centre of power after the Second World War and the dissolution of Empire. The Anglo–American special relationship cushioned the decline for some years; as chief Washington correspondent of *The Times* during the 1960s I still had easy access to high places, but it was no longer the world's top newspaper. It remained a good newspaper, in some ways a better one, and was still widely read abroad but the emergence of America as a superpower placed the *New York Times* at the top of the international league. This was also a good newspaper although different from its namesake in London. The editors in West 43rd Street were more interested in news than opinion.

The reputation of the London *Times* was of course built on its fine news service, but the editorials took pride of place. This was reflected in the organization of the editorial staff. The editor was responsible for all sections of the paper, but his prime concern was the editorial page. The assistant editors, those responsible for foreign, home and business news, were until recently expected to write editorials and some of them paid less attention to news-gathering than they should have done. That was largely left to the next layer of executives, the news editors. The news columns did not suffer, but the top men of the top people's newspaper saw themselves as moulders of opinion. Most of the modern editors were Establishment men first and journalists second. They were able men, but few of them had been reporters or foreign correspondents. The emphasis on editorials was also strengthened by the traditional independence of the editor. Except during the Northcliffe period, the proprietor had no say or influence on the paper's editorial content. In a very real way, the London *Times* was the editor's newspaper.

It had been different on the *New York Times* since Adolph Ochs (1858–1935) saved it from bankruptcy in the 1890s. The chief editorial executive, the managing editor, did not write editorials and was not responsible for them. His prime concern was news, and successive managing editors were former reporters and foreign correspondents and not editorial writers. The division between news-gathering and editorials, and the subordinate position of the editorial-page editor, was common to most American newspapers, but the emphasis on news was especially strong because of Ochs. His idea of a newspaper was summed up in the classic slogan, 'All the News That's Fit to Print.'

Ochs, a Jew of German origin, was from Tennessee. He had always wanted to be a newspaperman and Horace Greeley of the *New York Tribune* was his boyhood hero. He started in Knoxville at the age of 14, first sweeping floors and then working as a compositor and reporter. He was only 20 when he bought a failing newspaper, the *Chattanooga Times*, with a down payment of $250. Gay Talese wrote in *The Kingdom and the Power: History of the New York Times* that Ochs treated the *Chattanooga Times* as he was later to treat, on a much greater scale, the *New York Times*:

> He made it into a *news*paper and not a gazette of opinion, or showcase for
> star writers, or a champion of the underdog or topdog, or a crusader for
> political or social reform. Ochs had something to sell – news – and he hoped
> to sell it dispassionately and with the guarantee that it was reliable and
> unsoiled and not deviously inspired. Ochs wanted to be accepted in
> Chattanooga, to grow up with the town and help it grow, and he knew that
> one way to do this was not to criticize it but, inoffensively, to boost it.

Chattanooga did not grow as expected, but Ochs prospered despite some disastrous land speculation and with borrowed money bought the *New York Times* for $75,000.

The *Times* had been founded in 1851 by Henry Raymond (1820–69), who had worked for Greeley. He had taken the London *Times* as his model, and from the beginning its news service was extensive and balanced. Raymond was a good journalist but he was also actively involved in politics. He wrote the first Republican platform in 1856, and served as Lieutenant-Governor of New York and as a Congressman. The paper inevitably suffered, and the decline continued after Raymond's death in 1869. When Ochs bought the company (he was the publisher from 1896 to 1935) the circulation had dropped to 9000, less than it had been during its first year of publication. Pulitzer's *World* and

Hearst's *Journal* were between them selling more than a million copies a day. The *Sun, Herald* and *Tribune* were also doing well, but Ochs was not deterred.

Ochs was a businessman who wanted to make money, but there was no question that he would try to compete with the *World* and *Journal*. He did not want to rake muck or attack authority. He wanted to grow up with New York and help it to expand and mature. Greeley's *Tribune* had become an organ of the Republican party and was rather reactionary. Ochs concluded that there was a market, especially among the business community, for the kind of paper he wanted to publish; an impartial newspaper of record which would 'not soil the breakfast linen'. He wanted to give:

> . . . the news, all the news, in concise and attractive form, in language
> that is parliamentary in good society, and give it early, if not earlier, than it
> can be learned through any other reliable medium; to give the news
> impartially, without fear or favor, regardless of any party, sect, or interest
> involved.

As a statement on the duties of the press, it did not compare with the two magisterial editorials which appeared in the London *Times* in 1852 (quoted in part in Chapter 1) but it was wholly admirable. No less important, Ochs tried to live up to it. The editorial staff soon became the largest in the business, and reporters were expected to report exhaustively. Normal editing and compression were discouraged for fear of altering the meaning and balance of stories. Objectivity was taken to such lengths that the paper became known as the 'good, gray *Times*'; reliable, informative, balanced but dull. Little space was given to headlines, but every fire in the city was reported. There was no sugar on the pill, readers had to be interested in news or look elsewhere. Some of Ochs's men must have wondered if the paper would survive, but in 1901 when he cut the cover price from three cents to one cent the circulation was tripled in a year. It was in excess of 100,000 in the following year and more than 300,000 in 1915.

Ochs did not appear to be closely involved in the production of the paper. Unlike Bennett, Greeley, Hearst and other press barons, he did not spend a great deal of time in the newsroom but the managing editor and editorial-page editor did not enjoy the independence of the editor of the London *Times*. They generally knew what he wanted and did not want, and when in doubt they always referred to him. According to Talese, 30 years after his death the *Times* was still Ochs's paper, 'his words of wisdom being re-echoed by old sages still under his influence'.

In 1870 the *Times* had covered itself in glory by campaigning against William Tweed, the Tammany boss who over the years had robbed New York city of $200 million. There were no more campaigns after Ochs bought the paper. It was not that he was indifferent to corruption and malpractice, but crusading was not seen as a function of a respectable newspaper. The *Times* would report investigations but not investigate. That was the responsibility of the district attorney, the state legislature and Congress. Similarly critics were not expected to be too critical. Book reviewers were asked to treat books as news and to be courteous in their comment. Theatre critics were more difficult to discipline but while Ochs was alive the fate of a new Broadway show did not necessarily depend upon the *Times* review.

His approach to politics and business was also restrained. The paper stood for democracy and capitalism, the established order and middle-class values. The public had the right to know, but only up to a point. Ochs had a clear idea of what was in the national interest, and believed that discretion was necessary at times. (This view survived after his death and led, for example, to the decision to censor reports of the preparation for the Bay of Pigs Cuban invasion in 1961.) Discretion did not have to be exercised much during the early years. Washington DC was still a sleepy southern town, and the president had yet to assume great power. Out-of-town correspondents were few, and they could cover the White House, the Treasury and the State and War Departments in a couple of hours because there was little to report. The United States did not have a foreign policy as normally understood apart from the Monroe Doctrine. Foreign news was well covered, partly because of the exchange arrangement made with the London *Times* in 1900, but the *New York Times* was still essentially a metropolitan paper with a limited circulation area.

There was another reason why Ochs was content to report the news and avoid criticism. He wanted to belong, to be part of what eventually emerged as the eastern Establishment. This was natural enough for a second-generation American still uncertain of his place in society, and he was probably less secure than others because of his German Jewish background. His brother, George Washington Ochs, changed his name to Oakes because of anti-German sentiment during the First World War, and anti-Semitism was so strong at the time that Ochs posted an armed guard outside his office. This prejudice must have been doubly painful because he shared with other prominent New Yorkers of German Jewish origin a low opinion of Jewish immigrants from eastern Europe who had begun to arrive in their tens of thousands at the turn of the century.

The established Jewish community were ashamed of the newcomers, and perhaps a little afraid because they encouraged anti-Semitism. It resented their initial reluctance to come to terms with their new country, and their attachment to Yiddish and foreign customs. Some of the newcomers were also socialists, which was regarded as anti-American. Ochs wanted cultural assimilation, and believed that a Jew could be faithful to his religion and at the same time become a good American. He did not want the *Times* to be regarded as a Jewish newspaper, which explains why his managing editors were always Christian although many of the Jews on the editorial staff were superb journalists. This practice was followed by his successors, and the first Jewish managing editor, A.M. Rosenthal, was only appointed in 1969. It also explained Ochs's opposition to Zionism (which remained the policy of the paper until the state of Israel was established in 1948), and to anything that could prolong Jewish separateness.

Ochs made the *New York Times* as much an establishment newspaper as the London *Times*, but he was not accepted by the white Anglo-Saxon Protestant establishment because he was a Jew. The residual WASP prejudice emerged when he died in 1935, and President Roosevelt described the perfectly legal arrangement to ensure that heavy death duties would not be paid as 'a dirty Jewish trick'. In fact, Ochs had ploughed most of his earnings back into the company and the arrangement was intended to ensure the continued independence of the paper. Arthur Hays Sulzberger (1891–1968), Ochs's son-in-law, who succeeded as publisher – from 1935 to 1961 – believed that control of the company by the family was the only way to guarantee editorial independence, which might well have been threatened if stock had been sold to pay the death duties. He was probably right, but the arrangement also established a dynasty unusual in newspapers. It has lasted for four generations, and is likely to continue although the company went public in 1971.

Neither Sulzberger nor his successors tried to exploit the power of the paper for personal or political reasons. They were essentially modest men who regarded themselves a guardians of the paper's traditions. While they still had the last word, the editors were allowed to run the paper as long as they abided by its traditions. Greybeards in the newsroom also saw themselves as guardians, and probably made the paper greyer than it need have been, but for decades the link between the past and present was Ochs's daughter, Iphigene, and the wife of Arthur Sulzberger. Her son-in-law, Orvil Dryfoos, briefly succeeded her husband, and her son, Arthur Ochs Sulzberger became the fourth member of the family to be publisher.

Unlike Katherine Graham of the *Washington Post*, Iphigene Sulzberger did not play an active role and rarely came into the office, but her influence was all-pervasive. Talese described her as: 'the *grande dame* of the *Times*, its good gray lady, and the editors and executives were courtly in her presence and mindful in her absence'. That was one way of putting it; although *Times* men enjoyed enviable job security, they knew that promotion largely depended upon the Sulzbergers liking them. They also knew that the Washington bureau chief, James Reston, had as much authority in New York as the managing editor because of his friendship with Iphigene.

Reston, known to everybody as Scotty, was a superb journalist and a very likable man. His scoops were legendary, and in his prime he had no rivals. He was the confidant of every Secretary of State and most Presidents for more than two decades after the Second World War, and when he dined with ambassadors he was given the place of honour instead of a chair at the middle of the table where journalists normally sit. He was a child when his parents emigrated from Scotland, and as with most successful immigrants he was grateful and more obviously patriotic than most native-born Americans. He believed that the United States was God's Own Country, and assumed that its elected representatives were decent, altruistic men who sought office only to help make the country a more perfect republic. Or rather he wanted to assume that they were, which made him reluctant to criticize. He adopted in his later years a kind of avuncular approach to Washington, his column explaining rather than revealing its strange goings-on although he was still capable of writing block-busting scoops. This was why he was not the greatest journalist of his time, as his staff believed. That accolade must be awarded to Walter Lippmann, but it did him no harm with the Sulzbergers whose political and patriotic attitudes were identical.

Reston, for all his scoops, was also an Establishment man. Arguably he would not have scored so many if he had been otherwise, and there is a strong case for journalists to associate themselves with established authority. Fortunately, it is not accepted by every journalist, but it suited the *Times* and most of its readers. The United States had emerged from the war as the superpower, the only bulwark against communist imperialism, the bread basket for much of the world and the provider of foreign aid first to devastated western Europe and then to much of the Third World. The United States was seen to be the hope of the world, and the assumption was that the 'American Century' was about to begin.

The United States had certainly grown up, and as Ochs had hoped that the *Chattanooga Times* would grow with that city, so the *New York Times* grew with the United States. Circulation steadily increased, and by 1951 the paper was selling 500,000 copies a day and more than a million on Sundays. The number of pages also increased, and about 200 acres of forest had to be razed to provide newsprint for every Sunday edition. In the same year about 137,000 columns of advertisements were published, and revenue rose to $56 million. Profits remained relatively low, not much more than $2,500,000, because Sulzberger continued to plough money back into the paper. If there was an editorial budget, it did not inhibit the editors from striving to cover the world to an extent that other newspapers found hard to believe. The *Times* employed more foreign correspondents than any of them. The London *Times*, which for a hundred years or more had set the standards for foreign reporting, might send two or three men to cover an important international conference whereas the *New York Times* would send a dozen. On such occasions the competition was not always between the *Times* and other American papers, but between the correspondents of its daily and Sunday papers. Its Washington bureau was larger than the national news desk of the *Washington Post*. It was required reading in every capital, and the house magazine of the eastern Establishment.

The *Times* had become a very good newspaper, not particularly well-written but serious, even earnest, and comprehensive. No other newspaper published as many stories, but it was not and never had been true to the letter of its slogan, 'All the News That's Fit to Print'. Apart from the physical impossibility of printing every word that poured into the building from its correspondents and the news agencies, Ochs's concept of the national interest had always required a discretion in the selection of news which some journalists regarded as news management. This process was intensified in the era of Arthur Hays Sulzberger. A further difference was that in the past discretion had been exercised by the publisher on the advice of his editors or vice versa, but by the early 1950s Arthur Hays Sulzberger was listening to other voices.

He was, on his own admission, a patriot and conservative. Although a Democrat, he supported General Eisenhower in the 1952 presidential election when most of his editors favoured Adlai Stevenson. He courageously opposed McCarthyism, in public speeches and supported the editorial policy of the paper yet dismissed two employees who refused to say whether they were members, or former members, of the Communist party. Worse was to follow. Allen Dulles, the director of the Central Intelligence Agency (CIA), passed the word that the situation in Guatemala was very delicate and that he and his brother, John Foster Dulles, the Secretary of State, would be obliged if Sydney Gruson, the *Times* correspondent in Mexico City, was not sent to cover the story. It was hinted that Gruson was a dangerous radical. It was true that he was born in Ireland, and travelled on a British passport issued in Warsaw. Not that these irrelevant details had bothered Sulzberger up till now. The *Times* had in fact hired many Britons in the past, and one of them had been managing editor although officially he was only the acting managing editor because Ochs did not want to be regarded as pro-British, which he was. Nevertheless, he now followed the CIA's line and Gruson was ordered to stay in Mexico.

Gruson was not in fact a radical. The reason why Dulles did not want him in Guatemala was because the CIA was planning a coup against the leftist regime of Colonel Jacob Arbenz and did not want a good and well-informed correspondent such as Gruson to cover it.

In retrospect, it is difficult to explain why Sulzberger acted as he did. Foreign correspondents are vulnerable, and cannot operate efficiently if they are not supported by the head office. Once in my own career I was accused of being a communist, and the London *Times* was requested to remove me. The editor, Sir William Haley, quite rightly refused. Harrison Salisbury, a former *New York Times* foreign correspondent and national editor, suggested in his book *Without Fear or Favor: The New York Times and Its Times* that Sulzberger was a creature of his times. CIA and *Times* men belonged to what

Vice-President Spiro Agnew excoriated as the 'eastern elite'. For the most part, they had gone to the same schools and universities. They shared not only a cultural and social identity but also a common view of the world. Together they had fought the Germans and Japanese, and it was natural that they should continue to work together against the Soviet Union, a new and more dangerous enemy.

Salisbury's explanation is not wholly persuasive. Ochs's pronouncement that the *Times* would give the news impartially regardless of any party, sect or interest involved had been compromised. It is true that foreign correspondents of all nationalities generally get to know their own, and other, intelligence people, because they tend to know more about the countries in which they are stationed than the diplomats do. Oddly enough these contacts are also more inclined to talk. When I arrived in a strange capital I often sought out the 'spook' at both the British and American embassies. They had access to information, and information is a marketable commodity; not to be paid for by working for them, but to be exchanged. They also tended to have a better perspective than the average diplomat, and they were interested in the views of experienced correspondents whose circle of contacts was nearly always wider than their own. Some of my best friends worked for the British Secret Intelligence Service (SIS) and the CIA, but I never compromised the paper or my professional integrity. It was strictly business, like having a drink with the ambassador or interviewing the foreign minister.

Salisbury admitted that some of his colleagues had continued to cooperate with CIA men, whom they had met when serving in the Office of Strategic Services (OSS), the forerunner of the CIA during the Second World War. Wallace Carroll, Reston's deputy in Washington, was a close friend of Richard Helms who succeeded Dulles as the agency's director, and had been given leaves of asbence 'to undertake important psychological warfare and intelligence-related assignments'. Sam Hope Brewer had also served in the OSS, and was an old friend of Kim Philby. They had worked together as correspondents in Spain and the Middle East, and before the British traitor defected to Moscow the CIA formally requested that Brewer should also work for them. Presumably they wanted him to keep an eye on Philby, who was already under suspicion. The blatant request was refused, but Salisbury's conclusion was that he, Brewer, had served two masters – the CIA and the *Times* – for years.

The *Times* was not the only American paper with men who cooperated with, or worked for, the agency. In those days the CIA were still the good guys, and Richard Bissell, who ran the agency's department of dirty tricks or covert operations, once told a group of Washington journalists that it was their duty to cooperate. Unbeknown to him, I was present and to my astonishment not one of my colleagues demurred. It was therefore hardly surprising when the *Times* decided not to print the full story of CIA involvement in the Cuban invasion in April 1961.

The CIA (including, incidentally, Howard Hunt who was afterwards implicated in the Watergate scandal) had recruited and trained hundreds of Cuban émigrés in secret camps in Florida and Guatemala. Secrecy was impossible to maintain even after the Florida camp had been closed down, and Cuba, well-briefed by its spies, complained to the United Nations. It was denied, and President Kennedy pressed ahead. The *Times* was slow to react, but eventually sent one of its best men to investigate. Tad Szulc had many contacts among the émigrés and by early April had the full story, including details of how the invasion force was organized and led by the CIA. He also reported that the attack was imminent. (In fact it took place during 17–20 April.)

The night editors decided to lead the front page with it under a four-column headline. The paper was about to go to press when Orvil Dryfoos (who had taken over after Arthur Hays Sulzberger's retirement earlier in the year) came down to the newsroom and told Turner Catledge, the managing editor, that Reston, after talking to his sources in government, had advised him not to run the full story. There was no proof that the CIA was involved. Dryfoos was inclined to kill it, but Catledge protested that it was a major story and must be published. It was, but under a single-column heading and with all references to the CIA and the imminence of the invasion deleted. One of the night editors was shocked. The *Times* had always accepted the word of its correspondents, and Szulc was one of the best. He demanded to be told by the publisher why the changes had to be made. Dryfoos returned to the newsroom, and said because of national security. It was his newspaper, and the editor reluctantly submitted.

Dryfoos's action would not have raised many eyebrows in Fleet Street, but in the United States there are no such restrictions as the 'D Notices' which request British editors not to publish sensitive news, and no Official Secrets Act. The American press also enjoys the protection of the First Amendment, which states that Congress shall make no law abridging the freedom of speech or of the press. Dryfoos was free to publish the story, and it could be said that it was his duty to publish. The intention of the founding fathers was clear; they accepted the amendment because they saw a free press as a safeguard against arbitrary government, and the United States had no right under its constitution or the United Nations charter to organize an invasion to overthrow a sovereign government. Moreover, the *Times* should have known that the invasion could not succeed. Castro's spies living among the émigrés were better-placed than Szulc or any competent reporter to find out what was planned, and his troops were waiting when the invasion force landed. The invaders were ill-equipped and had little air cover. They were doomed before they sailed, and if the *Times* had published the full story the operation might well have been cancelled.

Certainly Kennedy told Catledge afterwards that if the *Times* had published what it knew 'you would have saved us from a colossal mistake'.

The Bay of Pigs was a turning point in the history of the paper although the new direction was not immediately apparent. Dryfoos agreed with Catledge that in future it would not abide by the wishes of the government except in time of war. An editorial, entitled 'The Right Not To Be Lied To', said that neither prudence nor ethics could justify any administration telling the public things that were not true. It went on to say that a democracy could not be lied to, but the editors were probably more offended because the administration had dared to lie to the *Times*. It was a terrible shock, but there was not much they could do about it because a strike closed down the paper for nearly four months. Then in 1963 Dryfoos, exhausted by the strike and worried by the loss of revenue, died and his death was a double shock. He was only 50, and his successor, Arthur Ochs Sulzberger (b.1926), was an unknown quantity.

Punch, as he was known by all the senior men, was only 37 and few of them had bothered to get to know him because of the assumption that Dryfoos would be in charge for at least another 15 years. What they did know was not reassuring. He was a modest and affable man who had shown little interest in the paper, or anything else except mechanical gadgets. He had done badly at school, and had been transferred from one expensive establishment to another as each admitted defeat. He had volunteered for the Marine Corps at the age of 17, had served in the Pacific war, but was mustered out with the lowly rank of corporal. His early career on the paper had also been undistinguished. He was a disaster as a cub reporter and not much better when he was attached to the Paris office. Any other young man would have been fired, but he was a Sulzberger and was given a minor executive job where he could do no harm. He afterwards said: 'My career didn't look very promising. I'd go up to Orv [Dryfoos] occasionally and ask him to give me something to do. I was in charge of the cafeteria and purchasing. Nobody wanted to give me anything to do – no honest-to-God job.'

The editors were understandably worried because a strong publisher was now more than ever necessary, even vital. Dryfoos had carried on the Ochs tradition, but that belonged to another age – almost another country. The Cuban invasion had been followed by the missile crisis, the assassination of Kennedy, racial violence in the South and increasing American involvement in Vietnam. The new generation of *Times* men were impatient with the old restraints. The strike had gravely weakened the company financially, and the flight to the suburbs was beginning to affect circulation and advertising. The new western edition of the *Times*, printed in Los Angeles, was also losing circulation and money.

It was not a good time to be landed with a young and inexperienced publisher, but they had misjudged their man. He, also, was ready for change, and the fact that he did not know most of the editors and business executives made innovation easier. He fought off a family attempt to give him advisers, and shut down the western edition. Only Catledge had been friendly in the past, he and Punch often having a drink together. Catledge was appointed to a new post: executive editor in charge of all news operations, including the Sunday paper and the Washington bureau. Clifton Daniel, another former foreign correspondent, was appointed managing editor, and soon after gave a speech in which he described in great detail the night when Dryfoos censored Szulc's Cuban story. That was remarkable in itself, the *Times* rarely discussed its internal affairs in public, but without his knowledge the speech was run verbatim and across six columns. It was a signal that great changes were about to be made.

Catledge knew what he wanted to do. He had made a number of improvements over the years, but the *Times* had grown so big that the news operations were beyond his control. He was determined to impose a chain of command (an idea which Punch Sulzberger understood and approved after his Marine service), and also make the Washington bureau accountable. Unlike editors of other great newspapers, Catledge and Daniel had little or no control over national news because Reston had been allowed to run his bureau as if the editors in New York did not exist. It was an impossible situation, as if the London *Times* were based in Birmingham and the political staff at Westminster were given a free rein to report the capital. Moreover, Catledge believed that Reston and his men had identified themselves too closely with the White House, the State and Defence departments and other government agencies, and that their news judgments had suffered. This was to lead to a bruising conflict, but while the preliminary rounds were being fought Catledge advanced the man who was to transform the paper. He was A.M. Rosenthal (b. 1923), universally known as Abe, another former foreign correspondent, who had reluctantly come in from the cold to be metropolitan editor.

Rosenthal was not one of those *Times* men who, according to Salisbury, were charter members of the eastern Establishment. Few of the new generation were; the majority had come up the hard way, and Rosenthal had had a tougher climb than most. The son of a Russian Jewish immigrant, who died when he was young, he was brought up in the Bronx and attended the local elementary and high schools. He had suffered from osteomyelitis as a teenager, and might have been permanently lame if the Mayo Clinic had not accepted him as a charity patient. He went to City College, the Alma Mater of all poor Jewish kids, and became the campus correspondent of the *Times* in 1943, being unfit for military service. He went on to cover the United Nations, India, Poland and Japan, and developed into a superb reporter and a good if occasionally schmaltzy writer.

Rosenthal, although a likable man, was not liked by most of the New York staff because he made them work hard. New York City was covered as it had never been before, and his promotion was rapid; first to assistant managing editor and associate managing editor, then managing editor and executive editor. During that period the *Times* scored some notable scoops, including Salisbury's eyewitness reports of the American bombing of Hanoi. Salisbury was one of an increasing number of *Times* men who believed that government statements about the Vietnam war could no longer be trusted. Their belief was confirmed when he reported that instead of bombing military targets as claimed, the US air force was dropping an enormous weight of explosives on purely civilian targets. Dean Rusk, the Secretary of State, complained, as four years earlier President Kennedy had complained about David Halberstam's reporting from Saigon, but Punch Sulzberger remained unmoved. He had grown up very quickly, which was just as well for the *Times*. It was about to plunge into the greatest crisis in its history.

In the late 1960s the situation inside the United States continued to deteriorate as casualties in Vietnam increased and President Lyndon Johnson prevaricated over his intentions. There were student riots and draft-card burnings. The three Civil Rights Acts had done much to remove the legalized oppression of the blacks, but both Dr Martin Luther King Jr and Senator Robert Kennedy were assassinated. It seemed that the country was tearing itself apart. The old consensus was fast dissolving, the government was suspect in many middle-class eyes, and Washington correspondents who had long enjoyed cosy relationships with government officials began to distance themselves. Even Walter Lippmann, who had written his magisterial columns from Washington for decades, quit because Johnson lied to him.

His going alerted me to this journalistic crisis. I had always assumed that politicians and civil servants were not to be trusted. As a young reporter I had been advised to ask myself 'Why are these lying bastards lying to me?', advice that had stood me in good stead in many capital cities of the world.

James Gordon Bennett and Joseph Pulitzer had been similarly sceptical, but the American press had come a long way since they and other piratical journalists had created the popular penny papers and in so doing had articulated the traditional American suspicion of authority. The old muckrakers still survived to remind readers of official corruption and calumny, but for the most part the American press had become respectable and what was known in the schools of journalism as responsible. The old stereotype of the drunken hack who would do almost anything to get a good story had been replaced by another stereotype, the tweedy graduate who had never stood for hours in the rain on some newsworthy person's doorstep but who lived in Washington's fashionable Georgetown and knew senior government officials by their first names. Most members of the Washington press corps believed that they enjoyed a special status. They did indeed, but the First Amendment was no protection against official lies and the subsequent attempts of President Richard Nixon and Vice-President Spiro Agnew to denigrate them as wet liberals or worse. Nixon's televised appeal to the silent majority was a declaration of war. This was the background to the Pentagon Papers, publication of which by the *Times* was to have far-reaching consequences for the country as well as the paper.

Pentagon Papers was a useful journalistic label attached to an official study of the Vietnam war ordered by Robert McNamara, the Defence Secretary. McNamara, who was also the chief architect of the war under Kennedy and Johnson, began in 1966 to have doubts as to the efficacy of American strategy. The reason for the study was therefore praiseworthy. He wanted to know what went wrong, how the United States got involved in Southeast Asia and what were the origins of the war. Most of the answers were fairly well known by experienced journalists, but the study, or encyclopedia as McNamara described it, proved to be a terrible indictment, not only of Johnson and McNamara, but the entire national security apparatus devised by Kennedy. It proved that the White House had consistently lied to the American people, and had relentlessly pursued a policy in Vietnam that could only end in disaster.

For instance, it established that plans were being made for the massive air bombardment of North Vietnam when Johnson was campaigning as a peace candidate against the hawkish Barry Goldwater in the 1964 presidential campaign. That was only one example of presidential and political perfidy. Another shattering revelation was that of the ignorance of the 'defence intellectuals' from Harvard and other Ivy League colleges. The men who made the decisions knew nothing about Vietnam and its people, or the origins of the war between North and South although the United States was directly responsible for the division of the old Indo-China in 1945. They were also apparently unaware of the strategic bombing survey carried out at the end of the Second World War which proved that in certain circumstances bombing could raise rather than lower civilian morale.

The man who leaked the study to the *Times* was Daniel Ellsberg, a Harvard defence intellectual and a hawk who had become a dove, and he presented the paper with a problem. It was a wonderful scoop, but was publication in the public interest? Ochs, Arthur Hays Sulzberger and Dryfoos would have rejected it without a second thought, as did the company's lawyers. As they saw it, publication would be tantamount to theft of government property. The editors were more or less evenly divided, but Rosenthal was prepared to resign if the study was not published. Punch Sulzberger was in a quandary, which would have surprised the earlier American press barons. They had flourished long before newspapers had become respectable and responsible. They did not care what the President or anybody else thought of them as long as they sold newspapers. They had the journalist's atavistic urge to publish and be damned, and to humble the mighty.

[133]

The *Times* was different. Ochs, Arthur Hays Sulzberger and Dryfoos had created a great newspaper by joining the Establishment. They, and now Punch Sulzberger, saw themselves as defenders of a great family tradition. The history of American journalism is in part a series of revelations of official corruption and wrongdoing, but the *Times* had rarely indulged in muckraking. Since the emergence of the United States as a superpower the *Times* had seen itself as a paper of record, the first newspaper in the world which while maintaining its independence had sought the closest possible relationship with the government. Now Punch Sulzberger, still a relatively young and inexperienced man, had to decide whether or not to publish a story that would gravely damage the reputation of the United States, and at a time when it was trying to extricate itself from an unpopular war.

He was worried by the divided opinion of the editors and the stern reaction of the law firm which had represented the *Times* since before he was born. He was unhappy with the early drafts of the series, and requested rewrites. To that extent he was a chip off the old block, cautious and respectful of journalists dedicated to the paper, but almost from the beginning he was disposed to publish. Ellsberg may have betrayed his trust by making the study available, but it was clearly authentic. The Cuban invasion and Salisbury's reports of the bombing of Hanoi were sufficient reminders that Kennedy and Johnson had been capable of monumental errors of judgment and had been less than truthful. He eventually gave the go-ahead, and on 13 July 1971 the first instalment appeared under a four-column but typically sedate headline: 'Vietnam Archives: Pentagon Study Traces Three Decades of Growing US Involvement'. Reston's column was no less sedate. After quoting Edward Gibbon, 'history is little more than the register of the crimes, faults and frailties of mankind', he observed that the study provided 'compelling new evidence of this melancholy conclusion'. The *Times* had slipped its safe mooring for uncharted waters, but the editors were determined to maintain the old decorum.

The Pentagon Papers were a sensation, and John Mitchell, the Attorney-General, requested the paper to cease further publication. Sulzberger refused, and his defiance was reported on the front page under a five-column headline. Mitchell successfully sought a temporary restraining order, although the New York district judge was clearly sympathetic to the *Times*. Referrring to Sir William Blackstone, the eminent eighteenth-century jurist, he said:

> From the time of Blackstone, it was a tenet of the founding fathers that precensorship was the primary evil to be dealt with in the First Amendment . . . The Security of the nation is not at the ramparts alone. Security also lies in the value of our free institutions. A cantankerous press, an obstinate press, an ubiquitous press must be suffered by those in authority in order to preserve the even greater values of freedom of expression and the right of the people to know . . .

The Supreme Court eventually agreed, and the *Times* completed its publication of the Pentagon Papers.

It was a famous victory, and was to have historical repercussions. President Nixon, convinced that it was part of a conspiracy against his re-election, ordered into being the group known as the 'plumbers'. They were to plug all information leaks by fair means and foul. Even the office of Ellsberg's psychiatrist in Los Angeles was burgled. These could be said to be the first steps down the slippery slope which led to the Watergate scandal and Nixon's resignation. What was certain was that the liberal press, already suspicious of Nixon, were emboldened to pursue inquiries which helped to bring about his downfall. The *Times* achieved more than it knew at the time.

The Pentagon Papers is what most people have in mind when they think of the power of the press. The story established what had long been suspected; that in the conduct of the Vietnam War the Johnson and Nixon Administrations had deceived the Congress and the public. Its publication had far-reaching consequences. Subsequent congressional hearings led to the passing of the War Powers Act, the first attempt to limit the war powers of the President, and to congressional oversight of the Central Intelligence Agency. It discredited President Nixon, and with Watergate (see Chapter 10) helped to bring down one of the most powerful men in the world. So much is self-evident, but Harrison Salisbury (whose book *Without Fear or Favor* is the best account of the decisions which led to the publication of the Papers) and his peers on the *Times* and other worthwhile newspapers thought that it revealed the weaknesses of the press.

Richard Harwood of the *Washington Post*, a capable and serious journalist (who was not carping at a rival newspaper), concluded that the Pentagon Papers only proved that the impact of the press, including television and radio, was tragically limited. Many of the revelations in the Papers were in fact repetitions or confirmations of what had been reported earlier, but which had been largely ignored by Congress and the American people. According to a Gallup Poll in 1964, 63 per cent of those polled had no opinion about the Vietnam war, and were paying no heed to it or reading about it. Another poll reported six months later that 25 per cent did not even know that a war was in progress.

Presumably those percentages did not apply to readers of newspapers such as the *Times* and the *Post*, but they were not entirely blameless. It used to be said that good novelists wrote stories with a beginning, a middle and an end, but that rarely applies to journalists whether they work for the New York or London *Times*. Today's scoop is tomorrow's cold type, and although follow-ups are attempted they are invariably dropped when the next big story is written. The lack of continuity inevitably diminishes the impact of the first headlines, and Salisbury ruefully admitted that the *New York Times* even mishandled the follow-up to the Pentagon Papers: 'Although they now possessed a frame of reference as to how the US conducted its military business in Southeast Asia this knowledge was not integrated into the field reports (or) the characteristically bland statements of the government press agents in the Pentagon, the State Department or in the US establishments in Vietnam.'

Another critic, James Thomson, curator of the Nieman journalist scholarships at Harvard, put it another way. As quoted by Salisbury, he said that the reason for public indifference was that the press had not been: 'doing its job, was simply responding to government, showing the herd instinct, and seldom staying long enough with one central story'. No less telling, he went on to say that the Washington press had in large measure become part of the establishment, and had been co-opted into what he described as the 'National Security State' with its phobia for classification and secrecy.

So much had been obvious since the United States became a superpower. The American press had censored itself, and at a time when the growing power of the government more than ever demanded a watchdog press. For instance, the Alsop brothers, Joseph and Stewart, whose widely-syndicated column also appeared in the *Washington Post*, happily cooperated with the CIA and the Defence Department. They regarded themselves as very superior reporters, and were certainly well informed, but appeared to see themselves as captains in the forefront of the battle with communism. They were brave and honourable men, and Stewart even volunteered for active service with the British army in 1939. They were genuine patriots, but a disgrace to their ancient disreputable trade and the memories of the pioneers such as Defoe and John Zenger (whose successful battle for press freedom was described in Chapter 1).

Sulzberger and Rosenthal were also patriots, and very much aware of the Ochs traditions. One reason why Sulzberger agreed to publish the Pentagon Papers may well have been his comparative youth. He was not a member of the generation which fought the Second World War as commissioned officers or OSS men, and his service as a corporal must have given him a different view of the war. Nor had he been trained to become a publisher; he had taken over the paper with an open mind and a determination to run it his way. Rosenthal was also different. The poor boy from the Bronx, medically unfit to fight in the war, was a born reporter. He knew a good story when he saw one and was prepared to give up the best job in American journalism if he had not been permitted to publish it.

Both of them earned their niche in the pantheon of great journalists, and they also made serious journalism profitable. They were helped by the unique position of the *Times*, which also enjoys a near-monopoly in its circulation area – but it could have been otherwise.

KATHERINE GRAHAM AND THE 'WASHINGTON POST'

When I first met Mrs Katherine Graham (b.1917), the publisher of the *Washington Post*, in the early 1960s, she was a fragile-looking lady with a perpetual Florida tan. He voice was soft and cultivated, and she could make a well-spoken Englishwoman sound raucous. She looked too delicate to rule a large publishing and television empire, but was probably the most influential woman in the United States. She was accused of being its most ruthless press baron, and there was a time when she hired and fired so many executives that even the ambitious regarded her offers of highly-paid jobs with caution. She once broke a long printing strike by hiring scab labour from the South and by flying 'flongs' (from which pages are cast into semi-circular plates for the rotary presses) by helicopter from the roof of the *Post* building to an out-of-town printing plant. She even walked through a violent picket line during the strike so that she could work in the mailroom. That said, she was not a barracuda of the executive suite but a very courageous woman.

The Watergate scandal was to prove her courage, as would the decision to print the Pentagon Papers after the story had been broken by the *New York Times* although the Justice Department warned that the paper was liable to criminal prosecution and threatened to revoke its profitable broadcasting licences. The threat was very real. The Nixon White House hated and feared the *Post*, and under federal law convicted felons cannot hold broadcasting licences but Mrs Graham overruled her own lawyers and published. Her courage was all the more surprising because, being the capital's only morning newspaper, the *Post* enjoyed a unique monopoly. With her other successful properties such as the television and radio stations, *Newsweek*, the *Trenton Times* and an interest in the *International Herald Tribune*, Mrs Graham could have joined the majority of American newspaper publishers and cut news-gathering costs to maximize profits.

It was not always so. The *Post* was launched in 1877 as the voice of the Democratic party, and after one change of ownership was bought in 1905 by John McLean, a Middle West publisher and a power in the party. The paper was distinguished by having Sousa compose a march for it, and for little else. It had seen no news value in the Wright brothers' first flight, and published more short stories – admittedly by Conan Doyle, Bret Harte and Emile Zola – than foreign news, but was moderate in tone and outlook. It looked with disfavour on the Spanish–American War of 1898 although one of its cartoonists coined the rallying cry 'Remember the *Maine*'. (It was the mysterious sinking of the USS *Maine* in Havana that led to the declaration of war.) McLean changed all that and concentrated on crime, sports and comic strips. No reporters were sent to the party conventions, and it was one of the few newspapers on the east coast to be pro-German in the First World War. It also helped to provoke the 1919 race riots. McLean's son, Ned, supported Republican Warren Harding for the presidency and was involved in the Tea Pot Dome oil scandal. This was perhaps the worst of the many scandals which rocked the Harding Administration. The oddly-named oil field was reserved for naval use, and a high official leased it to a private company in return for a $500,000 bribe. Generally regarded as a contemptible sheet lacking moral integrity, the *Post* lost circulation, advertising and money and was sold to Eugene Meyer in 1933 for less than $1 million.

It was not a good time to buy a newspaper as the Depression was devastating the American economy, but Meyer was prepared to spend money. He was an immensely rich investment banker and the founder of Allied Chemical, and could afford to sustain losses while gradually improving the newspaper and modernizing the plant. By 1938 the *Post* was selling 100,000 copies a day. It still depended heavily upon the news agencies and staff reporters rarely made the front page, but Meyer was more interested in the editorial page. Walter Lippmann was one of the columnists hired to give it lustre, and the *Post* became a Liberal paper. By 1945 the paper was in profit, if barely, and Philip Graham, who had married Meyer's daughter, Katherine, was appointed associate publisher.

Philip Graham (1915–63), a former law clerk to Justice Felix Frankfurter of the US Supreme Court who had served in military intelligence during the war, was by all accounts a prodigy; a brilliant young man, handsome and with all the social graces. Young Katherine was happy to be the adoring wife and to leave the running of the family business to him. He had a lot going for him. The *New York Times* covered national politics much better and its Washington bureau was much bigger than the *Post*'s national affairs desk. There was no real comparison between the two newspapers, but Washington was an expanding city with suburbs enjoying the highest average incomes in the country. The *Post* was a local paper, and covered the suburbs and the concerns of the tens of thousands of civil servants more diligently than national or international affairs. All this attracted advertising, which filled two-thirds of the paper. Graham used this revenue to start buying radio and television stations, and in 1954 bought up his only morning rival, the *Washington Times-Herald*. Graham managed to retain most of its readers for his *Post* by publishing the *Times-Herald*'s comic strips and hiring its best sports writers. The *Post* began to look less and less like the *New York Times*. It ran more comic strips than any other paper in the country while the *Times* had none – but the *Post* was making more money.

Not that Graham ploughed much of the profits back into the paper. The *Post* did not appoint its first foreign correspondent until 1957, although Graham said in a magazine interview that he wanted to make the *Post* as internationally famous as the London *Times* and the *New York Times*. He was intensely ambitious politically. He saw himself as the *éminence grise* in the new world capital, and was prepared to use the paper to realize his ambition. He was a Democrat by inclination, but supported the Eisenhower-Nixon Republican ticket in the 1952 presidential election for understandable reasons. The Korean war had reached a stalemate. The Cold War dragged on, and Senator Joe McCarthy had divided the nation. General Dwight Eisenhower was a national hero and Graham, who hated Soviet imperialism as did most Americans, believed that the former Supreme Commander would make a better President than Adlai Stevenson, the Democratic candidate. Nixon was harder to accept because of his involvement in McCarthyism. The *Post* had courageously fought McCarthy's campaign of smear and character assassination, but as the election approached Graham stopped publication of a Herblock cartoon depicting McCarthy and Nixon with pots of tar in their hands. Meyer, who had become board chairman, flew to NATO HQ (North Atlantic Treaty Organization) to persuade Eisenhower to run, and Graham cultivated Nixon and praised him in the *Post*. It was a classic example of a newspaper publisher meddling in politics.

Whether or not Graham would have become the power broker he wanted to be is impossible to tell because he became mentally ill. He had lucid periods when he was as brilliant as ever, but they were increasingly interrupted by drinking bouts and womanizing. He was said to have a mistress in Europe, and would disappear without warning. The similarity with Northcliffe's growing madness was striking. When in Washington he was deeply involved in high politics. He knew about the flights of the U2 spy-plane over the Soviet Union long before the shooting down of Gary Powers in 1960 destroyed the summit conference in Paris, but chose not to publish. He was too close to the government, as were many of his senior journalists. The *Post* was perhaps no worse than the *New York Times*. Both were silent over the preparations for the Bay of Pigs invasion of Cuba in 1961. But Graham's silence was as much a personal issue as a mistaken belief that he was serving the national interest.

Graham had become a close friend of John Kennedy, and their intimacy was such that when the 1960 Democratic national convention in Los Angeles nominated Kennedy as the presidential candidate Graham persuaded him to accept Lyndon Johnson as his running mate. Kennedy's brother, Robert, was violently opposed to this, but Kennedy took Graham's advice. It was a wise

decision. The first Roman Catholic President was not liked by many funda-
mentalist Protestants, especially in the South, and the political experts
subsequently agreed that Kennedy would have lost the election but for
Johnson. As it was, he scraped through to victory only because he won Illinois
with the help of Mayor Richard Daley of Chicago who controlled Cook County.
This was political influence of a special kind, and based as it was on shrewdness
and acumen Graham might well have become a power in the land had he not
committed suicide in 1963. It was only then that his heartbroken wife became
publisher of the *Post*.

Mrs Graham had no experience of running a communications empire. She
had worked briefly for a San Francisco newspaper, but so had many other
bright young things after coming down from university. Fortunately she had
good advisers, and after a wobbly start – President Johnson tried hard to win
her over – began to transform the *Post*. Much of the credit for this went to Ben
Bradlee, who was appointed executive editor, but he always referred important decisions to her.

Bradlee and Philip Geyelin, the editorial-page editor, were in their forties
when appointed, and European head waiters would have recognized them as
Americans who did not need to have the menu translated. As newspapermen
they were superior in both senses of the word. Carl Bernstein and Bob
Woodward, the two young *Post* reporters who broke the Watergate story,
revealed an un-American class consciousness when they described Bradlee in
their book *All the President's Men*:

> There was an alluring combination of aristocrat and commoner about
> Bradlee: Boston Brahmin, Harvard, the World War II navy, and press
> attaché at the US Embassy in Paris . . . Howard Simons [the managing
> editor], as restrained as Bradlee could be hard-charging and obstreperous,
> liked to tell of watching Bradlee grind his cigarettes out in a demitasse
> during a formal dinner party. Bradlee was one of the few persons who could
> pull that kind of thing off and leave the hostess saying how charming he was.

I doubt that all the hostesses were charmed, but if Bradlee was a Boston
Brahmin he did not behave like God's elect were supposed to behave. Unlike
the new generation of earnest young journalists, he smoked and drank more
than was good for him, and his shirt collars always seemed to be frayed and
grubby. He had worked as a young reporter on the *Post* and as Washington
bureau chief for *Newsweek*, and he knew his way about town. He had a fine
house in Georgetown, the capital's fashionable neighbourhood, and was one of
Kennedy's closest friends. Whenever the President was free the two couples
met at the White House for drinks and supper, and the way Bradlee told it in his
book *Conversations with Kennedy* the evenings were no different from those
enjoyed by any close friends in Georgetown, except that they rarely discussed

politics. The two men had both gone to Harvard and served in the navy and their personal interests were similar. The nature of their friendship might have changed if Kennedy had not been assassinated before Bradlee was appointed editor, but Bradlee was more interested in news than in playing at politics. And unlike her husband, Mrs Graham was prepared to spend money to improve the paper's news service.

The editorial budget was more than doubled in the first four years, and Bradlee hired all the talent available. Its corps of foreign correspondents was increased, and the international news service established with the *Los Angeles Times* further broadened the coverage. The size of the national affairs desk eventually outnumbered the Washington staff of the *New York Times*. Not that Bradlee imitated his illustrious rival. His circulation area was smaller, and he knew that readers do not live by news alone. The new *Post* was still very much in the tradition of American newspapers in aiming for a general readership. While many of his customers were politicians, government officials and diplomats, and the paper was read very closely in the White House, the vast majority of readers were still civil servants and ordinary Washingtonians. National news was improved, but the style section, which as its name suggests deals with more ephemeral things, was given more space, as was sport. Comics and non-political features were treated more generously than foreign news. The formula was immensely successful; circulation, advertising and profits rose dramatically, but it was Bradlee's attitude to news that really transformed the *Post*. He was responsible for breaking up the cosy relationship between government and the press, and because he was more aware of the particular dangers of working as a journalist in Washington he began the good work before Rosenthal set the *New York Times* on its new course.

The concentration of power in Washington is universally acknowledged. What is not always appreciated is that for all its recent growth it is still a small town. Good restaurants and bookshops are few, and the cultural life, despite the pretensions of the Kennedy Center, does not compare with that of New York, London or Paris. In power terms, it is rather like trying to pour a bottle of cognac into a tea-cup. The power overflows and the smell is all-pervasive. There is little escape from it, and few would wish to escape because power is the town's main attraction.

Journalists who spend their days patrolling the White House, Congress, or the departments of State, Defence and Justice, talk shop over lunch – sources always demand their pound of flesh, generally *filet mignon* – and dinner. You can talk to an Assistant Secretary of State in his office during the day and meet him over somebody's dinner table in the evening. Light conversation is almost non-existent. Shop and more shop is served with the vichyssoise and rib roast. The intimacy has its uses. Journalists can cultivate sources with the minimum of effort. But it also has dangers. Some of the newspapermen came to believe that they were helping to make policy, and in a way they did. The *New York Times* and the *Washington Post* were the 'house magazines' for the powerful. The government could not function effectively without them. Official channels existed, but not for the nods, winks, leaks and kite-flying of politicians and officials anxious to promote their programmes. A sure way of attracting White House attention was to get a story into one of the two house magazines. The White House also needed the press, and some presidents spent more time with reporters than with their Cabinet. Other newspapers and even foreign correspondents were used, but none could hope to compete with the *Times* and *Post*. They were carefully fed and read by every man and woman of consequence in Washington.

The intimacy was further enhanced by Kennedy, whose promised reforms at home and vigorous policies abroad were immensely attractive to the journalistic majority. They embraced the Kennedy team with abandon, and the dangers of this intimacy soon became evident. Kennedy was easily forgiven for the reckless and abortive invasion of Cuba. Much was made of his immediate acceptance of full responsibility although none but the President could be held responsible. Few questioned the wisdom of the growing involvement in Vietnam and Laos. Instead, the urgency generated by the White House was communicated to readers without much comment. The majority accepted that the American frontier was on the Saigon River because that was where Kennedy and his national security advisers had put it. The assumed need for more military advisers – the vanguard of the hundreds of thousands of American troops who followed – became an urgent imperative because General Maxwell Taylor, the President's military adviser, said it was. Few protested when in effect the President signed the death warrant of President Diem by suggesting that a change at the top was required in Saigon. No influential journalist questioned the wisdom and morality of the Cuban missile crisis. Nobody asked what would have happened if Kennedy's challenge had not worked, if, to use the chilling euphemism, there had been a nuclear exchange. Looking back on that ghastly week in 1962, it is clear that Washington journalists were losing touch with their readers.

They were not lap-dogs of the government, as Jack Anderson, the muckraking columnist once sneered. The vast majority were honest and honourable men. Most of them were good journalists. They were hardworking, and the competition between them was genuine – which was exploited by their sources. A journalist who did not cooperate, or asked too many searching questions, was put in the White House 'doghouse'. He could not get in to see anybody and his phone calls remained unanswered until he made amends. Not that many had to be punished. The majority had been seduced by power, and those who regularly covered the White House or the State or Defence departments became part of the imperial presidency.

Bradlee was determined to reassert the old healthy scepticism of government and officialdom when he became editor, but not because, as some of his critics claimed, he resented Kennedy's successor. It might have been difficult if his old friend had lived, but he really was more interested in news than in playing politics. He was not obstreperous, as Bernstein and Woodward said, but was not afraid of a fight. He and his senior men began to distance themselves from the White House and other seats of power. Reporters avoided off-the-record press briefings which, like the 'lobby' briefings in London, enable the government to manage much of what is reported in the press and on television and radio. The questioning became more searching, the reporting sharper. The new recruits, men such as David Broder who was hijacked from the *New York Times*, were given their head and scoops became almost commonplace. Old-timers such as Chalmers Roberts gave the coverage a perspective which made it all the more valuable.

The 1960s were the dreadful years when the country was torn by the civil rights campaign and violence in the South and then by the Vietnam war. In truth they were wonderful years for journalists and not simply because bad news makes headlines. The civil rights campaign was a historical movement which righted ancient wrongs and freed the blacks from institutionalized prejudice. Resistance to the war was ugly at times but was nevertheless the response of a democratic people to a government waging a war nobody wanted, and regardless of cost. History was being made, and the *Post* wrote it better than most other newspapers because of Bradlee's demand for hard news and reporting in depth.

The war was still on when President Nixon came to power. He was a secretive man who held the press responsible for his defeat in the 1960 presidential election and in his bid to be Governor of California two years later. He declared his own kind of independence by rejecting rather than courting the press. The frequency of presidential press conferences was drastically reduced, and he gave briefings to newspaper editors to which the *Times* and *Post* were not invited. Exclusion was reinforced by structural change in the White House. For as long as anyone could remember the West Lobby had been the waiting room for correspondents. They waited there for the twice-daily briefings and to interview the president's visitors. There was easy access to the press secretary's office, and from time to time they discreetly slipped behind the scenes to talk to presidential assistants. It was an uncomfortable place until Johnson had it refurnished with green leather seats and chesterfields reminiscent of an expensive bar. The old-timers thought that they would at least be able to sit at ease until retirement, when suddenly the correspondents were banished to the basement where earlier Roosevelt had had a swimming pool installed. The new press room was said to be more efficient. It was, but it was also completely shut off from the rest of the White House. The correspondents could now be compared to goldfish in a bowl hungrily waiting for crumbs of information thrown to them by Ron Ziegler, the press secretary.

The significance of Nixon's appeal to the 'silent majority', first made in a 1969 television broadcast, was not at first appreciated by most Washington journalists. Most of them saw it as a blatant attempt to rally the extreme right wing in support of prolonging the war, but it was more than that. With one speech, Nixon had outflanked the press. Spiro Agnew, the Vice-President, led the subsequent attack and proved to be a formidable adversary. His charge that the media were controlled by a small eastern elite was successful because it struck several chords. The cultural domination of New York was widely resented. Some who watched the presidential press conferences on television were genuinely shocked by the behaviour of the journalists, and thought that their questioning was disrespectful if not downright insulting. Perhaps the greatest response came from men and women who hated the war but did not want to be told that their sons had died in vain.

Nixon continued to appeal directly to the nation by exercising the presidential prerogative of television free time. He skilfully used the anti-war demonstrations to his own advantage, and was so effective in this that even the notorious shooting of students at Kent State University in 1970 failed to outrage the majority. It was an extraordinary performance, and he achieved a position usually attained only by dictators once they have succeeded in muzzling the press. Attacks were pressed home on other fronts. Reporters' notebooks were subpoenaed, which amounted to an attack on the confidentiality of conversations between journalists and their sources without which investigative reporting would be impossible. The practice spread, and at least one reporter who refused to divulge the contents of his notebook was jailed for contempt.

Nixon's success depended upon his access to television, but the networks did not escape Agnew's attacks either. They were criticized not only for a lack of balance in their news programmes (an allegation which was patently not true) but also for the instant commentaries which were given after presidential broadcasts. These were less easy to defend and many journalists had doubts about the propriety and usefulness of the practice. Editorial writers had time to think before sitting down to their typewriters; but even experienced television commentators such as Eric Severeid could hardly give of their best without time for consideration. It was questionable journalism, but Nixon was not just concerned about the quality of their commentaries. He was bothered by the fact that instant analysis reduced the impact of his speeches, and he was determined to establish a rapport with his huge audiences on his own terms. The media were the enemy, and despite the First Amendment he was determined to make them ineffectual.

The major enemies, however, were the *Times* and the *Post*. They were the epitome of what Agnew described as 'the effete eastern elite', a comment which almost certainly explains much of the violent response to their publication of the Pentagon Papers. Mrs Graham's decision to publish after the *Times* had begun its revelations was courageous, and not only because her television stations were at risk. The *Post* was about to become a public company, and the flotation of stock might have failed had the courts not upheld the right to publish. Mrs Graham and her managers must have had some sleepless nights. It is impossible to say how far this unprecedented campaign to diminish the press would have gone had Nixon and Agnew been reasonably honest politicians, not impeccable but no worse than any others. As it turned out, only the Watergate investigation by the *Post* put a stop to their calculated attempt to emasculate the American press.

The story of how two young reporters, Bernstein and Woodward, investigated the burglary of the Democratic national headquarters and followed a trail that eventually led to Nixon's resignation is too well known to be repeated. It has been the subject of a bestselling book and a successful movie, but neither explained why it was only these inexperienced local reporters who pursued the story in its early stages. One reason was that they had the full support of their publisher and editor, but there was more to it than that. Older and more experienced journalists representing other newspapers had been too close to the government for too long. The old habit of going along with the administration persisted even after Nixon had launched his anti-press campaign. In spite of his chequered past, they could not bring themselves to suspect that the President of the United States could be a crook.

The excitement of covering the Watergate hearings in Congress and the eventual resignation did not leave any time for journalists to think about the significance of Nixon's anti-press campaign, and those who did thought that he had offended the First Amendment. He had not, as Justice Potter Stewart of the US Supreme Court made clear in a speech at the Yale Law School. The Amendment, one of the ten which make up the Bill of Rights, is straightforward enough: 'Congress shall make no law respecting the establishment of religion, or prohibiting the free exercise thereof; or abridging the freedom of speech, or of the press . . .' The Justice first said that the Amendment was broader than generally supposed. The Bill of Rights protected the specific liberties and rights of individuals, such as free speech, but the free press clause extended protection to an institution. The press was the only organized private business given explicit constitutional protection.

But Stewart added an important rider: 'So far as the Constitution goes, the autonomous press may publish what it knows, and may seek to learn what it can.' But the autonomy cut both ways. The press was free to do battle against secrecy and deception in government, but the press could not expect from the Constitution any guarantee that it would succeed. There was no constitutional right to have access to particular government information, or to require openness from the bureaucracy. The Constitution was neither a Freedom of Information Act nor an Official Secrets Act. The Constitution established the contest, but not its resolution.

The Supreme Court had done more than define the contest between the press and government. The Pentagon Papers decision was an obvious example, as was the 1964 *New York Times Co.* v. *Sullivan* decision which declared that public men were not entitled to complete privacy. The press had a friend in the Supreme Court, but what Justice Stewart said, if not in so many words, was that the press did not have a constitutional right to know. This turned upside down the old easy assumption, trumpeted at so many publishers' and editors' conferences, that the press had almost a divine right to know everything. It could not be otherwise, of course. An absolute right to know would give the press, which after all is a group of commercial companies run for profit and not necessarily for some high public duty, a power superior to that of freely-elected governments. The press does not possess, and should not possess such a right. The only right it has is, to quote the Justice again, 'to seek to learn what it can.' The Freedom of Information Act to some extent helps the American press in its search, but it has strict limitations. The contest between press and government remains, for which thank Heaven. Without it journalists would not have developed or enhanced their curiosity and scepticism which are the true basis of a free press. And, if only to avoid sounding too pompous, it makes reporting fun.

Investigative journalism, such as the Watergate story, was not a new development in American journalism. Muckraking, as it was once known, had a long and honourable past. The best known of the early muckrakers was Lincoln Steffens, but there were many others. His exposures of the injustice and corruption of city governments were equalled by Ida Tarbell's investigation of Standard Oil, Ray Stannard Baker's inquiries into organized labour, and Upton Sinclair's book on Chicago and the meat-packing industry, *The Jungle*. They were admired by political reformers, including Theodore Roosevelt, but became an embarrassment to the latter when he succeeded to the Presidency. Steffens and the others were impatient for reform, but Congress was conservative and slow to move. Roosevelt was caught in between, and disavowed his journalist friends in a speech to the Gridiron Club, of which all prominent Washington journalists are members. Quoting from John Bunyan's *Pilgrim's Progress*, he complained of writers concerned only with 'the filth on the floor.' He returned to the theme later saying:

In *Pilgrim's Progress* the Man with the Muckrake is set forth as the example of him whose vision is fixed on carnal instead of spiritual things . . . Now, it is very necessary that we should not flinch from seeing what is vile and debasing. There is filth on the floor, and it must be scraped up with the muckrake; and there are times and places where this service is the most needed of all services that can be performed. But the man who never does anything else, who never thinks or speaks or writes save of the feats with the muckrake, speedily becomes not a help to society, nor an incitement to good, but one of the most potent forces of evil.

Steffens was deeply wounded. For him investigative journalism was one of the most potent forces of good, although his judgment was not always sound. (He visited the Soviet Union after the Revolution, and claimed that he had seen the future and it worked.) The investigative reporters who came after him accepted with pride what was intended to be the damning charge of muckraking. An obvious example was Drew Pearson who wrote his syndicated column *Washington Merry-Go-Round* from 1932 to his retirement in the 1960s. Few other American journalists have been so influential or so widely read. Walter Lippmann was generally believed to have been the most influential American journalist in recent history, but Pearson cast a larger net. He was not as welcome at the British or French embassy, but he knew, as Lippmann did not know, the men who ran American politics: the ambitious and the time-servers, the do-gooders and wheeler-dealers, the honourable men and the crooks.

Pearson was not a roughneck, although he had to keep some curious company. With his moustache and trim tailoring he looked like an irate British colonel of the old school, a misleading appearance for he was, in fact, suspicious of the British because of their colonial past. He was a genuine American patriot, not a flag-waver but a patriot as often as not angered by men who sinned against the United States and mankind – in that order. An admirer of President Wilson, he really believed in making the world safe for democracy. He was shrewd, and knew everybody worth knowing in Washington: Presidents, Chief Justices, Congressional leaders, lobbyists, influence pedlars – the lot. Many hated or disliked Pearson. President Truman called him a son of a bitch and Senator McCarthy physically assaulted him. He was sued and investigated, but his sources rarely dried up. They were not only discontented civil servants and politicians on the make; his relations with top people were often intimate and they no doubt found him useful when they had policies and programmes to push or obstruct. His legmen were a kind of private FBI, and what they uncovered was not always resented.

Experience, sources and exclusive information were Pearson's main strength, and everybody knew that his daily column was published by hundreds of newspapers across the country. He also had his own syndicated radio programme, and for many years his own television show. He brought a good deal of trouble upon himself because of his private vision of what the United States should be. His Quaker background probably led him to expect too much of his fellow Americans, and he was inclined to jump to conclusions. He bequeathed his column when he retired to an assistant, Jack Anderson, a fierce and dedicated muckraker who burned with a passion to get at the truth and expose scoundrels. A devoted Mormon, he was convinced that power corrupts, that even decent men lie and cheat for power. As he saw it, the American political system invited corruption. Put at its simplest, candidates for public office had to seek campaign funds – those running for the US Senate needed at least $1 million – and the fat cats expected a return on their investment. Once elected, senators had to cooperate with the special interests which met their campaign bills while preaching the public interest.

Anderson was contemptuous of most Washington journalists, being convinced that they, too, were seduced by power. Hence his dismissive sneer that they were lap-dogs and not watch-dogs of government. They in turn tended to regard Pearson and Anderson as anachronisms. There were more important things to report than corruption. The Pearson–Anderson column never appeared on the main feature page of the *Post*. Instead, it was relegated to the comic strip section. Muckraking was frequently tedious when it produced endless stories of petty corruption, and some of the lesser practitioners could see little good anywhere. To that limited extent Theodore Roosevelt was right. As the power of the imperial presidency grew, however, and the White House and Defence department lied more and more about the Vietnam war, other journalists began to get a taste for investigation. Seymour Hersh, a freelance who afterwards joined the *New York Times*, uncovered the My Lai massacre singlehanded. It was a dreadful story of an ill-led and half-trained infantry platoon which wantonly slaughtered the men, women and children of My Lai hamlet. He had photographs and the sworn affidavits of the soldiers, but no American newspaper would publish the story until it appeared in the London *Times* of 25 November 1969. In desperation Hersh had sold me the story for $100, and only after it had been reported back from London did the American press and television show an interest.

The American editors no doubt believed that they were acting responsibly. They must have told themselves that My Lai was an aberration, and that publication would have brought unwarranted shame on the army as a whole. The story did present a terrible dilemma. Journalists have many loyalties and one is to their country, but it is probable that some were influenced by their closeness to the men ultimately responsible for the war. This attitude changed abruptly after Watergate, and investigative reporters found themselves admired and respected. For a time they were regarded as the natural successors to the lone man on a white horse, the private eye battling alone against evil, and other heroes of popular mythology. One social scientist saw them as the defenders of morality and architects of national goals as the churches and the business community had once been.

Some of this was understandable: the thought of young reporters taking on the high and mighty was romantic, but the reaction to Watergate often went too far. Some of the Washington regulars previously content to go along with the government felt duty-bound to prove their manhood by questioning the most innocuous official act or statement. Calling the White House press secretary a liar was apparently regarded as muckraking. Sinister motives were seen everywhere, which was absurd. There were still piles of muck to be raked by the true professionals, but the prime task of the Washington press was to report the government. Much of it was routine, but essential. Equally much of the work called for a high level of expertise, in economics and agriculture for instance, as well as in politics, diplomacy and defence. This in turn required a working relationship with officials, but a sceptical and not an intimate one. In the patois of journalism, they had to be prepared to bite the hand that fed them with information.

Watergate was a catharsis for the press as it was for the government, and both were improved as a consequence. Mrs Graham was triumphantly vindicated. Bradlee could not have taken the *Post* as far as he did without her agreement, and she allowed him to bring about a great constitutional crisis when Nixon was threatening her with financial ruin. Nevertheless, some people questioned her right to take on the President of the United States, and without regard to due process of the law. She answered that question when she gave the prestigious Granada Guildhall Lecture in London in 1974.

What was at stake in the Watergate crisis, she said, was not due process in the ordinary narrow sense of the term. The offences comprised a massive pattern of corruption and abuse, offences so numerous and headstrong that they shook the foundations of public trust and confidence. The issue was whether and how the people, the Congress and the courts, could get at the entire truth, assess the damage and work out the remedies. It was due process in the broadest and most fundamental sense. She continued:

> In this context the most prejudicial thing the press could do would be to cease publishing and stop broadcasting some arbitrarily chosen part of what it learns. Without a free and probing press, the events and import of Watergate would, in all probability, never have been revealed. Without the same thorough, persistent, independent press, public debate could not proceed, and the clamour and clash of opinions might never be distilled into that 'deliberate sense of the community' which decides the matter in the end. When the American press eases up on its vital adversary role, who is to determine how much it should ease, where it should stop short, what it should keep to itself – and for what purpose? Surely not the government. Surely, in this case, not the President . . . If any lesson has emerged from the turmoil and the tragedy so far, it is that the press in America should be

more free, not less. More vigorous and probing. More alert to its larger responsibilities – and less satisfied with its own performance.

Mrs Graham was one of the few press barons who changed the course of history. The *Post* did not do it alone, as she would be the first to admit. Other newspapers joined in, if belatedly, but Nixon was not hounded out of office by the press. He resigned to avoid impeachment – that medieval instrument in disuse since 1848 in Britain but included in the US Constitution by the founding fathers – because first the courts and then Congress began to move towards it, reluctantly but inexorably. The rule of law was applied against the most powerful man in the world. The American system worked, but it was the *Post* that first sounded the alarm and produced the evidence which set the wheels in motion. Almost certainly nothing would have happened if Bernstein and Woodward had not investigated clues suggesting that the White House was involved in the Watergate burglary and other crimes that were beyond their comprehension. Nixon would have served out his second term and taken the now infamous tapes with him into retirement.

Re-reading their early stories, incomplete and tentative because they were literally groping in the dark, one can only wonder how they achieved their cataclysmic result. It did not make exciting reading for many weeks, the evidence was too fragmented and there was always the reluctance to believe that a president could behave as Nixon did. Moreover, it should have been clear to even a political moron that Nixon would be re-elected in 1972, and that vast sums of money did not have to be raised and criminally spent to ensure his re-election. Hair-raising schemes were devised for 'mugging squads, kidnapping teams, well-trained prostitutes and electronic surveillance' to be used in the election campaign. The public was not impressed by the early stories. Nearly five months after the burglary, when the *Post* finally established that it was connected to 'an extensive campaign of political sabotage conducted by the White House', the Gallup Poll reported that only about half of the electorate had heard or read about Watergate, of whom eight out of ten saw no reason to blame Nixon. The *Post* persisted, and eventually the judges and congressmen did what was required of them.

That was not all. The first congressional hearings were followed by others which established that since the inauguration of Kennedy in 1961 the presidency had indeed become imperial. In the name of national security the Central Intelligence Agency had been used as a presidential hit squad. The CIA planned assassinations of supposed enemies abroad and, although forbidden by law, operated inside the United States. It even provided disguises for Nixon's accomplices when they broke into the office of the psychiatrist of Daniel Ellsberg who gave the Pentagon Papers to the *New York Times*. The catalogue of crimes is too long to be listed here, but in Bradlee's words the Nixon administration 'lied, lied and lied again'.

The hearings led to a readjustment within the American government. Congress, which had lost ground to the Presidency, tried to reassert itself as a co-equal arm of government. The CIA was made more accountable, at least as much as any secret service can be made accountable, and legislation was enacted to define and limit the president's war powers. Few Americans were naïve enough to believe that the modern presidency could be confined within strict constitutional limits, but they were reminded that the world's most open society still depended upon a free and probing press.

The question has often been asked if the Fleet Street press could expose a British Watergate. The British press is certainly not as free as the American press. Apart from the Official Secrets Act, the laws of contempt and libel are much stricter in Britain than in the United States. That said, Watergate began with a simple burglary, and if the Conservative or Labour party headquarters were burgled it would not escape the attention of Fleet Street news editors. Unlike Washington, London has many local newspapers which keep a close watch on police stations. Once alerted, the crime reporters of the national newspapers and what is known as the heavy mob would move in. The heavy mob are men prepared to stand watch on doorsteps for days if necessary, come rain or shine. They are not admired by the critics of the British press, but in my opinion are unbeatable. They may use cheque-books to buy exclusive information, which is also frowned upon, but they get the story. They are like the old-time Chicago police reporters immortalized in Ben Hecht's play *The Front Page*. British police stations do not have press rooms, but when I saw the movie of *The Front Page* I was reminded of some of my competitors when I was a young crime reporter.

British reporters working on a Watergate-type story would not be praised for their pains. The London *Daily Express* was accused of intrusion of privacy when its reporters trailed Mrs Donald Maclean, the wife of the British traitor, and no apologies were forthcoming when she joined her husband in Moscow. Today complaints would be made to the Press Council, questions would be asked in the House of Commons, and the law would also set up obstacles because in Britain nothing can be reported about a crime once the suspect has been charged. All that can be said is that 'a man is helping the police with their enquiries'. This is generally accepted as reasonable; in democratic societies rights frequently conflict and most journalists agree that the rights of a suspect should be honoured until he is tried. During the trial only what is said in court can be reported, but if the suspect is found guilty the newspapers can print all they know about the case. There would be no way, ultimately, of hushing up such a crime. Burglary is an offence, and if reporting restrictions were imposed, as occasionally happens in cases involving national security, questions could be asked in the Commons. It is not an uncommon practice for journalists to ask Members of Parliament to table questions to elicit information. John

Profumo, the former Minister for Defence who frequented the same prostitute as a Russian diplomat, was exposed by such a question.

A Watergate situation is extremely unlikely in Britain, not because politicians are any more law-abiding than in the United States but because the political systems are different. It is illegal to spend vast sums of money on election campaigns, which can be called at any time and last only three weeks or so. The prime minister is not elected as such. He or she runs as a normal candidate and is elected leader by the party. The electorate knows which leader will become prime minister should his or her party win, but an incumbent would hardly be able to behave as Nixon did. The prime minister's office is small and is not a co-equal branch of government. The modern White House is almost a government within the government and has much more power and freedom of action. Washington is a more open city than is London as far as the press is concerned, but the record shows that the White House can keep a secret if it wants to.

This of course made the Watergate revelations a greater achievement than is perhaps generally realized, but the *Post* is still not as good a newspaper as the *New York Times*. James Reston (the *Times*'s Washington bureau chief) told Mrs Graham that she had inherited a mediocre and erratic paper with no discipline. It is no longer mediocre, but in 1981 a *Post* reporter won a Pulitzer Prize for a story that was subsequently established to have been untrue. The paper also had to apologize for falsely reporting that President Jimmy Carter had bugged the President-elect Ronald Reagan. All newspapers make mistakes, but better editing would have kept these stories out of the paper. By all accounts, the *Post* has learned the lesson, but whatever its place in the list of the world's greatest newspapers Mrs Graham remains one of the very few press barons who changed the course of history.

THE BRITISH OVERSEAS, THOMSON 'OVER HERE', MURDOCH EVERYWHERE

British newspapermen were no less adventurous than the American journey-man printers who joined the wagon trains in the period when the West was won in the hope of becoming press barons. It could be said that they had a greater influence in the development of the English-language press. In the days when much of the globe was coloured red and the sun never set on the British Empire, trade followed the flag and the newspapermen were not far behind. The *Straits Times* was launched in Singapore before Ochs bought the *New York Times*, as was the *Statesman* in Calcutta. They are still good newspapers, serious and non-parochial. The *Straits Times* publishes five pages of foreign news every day, and must be one of the world's most prosperous papers.

Similarly in Australia, Canada, New Zealand, the West Indies and Africa. The tide of empire swept adventurous or discontented British newspapermen almost everywhere. The Commonwealth Press Union now has some 600 member newspapers in more than 30 erstwhile colonies. Few of them are still British owned, but most are unmistakably British in origin. The one major exception is Canada where the English-language press was strongly influenced by its neighbour south of the border. Nevertheless, the *Winnipeg Free Press* was very British under its great editor, John Dafoe (1866–1944), who took for his example Thomas Barnes of the London *Times*.

South Africa has quit the Commonwealth and is the pariah of the United Nations, but an independent and lively press still flourishes despite repressive press laws. The *Times* of Cape Town also modelled itself on the London *Times*, as did the *Argus* which imported a complete editorial staff from Britain. Cecil Rhodes was one of the press lords who owned the *Argus*, and he bought the *Johannesburg Star* in 1886 when gold was discovered on the Rand. He also launched the *Herald* in what was then Salisbury, Rhodesia. Rhodes was a mining magnate as well as an empire-builder, and the newspapers he owned with other magnates such as Barney Barnato and Solly Joel served their commercial and political interests, but they also helped to establish a free press. For many years papers such as the *Rand Daily Mail* have fought apartheid more vigorously than most newspapers in the American South fought segregation.

[153]

The first newspaper in Australia was the *Sydney Gazette*, a four-page weekly which first appeared in 1803. It was printed by George Howe, a convict, under the direction of the governor of New South Wales. Along with other newspapers subservient to authority, it became known as the convict press. Subservience is most un-Australian, and the first independent paper, the *Sydney Herald* was launched soon after censorship was lifted in 1824. Others followed, among them the *Melbourne Age* in 1854, a progeny of the gold rush which began in 1851. Tens of thousands of diggers and potential newspaper readers arrived, and the population more than trebled in the decade. It was a good time to launch a paper, but not a radical one.

The *Age* became the spokesman for the new immigrants, most of whom were denied the right to vote because they could not meet the property qualifications. It also supported the gold miners in their struggle against the exorbitant mining licenses issued by the colonial government, and when this led to violence the paper was boycotted by advertisers. The owners sold out to the printing staff, who each subscribed £25, but the paper continued to lose money. The workers' cooperative, probably the first ever to run a newspaper, sold it in turn in 1856 to Ebenezer Syme, who had been appointed editor.

Syme (1826–60) was an immigrant who had written for the *Westminster Gazette*, and as a liberal journalist had campaigned for electoral and social reforms in the old country. He must have been surprised on arrival to discover that he had exchanged one class-struggle for another. The landowners, originally squatters, owned vast acreages and dominated the upper house of the colony's legislature. They resisted reform as vigorously as did the aristocrats in London. In theory the governor was answerable to the Parliament in London, but from Pitt the Younger onwards there had been little or no disposition to intervene. In any case, Australia was half a world away and the telegraph had yet to be invented. The British government may also have remembered the earlier mistaken belief that the American colonies could be controlled from London.

The American War of Independence was responsible for Australia becoming a penal colony. Convicts could no longer be transported to America, and on the advice of Joseph Banks, who had accompanied Captain Cook on his voyage of discovery, New South Wales was designated as an alternative. The first convict ships sailed to Botany Bay in 1787. In fact, conditions in Australia were very different from those of pre-revolutionary America. There the colonies had enjoyed local autonomy for many years. Virginia's House of Burgesses was more than 150 years old when Thomas Jefferson wrote the Declaration of Independence. The US Constitution is living proof of the intelligence and wisdom of their political leaders. No such men had emerged in Australia at that time, and new settlers were denied the right to buy land and were generally exploited.

This was the situation which confronted Syme, and he was determined to change it. He campaigned for universal male suffrage, land reform and free secular education, but with little success. The advertisers' boycott continued, and not many settlers could afford to buy a newspaper costing sixpence. Syme also had to contend with the competition from British newspapers, copies of which arrived with every ship. The *Age* owned a whaleboat which sailed out to meet the ships to gather news from home, but the British papers were generally on sale by the time the *Age* appeared. On top of all this Syme had to carry a gun because his life was at risk, but he was not deterred. When his political opponents organized a second and more effective boycott, he declared: 'We shall go on as we have begun, calling a spade a spade, exposing imposters, unmasking hypocrites, denouncing falsehoods, gibbeting shams and showing no quarter to men who have been guilty of political infamy and who seem to glory in their shame.'

The circulation was down to 2000 when he died and his brother, David Syme (1827–1908), became editor. He had worked as a building contractor to help keep the paper alive, and was equally determined to campaign for reform. He was subjected to further advertising boycotts, and decided to fight them by reducing the cover price. When it was finally cut to a penny the circulation rose to 22,000, and the battle was essentially won. David Syme became a political power, in Canberra as well as Melbourne, and the *Age* became an influential newspaper although it lost much of its early radicalism in the process. Nevertheless, it had played its part in helping to transform the former penal colony into a country more democratic than most.

The Syme brothers and the *Age* also helped to establish a journalistic tradition that is quite extraordinary for such a sparsely-populated land. Australia has done well in many fields. Besides producing great cricketers, yachtsmen and opera singers, it has had more than its fair share of first-class journalists. There was a time, or so the story goes, when a young Australian could walk into a Fleet Street newspaper office, announce that he had just got off the boat at Tilbury, and be given a job immediately. Such was the reputation of Australian journalists. The best known was George Morrison (1862–1920), who worked briefly for the *Age*. After wandering about the world for years, during which time he took a doctor's degree at Edinburgh and was court physician to the Shereef of Wazan in Morocco, he became the Peking correspondent of the London *Times* in 1897. At least, *The Times* paid him and published his dispatches, but Chinese Morrison, as he became known, was very much his own man.

Morrison was a superb journalist, who knew everybody and travelled everywhere, and in the words of the statesman, the 1st Lord Curzon, had a remarkable capacity for 'the intelligent anticipation of events'. Hugh Trevor-Roper, in his book *Hermit of Peking*, said that Morrison was more than a

ist; he was a radical imperialist who believed that British power was
__ⅉ to govern and modernize the world because it was beneficent. He was
not interested in China as such, and did not bother to learn the language. What
interested him was China as a theatre of competing imperialisms. From the
moment of his arrival in Peking, he threw himself into the great game of
imperial power politics: 'He did not intend merely to report events: he
proposed to make them . . . From the beginning, he worked openly to promote
a Russo–Japanese war, and when that war came, it would be known as
"Morrison's war".' He was Australia's most swashbuckling journalist until the
appearance of young Murdoch.

Rupert Murdoch (b.1931) is not a dirty digger who with a tube of Fosters' in
each hand shambled out of the Outback in search of a Page Three nude. Many
of his critics in Britain and America would like to think so, but his grandfather
was a Presbyterian minister from Scotland and his father a successful and
respected newspaper publisher. Sir Keith Murdoch sent his son to Australia's
most exclusive boarding school and then to Oxford where he read politics,
philosophy and economics – and was converted to socialism. His father also
arranged with Lord Beaverbrook for Rupert to learn the trade of sub-editing in
London at the *Daily Express*. He was said not to be popular with the other
subs, mainly because he stayed at the Savoy Hotel while they had to commute
to the suburbs. This portrait of a member of the privileged classes is in no way
diminished by the fact that in Australia he had to live in an austere hut during
school vacations. Sir Keith, who was a war correspondent at Gallipoli, was
determined that his only son would not be softened and corrupted by a life of
ease and wealth.

Whether or not this conditioning did the trick, young Murdoch was more
than ready to take over after the death of his father. One American said that he
rode into an unsuspecting publishing world like a gunslinger from the Wild
West. Whatever the metaphor – dirty digger, gunslinger or a modern Ned
Kelly – hard living in a hut for a few weeks of the year could not entirely explain
his ruthless ambition. Another reason has been suggested. Sir Keith was
chairman of the large *Herald* and *Weekly Times* group when he died in 1952, but
owned few shares in the company. After the payment of death duties his widow
inherited only two small newspapers, the *News* and *Sunday Mail* in Adelaide,
South Australia. Rupert Murdoch may have felt that he had been manoeuvred
out of a large inheritance, and been determined to seek revenge. Even so, the
two Adelaide papers were a better patrimony than most ambitious journalists
can hope to inherit.

As Michael Leapman points out in his biography *Barefaced Cheek*, Murdoch
was only 21 when his father died, and had a lifetime before him in which to
expand the family business. He made a flying start, and before he was 50 had
expanded it into one of the world's largest media companies, with newspapers

on three continents, television stations, a publishing house and part-ownership of an airline. His newspapers included such contrasting publications as the London *Times* and the *Sun* – Britain's great pioneering tabloid (it was the first newspaper anywhere to print the photograph of a nude every day on its third page). The youthful socialist had become a conservative, which would have pleased his father, a pillar of the old Australian establishment. Rupert Murdoch, by his own choice, remained an outsider more comfortable in the first-class cabin of airliners than in gentlemen's clubs in London, New York and Sydney. He constantly circumnavigated the globe visiting his properties and on the lookout for others to buy.

Few people could have predicted this when he returned to Australia to take over the *Adelaide News* and *Sunday Mail*. The Australian press is very competitive, and was then dominated by barons such as Sir Frank Packer (1906–74) and his younger son Kerry of the *Sydney Telegraph* and Sir Warwick Fairfax (b.1901) of the *Sydney Herald*. Both owned other properties, including television stations. Murdoch was green, and the *News* had a powerful rival in the *Adelaide Advertiser*. It was owned by another baron, Sir Lloyd Dumas (1891–1973), who had offered to buy the *News* after Sir Keith's death. Murdoch refused and Dumas launched a new Sunday paper to compete against the *Mail*, the more profitable of Murdoch's two papers. A truce was called after a couple of years of brutal and costly competition, and Murdoch bought his first television station in Adelaide. The profits provided capital for further expansion.

As Lord Thomson was to remark when he bought the Scottish station, television was a licence to print money. This was equally true in Australia, but the Sydney and Melbourne stations accounted for 60 per cent of the country's advertising revenue. Murdoch decided to break into the Sydney market by taking over a small suburban station and then buying the Australian rights to every available new American programme. It was an audacious move, and Sir Frank Packer was quick to admit defeat. He sold Murdoch a quarter-share in the Channel 9 stations in Sydney and Melbourne in exchange for the right to transmit the American programmes, but Murdoch was still not satisfied. He bought newspapers in Brisbane and Melbourne, and with printing plants in four state capitals launched Australia's first national newspaper, the *Australian*.

It was a bold and risky venture. Facsimile transmission was not then available so the page matrices had to be flown long distances, to the various printing plants, from Canberra which had been chosen as the main office because a national newspaper necessarily had to specialize in federal news. But the capital's airport was frequently closed by night fog which delayed the dispatch of the matrices. Canberra already had a paper of its own, and was too small to support a second. And as the proprietors of the *New York Times* were reminded when they first launched a West Coast edition, local news and small ads are the life-blood of newspapers, and a national newspaper could hardly compete with the established dailies in Sydney and Melbourne. The *Australian* was, nevertheless, launched in 1964.

Murdoch afterwards said that to produce a national paper his father would have been proud of proved to be his greatest challenge. It was a bigger job than expected and almost everything went wrong until central production was moved to Sydney and Adrian Deamer was appointed editor. By 1970 the circulation reached 143,000 and a tidy profit was reported. A Sunday edition was launched the following year under the editorship of Bruce Rothwell, a serious journalist who had been a distinguished Washington correspondent of the old London paper, the *News Chronicle*. The future looked bright, but not for long.

The intrinsic problems of producing a national daily paper in a country the size of Australia remained, and they were compounded by the relatively small circulation a serious newspaper can achieve when in competition with more popular rivals. The readers were mainly found at the top end of the market, especially on university campuses. Murdoch also thought that politically Deamer was moving the *Australian* to the left. To some extent this was inevitable because of its campus readership, whose opposition to the Vietnam war was strong. The *New York Times* was also accused of swinging to the left because of its war coverage, but the *Australian* was owned by Murdoch, not Sulzberger. Deamer was fired, and the paper was moved downmarket and to the right. Circulation did not improve, and editors were hired and fired with a rapidity that made recovery impossible. One of them, Colin Chapman, lasted less than 48 hours.

Murdoch justified his actions by saying that many journalists imposed their own political views on papers, rather than those of the publisher. He added: 'The public certainly has no duty to support newspapers. It is the duty of the publishers to provide the type of newspaper the public wants to read'.

The statement was widely condemned by Murdoch's critics, although very few editors enjoy the editorial independence of the editor of the London *Times*. Certainly no publisher in his right mind would produce a newspaper the public did not want to read. If there are more successful conservative than liberal publishers, it is perhaps because the majority want to read their newspapers. To state the obvious is not to defend Murdoch's behaviour. The *Australian* was a worthy if risky venture, for which he should be given credit. It was further proof of his courage, but it also revealed his contempt for journalists. He is said to love newspapers, but his editors are hacks to be hired and fired as the whim takes him. There can be no other explanation for his treatment of Chapman, who arrived one day and went the next. The *Australian* also revealed his restlessness. He enjoyed the initial excitements of the launch, but soon wanted to move on. His failure to make it a great and profitable national newspaper must have been a disappointment, and perhaps only pride and the memory of his father prevented him from admitting defeat. What is clear is that he already had another interest. Before the end of the 1960s he had moved to Fleet Street and taken over the *News of the World* and the *Sun*. His career as an international press baron had begun.

The move had long been planned. Murdoch was still only in his late thirties, and room for expansion in Australia seemed limited although he did return to buy a couple of television stations and the *Sydney Telegraph*. The English-speaking world was his oyster, and although the United States beckoned, Britain was his first choice. The old sentimental kith-and-kin bonds were no longer strong, but relations between the two Commonwealth countries were still close. The old country still attracted Australians when they made their European grand tour. Murdoch had worked in Fleet Street after coming down from Oxford, and had been impressed by Lord Beaverbrook. The success of Lord Thomson, another Canadian, had shown that shrewd Commonwealth citizens could still make it in Fleet Street. Murdoch also loved popular newspapers, and Fleet Street had become the mecca for popular or tabloid journalists.

Murdoch had been impressed by the *Daily Mirror*, and had secretly been buying its shares for years. It was the shining example of what could be achieved by mass-circulation newspapers. Founded by Lord Northcliffe as a paper written by women for women, it was transformed by Harry Guy Bartholomew (1885–1962), known as 'Bart', who began his career as a boy in one of Fleet Street's picture-engraving departments and fought his way to the top. He was a half-educated James Gordon Bennett, and shared the American's hatred of cant. Like Edward Wyllis Scripps, he drank more whisky than was good for him and instinctively knew what interested working-class readers. He was a brilliant production journalist who sought the advice of an advertising agency to improve the display of pictures and headlines. Bartholomew hated social injustice and under his guidance the *Mirror* became a genuine radical newspaper and a wonderful read. Winston Churchill threatened to close it down during the Second World War because of its forthright and independent views, but other official threats only persuaded the readers that it was *their* newspaper. Bartholomew had raised the circulation from 700,000 to more than four million when in 1951 he was deposed from the chairmanship of the *Mirror* group in a boardroom revolution led by Cecil Harmsworth King.

King (b.1901), the nephew of Northcliffe, could not have been more different. His father was a member of the Indian Civil Service and afterwards professor of oriental languages at Trinity College, Dublin. King, who went to Winchester and Christ Church, Oxford, was a tall man who looked and behaved like a Roman patrician. He collected fine furniture and silver, and always went to bed at half past nine in the evening. A portrait of Northcliffe hung in his office, but he had inherited the commercial genius of Rothermere, his other uncle. He was the financial and advertisement director when he led the *putsch*, and went on to create what was then the world's largest publishing empire, the International Publishing Corporation.

At the peak of its development, IPC controlled four national newspapers with a combined circulation of 15 million copies, and papers in Australia, Scotland, West Africa and the West Indies; 90 weekly magazines, ranging from *Woman's Own* to *Horse and Hound*; and 120 monthlies in Britain, France and the United States. It also controlled 19 printing works and eight book publishing companies, and had large holdings in television, a record company, a newsprint group and other properties.

There had been nothing quite like it before, but King wanted political power and devoted much of his time to the *Mirror*. He did not have Northcliffe's editorial flair, and Hugh Cudlipp was appointed as his editorial director. Cudlipp (later ennobled as were other senior *Mirror* executives by a grateful Labour prime minister) was another poor boy who understood the interests and aspirations of working-class people and had none of Bartholomew's failings. Together they pushed the circulation above five million a day by producing a paper the public wanted to read. But they had decided that their duty was to inform and educate as well as entertain. Under the shouting headlines and cheesecake they reported and discussed the serious issues of the day. Francis Williams (by then Lord Francis-Williams) wrote in his book *The Right to Know: The Rise of the World Press* that 'Barnes of *The Times* would, one feels, have appreciated its purpose and general strategy while being somewhat shaken by its methods – these James Gordon Bennett would have better understood.'

Alas, although King owned only one per cent of IPC's share capital he succumbed to megalomania like his uncles before him. Perhaps it was in the blood. He spoke about 'my newspapers' and 'my editors', and grandly referred to the readers as 'my people'. There can be little doubt that the *Mirror* helped the Labour party to win the 1964 general election; he confidently expected to be invited to join the new Cabinet, and was furious when the Prime Minister, Harold Wilson, only offered him a junior job at the Board of Trade. He declined a peerage because nothing but an earldom would do. Thereafter Wilson suffered as did Lloyd George at the hands of Northcliffe. Editorial criticism was justified, because the performance of the Labour government was, to say the least, disappointing. But King decided that Wilson must be removed from office – apparently by any means. In 1968, convinced that inflation would ruin the country, he called on Lord Mountbatten, wartime hero and a great-grandson of Queen Victoria. Cudlipp gave an account of the meeting in his book *Walking on the Water*:

> He [King] explained that in the crisis he foresaw as being just round the
> corner the Government would disintegrate, there would be bloodshed in the

streets, the armed forces would be involved. The people would be looking to somebody like Lord Mountbatten as the titular head of a new administration, somebody renowned as a leader of men who would be capable, backed by the best brains and administrators in the land to restore confidence.

King no doubt saw himself as one of the best brains who would run the country, but Mountbatten refused to become involved. Sir Solly Zuckerman, who was Churchill's scientific adviser during the war and had been invited by Mountbatten to attend the meeting, was horrified and charged King with treachery.

Wilson said long afterwards that he had feared a high-level coup at the time and Marcia Williams (Lady Falkender), his former political secretary, later claimed that Mountbatten was a prime mover behind the supposed coup. Whatever happened, King remained determined to get rid of Wilson and two days after the meeting a signed editorial appeared on the front page of the *Mirror*. Under the headline 'Enough is Enough', King wrote: 'We are now threatened with the greatest financial crisis in our lives. It is not to be removed by lies about our reserves, but only by a fresh start under a fresh leader.' The IPC board was appalled, in part because King had signed the editorial as the chairman of the corporation. Led by Cudlipp, the board now did unto King what he had done to Bartholomew. He was dismissed and given a year's salary in lieu of notice.

Murdoch did not know the background of King's dismissal at the time, but he had already decided that the *Mirror* was vulnerable. Not that he could do anything about it; the tabloid was IPC's golden goose and was not for sale. In any case, he had just acquired the *News of the World*. Once the world's largest-selling Sunday newspaper with a circulation in excess of eight million, it was just as much a British institution as *The Times*. The inside pages were largely devoted to stories of sexual crimes and indiscretions, but were reported with all the authority and objectivity of *The Times* parliamentary pages. The political coverage and the sports pages were very good, and the combination was irresistible for rich and poor alike. It ought to have made a great deal of money but the chairman, Sir Emsley Carr, enjoyed the good life too much to give the company proper attention and circulation and profits had fallen. There was also a family feud, and after a fierce struggle with a rival bidder Murdoch eventually won control.

Murdoch's methods did not endear him to his peers; a member of the Carr family unsuccessfully referred the matter to the Takeover Panel, the self-regulating body of the Stock Exchange, and the President of the Board of Trade said that he was powerless to intervene. Murdoch became more unpopular by publishing the memoirs of Christine Keeler, the prostitute whose affair with John Profumo, then Harold Macmillan's Minister for Defence, had been a great and damaging political scandal. He was condemned by the Press

Council and church leaders. Even Murdoch admitted that it was a bad beginning. What galled him most was that the *News of the World* had one of the largest press rooms in western Europe, and it was used only once a week. The long lines of presses stood idle for the other six days when they could have been generating profits if he had a daily paper to print. The opportunity came when the IPC decided to sell the loss-making *Sun*.

Originally the socialist *Daily Herald*, it had been acquired when IPC bought Odhams Press. King wanted Odhams' magazines and not another newspaper. There was a strong case for closing it down, but King, who was still at that time the corporation's chairman, did not want to offend the Trades Union Congress, one of the original owners. Research indicated that there was a market for a paper written for affluent young people, and in 1964 the *Herald* was renamed and given a facelift. It was not a success and IPC lost £13 million in eight years. King was deposed soon afterwards, and the title was sold to Murdoch for less than £1 million. It was a terrible mistake, and cost the *Mirror* dear.

The researchers had got it wrong. Publishing a newspaper for one age group is a hazardous undertaking if only because young people, affluent or not, grow up. They had also ignored the change in reading habits since the war. One reason why the *Sun* had failed to attract sufficient readers was because essentially it was aimed at the middle range of the market long dominated by the *Express* and *Mail*. In the early postwar years such newspapers had won more than 60 per cent of the market, but they subsequently declined to less than half and were still falling when the *Sun* was launched. The *News Chronicle* had ceased publication, and the *Express* and other mid-brow papers were struggling to survive. There was no room for a newcomer. More people were reading serious newspapers, and the combined sales of the *Guardian, Telegraph* and *The Times* had doubled. Their share of the market remained modest, about 14 per cent, and Murdoch wanted a mass-circulation paper to keep his presses running. He knew that the tabloids' share of the market had nearly doubled and was still expanding. The *Sun* was therefore redesigned for the lower end of the market. In getting rid of an unprofitable newspaper, IPC had created competition for its most profitable property.

Murdoch proved to be a formidable and ruthless rival. In 1969 Larry Lamb, a former *Mirror* executive, was appointed editor and the two of them took the *Sun* to the very bottom of the market. Assuming that most people got enough news from radio and television, they mainly provided entertainment and sexual titillation. The Page Three nude became a daily feature, and an extraordinary circulation-builder. Sales surpassed those of the *Mirror*, despite the fact that it had taken fright and was displaying its own nudes. Some of its serious efforts to inform and educate were also quietly shelved, and it seemed that Murdoch had succeeded in trivializing the British popular press. The *Mirror* fortunately regained its nerve, the nudes were dropped, and it resumed its basic news service. It continued to be a good popular newspaper, essentially serious, and the Labour party's only foul-weather friend in Fleet Street, but the old spark had been extinguished. IPC, which had been over-extended by King, was sold to Reed International, a conglomerate based on paper and paint, in 1970. Thirteen years later Reed announced the sale of the *Mirror* and other newspapers. The *Mirror*'s circulation had crept up to nearly 3,500,000 but was still a long way from the five million plus it once enjoyed when King and Cudlipp had come close to producing the ideal tabloid. (After a boardroom battle the *Mirror* group was eventually sold in 1984 to the high bidder, Robert Maxwell, socialist millionaire and head of the British Printing and Communication Corporation.)

Murdoch was now known as the 'Dirty Digger', but he had also earned the reputation of being an expert at reviving failing newspapers. This stood him in good stead when London Weekend Television (LWT) almost went broke in 1970. He was invited to buy 40 per cent of the share capital and reorganize the company. This he did, and brought in as chairman John Freeman, the former Member of Parliament, editor of the weekly *New Statesman* and ambassador to Washington. LWT became one of Britain's best commercial television stations, profitable, entertaining but also serious and instructive – a kind of electronic *Mirror*. Not that this did Murdoch any good when he tried to buy the *Observer*. David Astor, the last of the great owner-editors, was getting old and his Sunday newspaper was expensive to run. He was prepared to sell to Murdoch, but led by the editor, Donald Trelford, the editorial staff were violently opposed, and the paper was taken over by Atlantic Richfield, the American oil conglomerate. Undeterred, Murdoch almost immediately announced that he had bought the *New York Post*.

Even before moving into the United States Murdoch had gained control of one of the largest newspaper and television empires in the world, and was still in his forties. He also had a host of critics, but remained an enigma. He lived well, but not ostentatiously. A lot of business was done in smart restaurants but he was a meat-and-potatoes man and drank very little. His first marriage collapsed, but he was obviously happy with his second wife, Anna Torv, and there was no hint of the kind of scandal in which many of his newspapers specialized. The Presbyterianism of his grandfather probably explained a great deal. He dressed modestly but well and when he was working, more often than not, the tail of his shirt would be hanging out. He was completely different from the earlier breed of press barons with their yachts, country houses, Rolls-Royces and mistresses. A good description of him was given in Harold Evans's book *Good Times, Bad Times*. They met in London when Murdoch was negotiating to buy *The Times* and *Sunday Times*, and Evans's wife, journalist Tina Brown, recorded a first impression in her diary:

I had to admit I liked him hugely. He was in an American country gentleman's three-piece suit and heavy shoes, and was by turns urbane and shady. His face seems to have been made for the cartoonist's distortion – the gargoyle lips, deep furrows in the brow, the hint of five o'clock shadow that gives him such an underworld air when he's sunk in thought. But when he was standing by the fire with one foot on the fender laughing uproariously he seemed robust and refreshing. There's no doubt he lives newspapers. They are not merely seen by him as assets, as Ken Thomson [who then owned *The Times*] sees them. At eight o'clock, when the first editions arrived, he fell upon them with childish excitement. I warmed to him when he read the *Observer*'s hostile account of his bid and instead of being cross burst into gales of laughter. 'The bastards!' he shouted, throwing it to the floor. The truth is that, although he'll be trouble, he'll also be enormous fun and H. [Evans] has had so many years of Thomson greyness this vivid rascal could bring back some of the jokes. 'I sacked the best editor of the *News of the World*', he said at one point. 'He was too nasty even for me.'

This side of his character – what I would describe as the buccaneer in him – was not widely known in London in the 1970s. His critics had conceded that he was not a boozy, uncultured Australian, but still suspected that he would use his newspapers for questionable political and commercial purposes. The suspicion was fed by reports from Australia where he was said to have played a disgraceful role in political manoeuvring which brought about a constitutional crisis. It began when his newspapers withdrew their support for the Prime Minister and Labour party leader, Gough Whitlam, having helped him win the 1972 election after many years in the wilderness. Within three years their support was withdrawn because, Whitlam alleged, the new government had not granted Murdoch a licence to develop bauxite reserves in Western Australia. Murdoch said he could no longer support Whitlam because his government was grossly inefficient. The climax came when the opposition, which had a majority in the Senate, refused to vote money supplies. The government machinery was brought to a standstill, and the Governor-General, Sir John Kerr, dismissed Whitlam. The part played by Murdoch in this unprecedented act was not clear, except that his newspapers had urged the Governor-General to dismiss the Prime Minister. Their news coverage of the crisis had also been slanted according to his instructions.

A murky episode, but in Britain there was little evidence to suggest that he was another megalomaniac in the style of Northcliffe, Rothermere or King. His nomadic life made it unlikely, and the *News of the World* and the *Sun* were hardly great organs of public opinion. The serious papers can help to mould public opinion, mainly by publishing news politicians would prefer the voters not to read, but not mass-circulation papers which print so little of it. They have to go along with the prevailing mood, understood so well by Bartholomew and Cudlipp – which explains why they were great tabloid editors. That said, popular newspapers can be politically useful. They are better placed to judge the prevailing mood in the broadest sense than the serious newspapers and most politicians because they can only flourish when in step with their readers.

The *Mirror*, the unofficial voice of the left, was outstandingly successful when the Labour party and the trade-union movement represented the aspirations of millions of readers. Its circulation dropped when the party and unions became unpopular among their traditional supporters and members. Other factors were involved of course, but the co-relation between the two was indisputable. Similarly with the *Sun*, which adopted a Tory populist stance at the right time. The nudes and sensationalism explained much of its success, but its crude political line undoubtedly attracted many working-class readers from the *Mirror*. Mrs Margaret Thatcher obviously thought so when she knighted the editor, Larry Lamb in 1980.

If Murdoch had political ambition it was largely to help maintain in power the party with the best economic policy for entrepreneurs such as himself. He was mainly interested in owning newspapers and earning profits. Certainly there was no evidence that he craved for personal political power, or a peerage. He remained an Australian, one of the new breed, and was more interested in the United States than the old motherland. There was plenty of room for expansion across the Atlantic, and he had a poor opinion of American journalists. He was convinced that his Australian and British editors and sub-editors could beat any opposition in New York and elsewhere. They were the true heirs to Bennett and Pulitzer.

Murdoch's American beginnings were modest. Earlier he had bought two small newspapers in San Antonio, Texas, which just happened to be available when he went on his first trans-Atlantic shopping spree. The application of the *Sun* formula – banner headlines, sex, crime, violence and the minimum of hard news – horrified the media critics as in Britain, but returned only a modest profit on his investment. The next venture was the *National Star*, which he launched to compete with the *National Enquirer*. The *Enquirer* was a weekly tabloid, sensational and successful probably because it had a number of Fleet Street men on its staff. Sold mainly in supermarkets, the circulation was about five million. Murdoch found the going rough at first, but persisted and after three years the *Star* was selling about 3,500,000 copies a week. The Australian carpetbagger, as he was known, had broken into the American market. But the *Star* was hardly a newspaper and he must have resented being treated as an unwelcome immigrant. Then he met Katherine Graham of the *Washington Post* and, although press barons tend to be suspicious of each other, she graciously introduced him to some of her peers in New York. Within a relatively short time he had acquired the *New York* magazine and *Village Voice* as well as the *New York Post*.

The *Post* was New York's only afternoon newspaper, but in sales and advertising ran a poor third to the other two, the *Times* and the *News*. It had been owned and run by Dorothy Schiff for 30 years, and the former socialite – she had been given the paper by one of her former husbands – had maintained its liberal tradition. The *Post* was one of the few American papers to stand up to Senator Joe McCarthy in his Red-baiting days, but it was not another *Guardian*. It was an indifferent paper with too many second-rate columnists and too little news. There was perhaps little to choose between Mrs Schiff and Murdoch, although the Australian specialized in sensationalism and Mrs Schiff in liberal causes. This suggested that they were worlds apart, but the *Post* could be just as strident and shrill as any of Murdoch's tabloids, and was not above slanting the news and publicizing scandals when dealing with political enemies.

Nevertheless, the *Post* was a big-city newspaper and with a loyal core of Jewish middle-class readers. Given shrewd editorial direction and a larger news budget, it could have become a good and profitable paper. New York was big enough to support three newspapers. It could also have given Murdoch an honourable place in American society, but apparently without a thought Murdoch brought in his Australian and British journalists, men with small regard for the proprieties or for the facts when they stood between them and a good story. They were great professionals who could if asked explain Einstein's theory of relativity in words of one syllable, and were handsomely paid to sensationalize crime, scandal and violence. Their golden opportunity came when a murderer, dubbed 'Son of Sam' by the rival *News*, began to shoot lovers in cars parked on quiet and respectable streets.

The story was as horrifying as that of Victorian London's Jack the Ripper, and just as fascinating. For urban dwellers generally thought to be inured to street violence the senselessness of the killing became the ultimate horror. The daily coverage was avidly read by everybody including, I suspect, the President and the Chief Justice of the United States. The hysterical rivalry between the *Post* and the *News* reminded some readers of Hecht's *The Front Page*. They probably enjoyed it immensely, and certainly both newspapers sold more copies, but others were appalled and blamed Murdoch for corrupting American journalism. The attacks on Murdoch and the *Post* continued long after the killer, a young postal worker, had been arrested and consigned to a lunatic asylum. The *Columbia Journalism Review* ran an editorial claiming that Murdoch was doing the devil's work by appealing to the basest passions and appetites. The *Post* was no longer merely a journalistic problem but a social problem, a force for evil. Murdoch, who appeared to be genuinely puzzled by the critics, dismissed them as elitists and wondered if there was any other industry in the country which 'seeks to presume so completely to give the customer what he does not want'.

Murdoch also moved the *Post* to the right, despite its liberal tradition. Bruce Rothwell of the *Australian*, who would have edited the London *Observer*, another liberal newspaper, if Murdoch had been allowed to buy it, was brought in as editorial-page editor. This swing was criticized, but apart from Murdoch's own political belief or prejudice the United States itself was moving to the right and many of his new working-class readers were natural Tory populists. Construction workers had supported President Nixon's Vietnam policy in the same way as British dockworkers had rallied behind Enoch Powell because of his opposition to coloured immigration. Rothwell's editorials supporting Ronald Reagan's bid for the Presidency were appreciated by the Republican candidate and subsequently earned Murdoch an invitation to the White House.

It did not earn him much more. The combination of sensationalism and right-wing politics helped to increase circulation, but the *Post* continued to lose money. New York newspapers depend heavily upon departmental store advertising – the *Times* could not be a great newspaper without Macy's ads – and the proud Jewish families who own many of the big stores had a poor opinion of Murdoch's *Post*. Although Murdoch was an ardent supporter of Israel, they seemed to resent the loss of its liberal voice. One of the better-known establishments was said to regard the *Post*'s new readers as potential shoplifters.

Americans are supposed to admire success and rugged individualism, and few businessmen could be more successful and rugged than Murdoch with his growing international conglomerate. The *Post* would eventually, like the *Star*, make a profit, but Murdoch had few admirers. The sensationalism of his papers was deplored, but I suspect there was more to it than that. Newspapers, including those with an international outlook and readership such as the *New York Times* and the London *Times*, are national institutions, and not only because until recently they were protected against foreign competition. (Papers such as the *International Herald Tribune* appeal only to tiny minorities and their own nationals living or working overseas.) Newspapers are part of a nation's life and political process. They reflect as well as influence the attitudes of their readers, and it was to be expected that the arrival of Murdoch and his band of Australian and British journalists aroused suspicion and resentment.

It was otherwise in Britain. Murdoch was not exactly admired, but from the early days of Empire and Commonwealth there had been an exchange of journalists between Britain and the old dominions. The Canadians Beaverbrook and Thomson were even ennobled, but the old Commonwealth bonds were stretched to the limit when Murdoch made a bid for *The Times* and *Sunday Times*. The editorial staff of the *Observer* had preferred the American Atlantic Richfield, once its guarantee of editorial independence was seen to be sincere and workable. Atlantic sold out after a few years, but as one of the paper's columnists with memories of the Second World War said afterwards, a well-bred GI's offer of marriage was preferable to the advances of a wild Australian intent on rape. The owners of Times Newspapers, the Thomson Organization, saw it differently. They had lost a great deal of money largely due to strikes and industrial unrest. The papers had been shut down for nearly one year in a vain attempt to introduce photo-composition. They had had enough, but closure would have cost them more than lasting ignominy – to be precise, over £40 million in redundancy payments. They decided that Murdoch was the only bidder capable of reviving *The Times*.

Roy Thomson (1894–1976), ennobled as Lord Thomson of Fleet in 1964, was born poor in Canada, and was bankrupted more than once before building up a chain of small newspapers and radio stations. He was in the minor league of dollar millionaires when his wife died, and at the age of 60 returned to the land of his fathers and bought the *Scotsman*. Within a few years he acquired the major holding in Scottish Television, the *Sunday Times* and many provincial newspapers. He introduced the Yellow Pages into Britain, launched a highly successful package-tour company with its own airline, and eventually struck it rich in North Sea oil. But the acquisition which really boosted his ego, to quote his own words, was *The Times* in 1966, only 13 years after leaving Toronto.

Thomson appeared to be a strange man to own *The Times*; he called himself a Canadian roughneck and apart from cowboy yarns only read balance sheets. He was obviously shrewd, but knew little or nothing about what are normally referred to as the finer things of life. He always flew economy class, and when staying at the Savoy in London ate breakfast in a nearby transport café. He was a natural and, I suspect, a bigoted Tory, but an immensely likable man and a benign publisher. Unhesitatingly, he accepted the tradition of the paper, that the editor would have complete editorial independence. He put it another way in his autobiography, *After I Was Sixty*:

> It was the oddest deal I had ever made. For I was negotiating an
> amalgamation of *The Times* and the *Sunday Times* under a new company,
> and at the same time I was agreeing to rule myself out of the new company.
> I was agreeing to give up the income of the *Sunday Times* and in return I
> wasn't even to have a say in the running of *The Times*. This was to be the
> new set-up of Times Newspapers Ltd.

He also undertook to provide the necessary means to enable the two papers to be edited in the national interest for 21 years. In other words, he pledged his personal fortune.

The old man deserved more than he got. The editorial staff was expanded so rapidly that many recruits were unsuitable. A business news section was launched which could have made *The Times* as profitable as the *Financial Times*, but was a shambles because too little time was given to planning and recruitment. A circulation drive in the late 1960s was successful but lost money because it did not attract advertising. The senior staff, the old *Times* men, rebelled against what they saw as a lowering of standards, and in 1970 the new management called a halt and for the first time began to do what they should have done in the first place – think. They were perhaps to be excused. The Thomson Organization had always been so successful that they presumably thought that methods suitable for the Sunday paper – which despite its sophistication was basically a mid-brow paper – and for promoting Yellow Pages and package tours could be applied to one of the oldest and most famous newspapers in the world. They had forgotten, or had not realized, that great newspapers have a corporate life of their own. There was a return to the old standards, and *The Times* began to recover. It had nearly always made a profit, albeit a modest one until the Thomson men came in spending money like drunken sailors. Gradually it began to move towards viability again when it was hit by the slump brought about by higher oil prices.

The management correctly believed that serious but relatively-low circulation newspapers such as *The Times* could only survive if they moved from the nineteenth-century technology of the Linotype machine to photo-composition, which could cut production costs by about half. They thought they had the agreement of the print unions, and then the National Graphical Association (NGA), the typesetters' union, dug in its toes. This led to the stoppage which lasted for almost a year, and publication resumed before new agreements had been reached. Millions of pounds were lost, and for nothing. The outcome might have been different if Lord Thomson had not died. His son, Kenneth, preferred to live in Toronto as an absentee landlord. Nevertheless, he was prepared to honour his father's pledge. The one condition was that the editorial staff should also remain loyal to the paper. Alas, some of the new men did not share that loyalty and the National Union of Journalists rejected a 22 per cent salary increase and went on strike. Thomson decided to quit, and Murdoch, who had once said that 'to buy *The Times* would be a highly irresponsible thing to do to your shareholders', became the publisher in 1981.

Although he was the publisher of the *Sun* and the *News of the World*, his bid was accepted because he was prepared to buy all the titles and not just the profitable *Sunday Times*. He was a Commonwealth citizen and not a foreigner, he had a good record for making unprofitable newspapers profitable and he accepted what appeared to be cast-iron guarantees to ensure the independence of the editor. Why he chose to buy a company which was losing millions of pounds annually was not as clear. Unlike Thomson, he appeared to have little or none of the residual loyalty of older Commonwealth citizens to Britain, and judging from his earlier statements did not think highly of *The Times*. The answer must be pure conjecture: he was an impulsive and impetuous man who bought newspapers whenever they became available.

The sale was not popular, and his critics believed that he had no intention of honouring the guarantee of editorial independence when he demanded the resignation of the new editor, Harold Evans, after little more than a year. There were charges of interference, but if that was the case Evans had not complained about it at the time. His successor, Charles Douglas-Home, was an old *Times* man, and if in the opinion of some readers editorial policy swung too far to the right it was because Douglas-Home was a Tory. He was also a capable journalist, and the circulation began to rise soon after he became editor. For the first time in some years it seemed that the old Thunderer would celebrate its bicentenary in 1985.

It would not be the paper of Barnes and Delane; no newspaper, not even the *New York Times* could now wield the power of those two giants even if it wanted to. Moreover, Britain had changed out of all recognition, and there was too much competition from other serious newspapers as well as television and radio for *The Times* to regain its former pre-eminence. It could hope to pursue the principles defined and applied by Barnes and Delane if it paid its way, and if Murdoch also accepted those principles. The future of the paper depended ultimately on whether Murdoch was another John Walter II or another Northcliffe.

Murdoch was certainly not another Walter; neither Barnes nor Delane would have survived under his proprietorship. He loved newspapers as much as Northcliffe did, but was more like the old American robber barons such as Jay Gould and John D. Rockefeller who wanted to lay their hands on every available railroad or oil well. His appetite for new titles was insatiable. In 1983, when cable and satellite television was becoming another passion, he acquired the *Boston Herald* and the *Chicago Sun-Times*. They were published in two of the few American cities with more than one newspaper and the competition in both was formidable. Their editorial staffs were appalled by the prospect of working for Murdoch, and some quit. One departing Pulitzer Prize-winning columnist, Mike Royko, said: 'No self-respecting fish would want to be wrapped in Murdoch's publications. He puts out trash.' Murdoch was not deterred.

With each new acquisition the question was asked 'What makes Rupert run?' He could not hope to achieve a monopoly in Australia, Britain or the United States, and there were easier ways of making money. He was creating a huge international chain of sensational and Tory populist tabloids, in part because he believed that he understood working-class readers no matter what their nationality. If he had a political purpose, apart from making the world safe for people such as himself, it was not immediately evident. He owned too many newspapers to run them effectively as a force for good or evil. There was no management structure or centralized editorial control. Operations in each country were run by a satrap, but they were rarely allowed to get on with the job. The international telephone made Murdoch ubiquitous, and he frequently interfered. That was his right, but because he did not have time to read all his newspapers the criticism was necessarily arbitrary.

The London *Times* was part of the British satrapy. The editor, Douglas-Home, had his guarantees of editorial independence and was expected to use them more effectively than his predecessor. He was a tough-minded journalist dedicated to the paper's traditions, but Murdoch was not another Thomson or Astor, content with the honour and glory of owning the world's best known newspaper. Like Northcliffe, he improved its commercial operations, and gradually reduced its enormous losses. His managers confidently expected to make a trading profit before the paper celebrated its bicentenary in 1985. Murdoch should be congratulated for that. A newspaper cannot be editorially independent unless it is economically independent, a truism that cannot be repeated too often. It was no less true that if Murdoch were to interfere again editorially, so that his second editor felt obliged to resign, *The Times* would lose all credibility. Murdoch had the power to make or break *The Times*. After cheapening his other publications, it was the only real power he possessed.

THE FUTURE – NEW JOBS FOR OLD?

The history of newspapers is partly the history of printing. There were no newspapers, apart from wall newspapers, before Gutenberg invented movable-type printing in the mid-fifteenth century, and no mass circulations before the Hoe family firm developed high-speed presses in the nineteenth century. Hand typesetting delayed production until the Linotype was invented in the 1880s. Illustrations were confined to line drawings and engravings until half-tone blocks became commercially available in 1897. Progress was slow, and if the nightly production of modern newspapers was a near-miracle it was because printing techniques were so primitive. Newspapers everywhere were still using the old methods halfway through this century. No other industry of comparable size and importance was dependent upon such archaic machines.

It was not seen that way even after the Second World War; indeed, the laborious production methods were part of the romance of the press which touched nearly everybody involved. It was buttressed by pride of craft and the nightly satisfaction of getting the paper out on time. I can remember as a foreign correspondent phoning in my stories from distant capital cities or wars, and when it was a big story sensing the excitement of the copy-taker and his eagerness to cooperate. When trying to make the last edition from Washington, where the five-hour time difference was not in my favour, I composed straight onto the teleprinter and in short 'takes' or sections so that the sub-editors and printers did not have to wait until the end before processing it. Often enough the first part of the story was in type before I had written the last paragraphs, and I knew that the presses would be running before I had finished a drink at the press club upstairs. On one occasion when I was writing right up against the final deadline, the copy-taker warned me how much time I had left. It was something like the countdown for the launch of a spacecraft: 'Ten minutes . . . five . . . two . . . sorry, squire, that's it.' It was always squire, and when the editor sent congratulations, known as herograms, the copy-takers invariably added one of their own.

On my infrequent trips back to London I would visit the composing room to chat to the Printer – a Cockney who was just as determined as the editor to get late news into the paper without delaying the presses – and watch the Linotype-operators setting the slugs of type and the stone hands putting the pages together and making last-minute corrections. They were calm men who worked swiftly but without hurrying. They appeared to be oblivious of the

[172]

clock, but invariably finished their demanding work on time. Each man knew what had to be done, and did not have to be told.

Before I was posted overseas as a foreign correspondent, it was decided that I should be attached to the night editor for a few weeks to make sure that I knew what had to be done after I had sent in my copy. The night editor had grey hair and a serene face, and he seemed to move in a portable pool of calm. All hell could break loose, but he was never flustered as he made room for late stories and wrote the headlines on the stone (the steel bench on which the pages of type were put together). One night he left early and put me in charge. I felt like the captain of a destroyer in action – I was in command, I told my 26-year-old self exultantly – until hell broke loose not once but three times. The light over the Printer's desk kept winking, informing me that another late story was coming down. I lost my nerve, but one of the stone hands said, 'All right, son. You write the headlines, and we'll do the rest.' They did.

I never wearied of the excitement of writing for one of the finest newspapers in the world with indisputably the best production departments in the world. That I would be read by important people almost everywhere, and perhaps influence their thinking, was secondary to making my contribution to *The Times*. I did not realize then that part of the excitement was generated by performing a twentieth-century task with nineteenth-century equipment. I was not alone in being seduced by the romance of newspapers. The first Royal Commission on the Press (1949) was appointed to investigate the charge that a few press barons were acquiring a monopoly of newspapers. It decided that the charge was unfounded, and admiringly reported:

A newspaper is one of the most remarkable products of modern society. To gather news from five continents; to print and distribute it so fast that what happens at dawn in India may be read before breakfast in England; to perform the feat afresh every twenty-four hours; and to sell the product for less than the price of a box of matches – this, were it not so familiar, would be recognized as an astonishing achievement.

The romance, alas, did not remain untarnished. High wages and newsprint costs drained away the profits of most Fleet Street newspapers, and industrial unrest led to delayed editions and the loss of complete issues. I was in charge one night and failed to get the paper out because the proof-pullers did not come to work. They were few in number and a moronic child could have done their job, but rigid demarcation lines drawn between the different unions did not permit anyone else to step in. All our work was in vain. The customers did not get their favourite newspaper, and the company lost tens of thousands of pounds in revenue. It could not be recouped because nobody wants to read yesterday's newspaper.

The print unions have been strong from the earliest days when their members were among the few workers who could read. Perhaps because printing was first associated with the Church, their shop stewards are called 'fathers of the chapel'. The senior shop steward is the imperial father of the chapel, and the women cleaners have a mother of the chapel. They have imposed a closed shop for as long as can be remembered, and controlled entry into the trade. They have also dictated staffing levels, recruitment and working methods. They have always been highly paid, especially the Linotype operators, and before the war most of them had middle-class values. They tended to live in the better suburbs, drive expensive cars, belong to good golf clubs and a few sent their children to private schools. The readers, who corrected the proofs and were once known as the 'Correctors of the Press', were well-dressed and wore dinner jackets at their annual functions. *The Times* was then probably the only newspaper to use Latin and Greek tags or quotations, and a few of these 'readers' were competent enough to discuss their usage with the editorial writers who tended to be classical scholars. I can remember going into the editor's room one night to say goodbye before going to the Middle East, and listening to the editor and the head reader arguing about some Greek quotation. A stranger might have found it difficult to distinguish between them, such was the erudition and good tailoring of the reader. It said something for the good manners which permeated all floors of the building – there were no employees on *The Times*, only companions and the publisher was known as the 'Chief Companion'. There had never been a strike before the 1950s, and that was called by the electricians who belonged to a large industrial union and not the traditional print unions. There was no picket line during the General Strike of 1926, and the journalists and managers were allowed to get the paper out.

This began to change after the electricians' strike. No doubt the changing social attitudes of the time played a part, but that did not explain the ruthless exercise of the printers' monopoly power. Linotype operators had always earned more than general reporters, but eventually some were earning more than the prime minister. Their pride in their craft was being eroded, and the number of typographical errors in the paper was shaming – but not for them. Their leaders seemed to enjoy damaging the paper; certainly they had no real reason for disrupting production. Apart from their princely pay, they had long had a 35-hour working week, six-week holidays, a generous pension fund and a heavily-subsidized canteen. When Lord Thomson bought *The Times* in 1966 he was told that he may own the paper but they ran it. This was true in more ways than one. *The Times* lost a complete issue in 1977 because they refused to print an article written by David Astor, the former proprietor and editor of the *Observer*, on their work practices, and other politically-motivated strikes amounted to a loss of press freedom much worse than the old stamp tax. They had in effect become the new press barons, and there was little or nothing the deposed barons could do about it.

[174]

One reason was that the barons' own union, the Newspaper Publishers' Association (NPA), was unable to present a united front. Fleet Street was too competitive. It was in fact the only centre of newspaper competition left in the English-speaking world, and the piratical nature of most of the publishers was still too strong to allow them to cooperate with each other. Another reason was the vulnerability of newspapers. They could not afford to lose issues, and a few might have secretly hoped to profit if a weaker newspaper went to the wall. Certainly they were not prepared to arouse the wrath of the unions by bringing in the new technology, the first major advance in printing in nearly a hundred years.

New technology is the label given to computer typesetting and other electronic innovations which amount to a revolution as fundamental as Gutenberg's. The revolution is still in its early phases, and the consequences can only be guessed at. They will not be confined to newspapers, but the press will be transformed and could be given a new lease of life. Experience in the United States and elsewhere proves that production costs can be more than halved. There are other benefits such as flexibility, expecially in the layout of pages, but low production costs could transform the newspaper industry in more ways than now seems possible. The capacity of systems currently available is such that they can produce national newspapers and have more than enough to spare for other publications. For instance, the British trade union movement, which believes it is not fairly reported in the national press, could launch its own newspaper at a fraction of the cost anticipated by the Trades Union Congress (TUC).

Fleet Street publishers were nevertheless cautious. They had millions of pounds tied up in existing plants, and some hesitated because the new technology could erode the dominance of Fleet Street. They were all convinced that the unions would fiercely oppose its introduction. What is known as hot-metal printing would disappear, and with it old crafts and most of the printers' jobs. The threat is posed by single-keyboarding. Instead of journalists writing stories to be set into type by the Linotype operators, they can write on a visual display terminal (a keyboard attached to a television screen) and at the press of a button the story is transferred to the computer to await sub-editing and page makeup. Journalists can also correct their own stories on these terminals, thus making both readers, who now do the corrections, and Linotype operators redundant. The composing room, with its smell of hot lead, and all the romance of printing would disappear. The unions were not much troubled by the loss of romance, but were determined to defend jobs. New technologies have in the past invariably created new jobs, but like the Luddites of old they declared war on the future.

This was the position when the 2nd Lord Thomson decided to install the new technology at *The Times*. Being a North American, he could not understand why anybody should want to resist progress, especially as he ruled out staff lay-offs. Older men would be encouraged to retire with generous redundancy payments, and staff levels would be gradually reduced by natural wastage. A number of men were tempted to accept, but the unions refused and the paper was shut down for nearly a year. It was an expensive time for the publisher but not for the union. Controlling recruitment as they did, hundreds of men were found jobs on other papers, and the National Graphical Association (NGA) imposed a levy on other members to pay *The Times* men. Efforts were made by the TUC and the then Labour government to resolve the dispute, but to no avail. The Minister concerned admitted later that in all his extensive experience he had never met any trade unionists as intransigent as the printers. They were determined to hold out even if it meant closing down *The Times* permanently. Thomson capitulated, the new technology was put into operation but with NGA men at the keyboards. The full potential of computer typesetting for cutting costs was thus vitiated by insistence on overmanning.

The closure of *The Times* for nearly a year was only one reason why the Conservatives were determined to reduce the legal immunities of trade unions when they were returned to power in 1979. The Employment Acts of 1980 and 1982 went some way to imposing legal restraints which unions in other countries had accepted for many years. The landslide victory of the Conservative party in 1983 was seen to prove that this policy had the support of the majority of the electorate, including union members. There were other indications, such as repeated public opinion polls, but this did not deter the NGA from trying to impose its will on the *Stockport Messenger* Group, a small new company publishing suburban weekly papers. The group refused to accept the closed shop because the majority of its employees did not want to join the union, and the NGA leaders behaved like so many medieval barons unwilling to accept the king's writ. In the ensuing struggle, comparable to a rebellion, they organized a massive and illegal picket of the *Messenger*'s plant and shut down Fleet Street although the national newspapers were in no way involved in the dispute. Mr Salim Shah of the *Messenger* group valiantly resisted, but the Newspaper Publishers' Association submitted when it failed to sue the union, thus giving a new meaning to the concept of the Yellow Press. Despite heavy fines and the sequestration of its assets, the NGA called for a general strike, which was narrowly averted by the courageous action of Mr Len Murray, the then general secretary of the TUC. Whether or not the union would eventually have its way, the incident proved that the history of newspapers was still largely the history of printing.

Beginning in the 1960s, many publishers unable to control rising production costs made economies on the editorial side. The fierce competition for hard news slackened perceptively, and with it went much of the power the barons could hope to wield. Cuts in the foreign departments were especially drastic, as

[176]

I realized, being a foreign correspondent. Unlike my colleagues on the *New York Times*, who had little or no competition, the rivalry I had to contend with before the cuts was intense. British foreign correspondents were then more numerous than other national groups, and I could not afford to ignore them just because I wrote for *The Times*. News was news, and its impact was just as powerful whether it appeared in *The Times* or the *Mirror*. Gradually the British became outnumbered by the Japanese and the Americans. Even the *Express*, which with men such as James Cameron and Sefton Delmer had rightly boasted of its foreign news coverage – the slogan was 'The Express Man on the Spot' – brought most of its men back to base.

Editors also had to contend with television. Objectively compared, television news programmes were rarely as good and comprehensive as a newspaper. Television was supposed to hold a mirror up to the world, but if the cameras were not there the world passed it by. It could be outstanding, performing a role beyond the scope of the printed word, when the cameras were in place but that was rare except on organized occasions. For the most part, television news programmes were dominated by 'talking heads', presenters reading news items which could be better explained in newspapers. The reporting staffs were small compared to those of national newspapers, and the words read by the presenters were more often than not provided by the news agencies. Television editors also depended upon the agencies and Fleet Street to alert them to breaking news stories, and they frequently milked the newspapers. So much was obvious to journalists. Moreover, the main television news programmes would only fill three or four columns of *The Times* or *Telegraph*, but apparently the majority of viewers did not mind as long as the news snippets were read off the Teleprompter by a sloe-eyed girl or one who looked like a games mistress.

Good or bad, comprehensive or incomplete, the significance of television was that it had finally broken the newspapers' monopoly of news. Radio had already eroded it but was never regarded as a serious rival. Arguably it was a better news medium than television, being more flexible, but its impact on Fleet Street had been minimal. Television was seen as a powerful rival almost from the beginning, but not by editors of serious newspapers. They believed that they provided an indispensable service to readers who wanted to know what was happening at home or abroad. Their confidence was not misplaced. Without making any fundamental adjustments, the circulations of the serious newspapers steadily if marginally increased, suggesting that the two media could be complementary. It was very different for the editors of the populars. They knew that most of their readers were only casually interested in news. Hence the sugaring of the pill, the wrapping up of hard news with features, human-interest stories, gossip, large headlines and pictures. The formula had successfully sold millions of copies a day since Northcliffe launched his halfpenny *Daily Mail*, but hard news had always been the *raison d'être* of newspapers. The professional pride of most of the editors and news editors had ensured that this was never forgotten, and now they were faced with a genuine dilemma. Assuming that readers who had watched the evening television news programmes would not want to read about it the following day, most of them reduced the news content to the minimum. Some newspapers looked and read like magazines and, ironically, gave more space to television than to hard news. They did not become completely frivolous as their critics claimed. Most of them remained watchdogs of the public interest; to that extent they still performed one of their traditional functions, but most journalists, including myself, regretted the change.

There was of course an argument for the defence. The British were used to reading more newspapers than Americans because publishers of national newspapers had given them what they wanted. From Delane's *Times* to Levy's *Telegraph*, from Northcliffe's *Mail* to Beaverbrook's *Express*, from King's *Mirror* to Murdoch's *Sun*, the search for readers had taken many papers down the social scale. In so doing, newspapers helped to broaden and strengthen democracy, and it was hardly their fault that despite nationwide availability and minimal price difference millions of readers, better-educated than ever before, did not want to read the more serious ones. If the majority of readers were content with television news programmes, if the press's monopoly of news had been shattered, there was little else they could do but to adjust to the new situation and perhaps hope for another change of taste or technology.

It became harder to defend popular newspapers when they embarked upon the so-called bingo war. Bingo, once known as housey-housey, is a simple game of chance played for as long as anybody can remember in the armed forces, church bazaars and more recently in bingo clubs which were opened in abandoned cinemas. No game could be more harmless, but its adoption to raise newspaper circulations raised howls of protest when £1 million prizes were offered.

Not that the prizes were so munificent when the *Daily Star* launched the first game in 1981. The then editor, Derek Jameson, thought that he was technically violating the Gaming Act but said, 'Who's going to sue us for giving money away?' The top prize was relatively modest, a mere £10,000, but according to Jameson 'it went like a bomb and circulation rocketed. It certainly put the wind up the *Sun* and the *Mirror*.' He later predicted that 'bingo fever and millionaire madness could produce blood in (Fleet) Street.'

For such a colourful editor that was a slight understatement. Within a month the *Sun* had distributed 20 million bingo cards and allocated £850,000 to be spent in prize money over a 20-week period. The *Mirror* scheduled its competition to last only four weeks, but two years later admitted that bingo was here to stay. The reason was obvious. The combined sales of the *Star* and

[178]

Sun were raised by nearly 500,000 within a few months. Other populars slow to compete suffered heavy losses, and were forced to join in. George Pinnington, the editor of the *Sunday People*, tried to call a halt. 'The bingo trap is like the poverty trap. You can't avoid getting into it and then you can't get out.' None of his peers listened, and eventually £1 million prizes were dangled before readers. There were no winners until Robert Maxwell, head of the giant British Printing and Communication Corporation, became the publisher of the *Mirror* group in 1984.

Maxwell, a Czech who served in the British army during the Second World War and was decorated for bravery, was another swashbuckling immigrant. Apart from making a great deal of money, he was Member of Parliament for Buckingham from 1964 to 1970 but had always wanted to own a newspaper. He must have been in his element after moving into the executive suite on the top floor of the *Mirror* building in Holborn Circus. Created by Cecil King when he was boss, the secretary's office was larger than the editor's room at *The Times*. The main office was huge and included a well-stocked bar, which when I was last there was manned by a bartender hijacked from the Connaught hotel. Then came a large private dining room run like a grand restaurant; no set meals, instead a long menu and wine list. Beyond was a bedroom with a double bed and a bathroom complete with bidet.

His arrival was resented by the editorial staff, but he was a member of the Labour party whose dislike for the hard left was shared by most of them. He also retained as editorial consultant Lord Cudlipp, the last of the great *Mirror* editors. He quickly proved to be as active as Cecil King. Signed policy statements immediately appeared on the front page, and he rewrote editorials to reflect his own views. His bingo game guaranteed regular £1 million prizes, and was called 'Who Dares Wins'.

This raised the ante. The *Express* claimed to be the first newspaper to offer a £1 million prize, but none had been won. As Jameson had said, 'the small print says only that you "can" win a million', and the permutations were such that the competition could have gone on for months without any one winning the glittering prize. Fleet Street assumed that Maxwell would give away the first million, but he was beaten to the post. The *Sun* announced the first £1 million winner under the front-page lead: WE SAID WE'D DO IT – BY GOD WE'VE DONE IT. Seven inside pages were devoted to pictures of the smiling recipient and self-congratulatory puffs for the paper.

On the other side of the world in Australia the *Sun*'s proprietor, Rupert Murdoch, must have allowed himself a smile. Two press barons were battling it out. This, I like to think he said, was what popular journalism is all about. Maxwell was not nonplussed. He claimed that 'the *Mirror* has made the first newspaper game millionaire – and it hasn't cost us a penny.' As he chose to see it, the *Mirror* was entirely responsible. The *Sun* knew that the first million

[179]

could be won in the *Sunday Mirror* and *Sunday People* that weekend and in a state of panic had raised its £40,000 prize to a million. The London management of the *Sun* was not amused and rather pompously said, 'if Maxwell says we are cheating, we will sue him . . . He has tried to bribe our readers away from us, but quite frankly his paper is not good enough.' No writ was issued of course, and the *Mirror* soon announced its first millionaire – or rather millionairess, a nice old lady who had obviously had to struggle all her life to make ends meet. Even the disappointed punters must have felt a glow of vicarious satisfaction.

The Times also launched its up-market game. Known as Portfolio, it was cleverly connected with the stock market. Readers were not given the usual bingo card but a 'portfolio' of investments. Prizes were modest, £2,000 for the daily dividend and £20,000 for the weekly dividend. The editorial staff was outraged, but most of the readers were delighted. I can recall dining with a peer, a former head of a great government department, who said that he checked his 'portfolio' every morning after reading the front-page headlines. The circulation rocketed.

The man who began it all, Derek Jameson, did not share the noble lord's pleasure. In an interview with the *UK Press Gazette*, he said that he was worried about his old newspaper, the *Star*. 'It's never made any money and it's hardly likely that Fleet Holdings [the proprietors of the *Star, Daily Express, Sunday Express* and *Standard*] is going to support a succession of *Star* millionaires. If a large section of its readership is there for bingo and larger prizes are being offered elsewhere on the Street then it bodes ill for the *Star*. It could be trampled underfoot.' It was self-defeating. Even with increased circulation, revenue would not be enough to support a millionaire winner a month. This applied to all newspapers involved, and eventually the proprietors would have to get together, as they did in the thirties, and end the circulation war.

This was a reference to the war declared by Lord Southwood of the *Daily Herald* who gave away complete sets of Charles Dickens to his readers. Its rivals felt compelled also to give sets of Dickens away, and when nearly every house in the kingdom must have had a set they offered cameras, cutlery, other household goods and clothing. According to Francis Williams, a family could be clothed from head to foot for only a few shillings. All they had to do was to switch from one newspaper to another. Neighbours who took different papers could equip their kitchens at little cost by ordering each other's paper and swopping over the garden fence. 'Journalism had reached its zenith as a public service.' The 'beneficial' war cost Fleet Street about £3 million a year, a great deal of money in those days. Four proprietors secretly met in the Savoy hotel to discuss a ceasefire, but Southwood refused. Perhaps it is apocryphal, but a story which is still remembered in Fleet Street has Lord Beaverbrook of the

Express saying, 'This is war – war to the death. I shall fight you to the bitter end.' He is then said to have drawn an imaginary sword to run Southwood through the body. Another version has Beaverbrook cutting Southwood's throat with an imaginary bowie knife. The details vary, but the drama is still fondly remembered. Journalists may not like press barons, but many cannot but admire the more colourful. Whatever happened at the Savoy, Francis Williams claimed that the circulation war was successful. The average daily circulation of national morning newspapers in 1930 was rather less than nine million, and ten and a half million in 1939. I am not convinced that sets of Dickens and cutlery were responsible for the increase. By the late thirties Britain was emerging from the slump, and more people could afford to buy newspapers. The worsening situation overseas and the prospect of war with the Axis powers must also have helped. There is nothing like war to sell newspapers.

What will happen in the eighties is anybody's guess, but a comparison of sales before and after £1 million prizes were offered suggests very little. During the six-month period, April–September 1983, the average daily circulation of national morning newspapers, excluding the communist *Morning Star*, was more than 15 million and the Sundays brought the total up to nearly 33 million. During the comparable period in 1984, the dailies had dropped to below 15 million but the Sundays had added nearly 600,000.

It would be dangerous to read too much into these figures. The *Sun* lost many copies because of industrial disputes as did some other newspapers. *The Times* increased its circulation by 20 per cent to a daily average of 424,893, but could not take full advantage of the success of its Portfolio competition because the printers demanded more to man an additional line of presses. The *Guardian* on the other hand increased its circulation by 6.7 per cent without the help of a competition. Bingo obviously helped the *Express, Star* and *Mirror*. The *News of the World* put on another half a million when it changed from broadsheet to tabloid format in May 1984, and bingo added another 300,000, bringing it up to about 4,800,000 copies. Jameson thought that the £1 million prizes had attracted about 250,000 floaters, readers who moved from one paper to another. Others probably bought two or three papers when previously they had taken one, and he thought that this would not survive the end of bingo when the proprietors were eventually obliged to call a truce.

He was almost certainly correct if only because saturation point had already been reached. A daily sale of 15 million suggests that nearly every family in the country already bought a newspaper. That said, the circulation war may not have been intolerably expensive for proprietors who publish more than one newspaper. For instance, Maxwell's game, Who Dares Wins, appeared in the *Mirror, Sunday Mirror* and *Sunday People*. The group had a combined circulation of more than 10 million, and arguably bingo did not cost much more than an extensive promotion campaign on television. The *Guardian* spent more than £1 million on television advertising, and its circulation was less than 5 per cent of that of the *Mirror* group. Bingo was also enormously popular among readers of all classes, and at least provided some light relief during a period darkened by high unemployment, the miners' strike and IRA bombing.

But I doubt that Francis Williams would have regarded bingo as a public service. During the circulation war of the thirties papers such as the *Express* still maintained a large corps of foreign correspondents, but this time all the indications suggested that the warring press lords had cut editorial budgets. The *Mirror* closed its New York office and reportedly saved £500,000 a year. The *Mail* closed its office in Washington. It was argued that such expensive outstations were unnecessary, that a reporter could be flown to New York and file a story for that night's newspaper. Perhaps, but the most enterprising reporter would not have the background knowledge of a resident foreign correspondent. His story might make the last editions, but perforce would be sketchy and shallow. More likely, he would only contribute his byline and sub-editors in London would rewrite news agency stories to run under it.

Towards the end of 1984 the Treasury let it be known that the Chancellor of the Exchequer was thinking of levelling VAT on newspapers. This could be the most damaging consequence of the bingo war. The enemies of a free press said that the populars were no longer newspapers but entertainment sheets and should be taxed along with theatres, cinemas and bingo clubs. The charge could not be made against *The Times*, despite its Portfolio competition. The populars still published more news than did the main television programmes. Moreover, future governments could use VAT to control or punish the press. It could easily become another stamp tax. That may have been the reason why a junior minister later in the year announced in the House of Commons that it would not be included in the next budget, but the threat was not completely withdrawn.

Critics on the far left, obsessed by what Tony Benn, the Labour 'Left' politician, described as 'distortion by the meejar', would welcome a tax which could make newspapers unprofitable for their capitalist owners. They really believed that newspapers reflecting their own views would flourish, but experience indicated otherwise. The *Daily Herald*, launched as a trade union and Labour party newspaper, failed despite the complete sets of Dickens given away to attract readers. They also ignored the decline of the *New Statesman*, the weekly magazine of the left, which despite its relatively small circulation was on occasions influential. For instance, its support for decolonization was a factor that no historian of the period can ignore, and Pandit Nehru, India's first Prime Minister, was one of its most loyal readers.

The *Statesman* was not a news magazine like the *Economist*, but it was required reading for journalists writing for national newspapers who followed developments within the Labour party. This also increased its influence. It was widely respected, earning the affectionate nickname of Old Staggers, until a new editor, Bruce Page, swung the editorial line to the far left. The civilized commentary on events, which was often amusing, was replaced by harangues and a shrillness which disconcerted many readers. The circulation plummeted, proving once again that the far left did not understand the functions of a free press. The damage done was fortunately not terminal. Peter Kellner, the political columnist, knew that neither the magazine nor left-wing politics could flourish in a vacuum. Duncan Campbell, an investigative reporter, produced stories that were picked up by the national press. This had long been another reason why Fleet Street news editors read the weeklies with close attention. (The *Spectator*, the rival Tory weekly, came to depend more upon lively writing to attract readers, in which it was modestly successful.) These political weeklies also deserved attention because they were nurseries for young and bright journalists.

The more specialized magazines such as *New Society* (launched in 1962) were also read in Fleet Street, but none more so than *Private Eye*, which was founded in the same year. Satirical and often very funny, the *Eye* had no sacred cows. No person or institution, including the Royal Family, was safe from its iconoclasm, and it also published investigative reporters such as Paul Foot whose stories were often worth following up by the national newspapers. An obvious example was the Thalidomide story, which the *Sunday Times* subsequently developed into a major story and won substantial compensation for the victims.

This did not impress the critics even when Foot joined the *Daily Mirror*, but their complaint that the prevalence of Tory-owned newspapers gave an unfair advantage to the Conservative party was not proven. Indeed, judging by the postwar election results the press had had little or no political influence. From 1945 to the mid-1970s, the Labour party was in power just as long as the Conservatives. Labour lost the 1979 election because of the 'winter of discontent' when widespread industrial unrest, much of it brutal, horrified even trade unionists. On the admission of Labour's leaders, the 1983 election was lost because of the party's internal divisions. Its drift to the far left was also unpopular, and even the loyal *Mirror* could not defend much of the party's programme. In any case, television and not the press was the chosen medium for electioneering. Even though it still could not hold a mirror up to the world, politicians of all parties preferred to campaign from the television studios at Westminster or on programmes such as LWT's *Weekend World*. More often than not, the press was reduced to reporting what was said on these programmes. The newspapers created by the great press lords, Northcliffe, Rothermere and Beaverbrook, played very little part in the elections. The press was powerless on this count.

Postwar developments for the American press were somewhat different.

The United States emerged from the war with its economy considerably strengthened, and the press benefited from the country's sustained economic prosperity. Newspapers grew fat with advertisements, and of course they had to assume a new role. Earlier they had largely reflected the isolationist policy pursued by many Administrations, although between the two World Wars a minority had been aware of the dangers of Nazism. A few had maintained some very good correspondents in Europe, but on the whole the press had not wanted to become involved. That changed when the United States became a superpower, with more space being given to foreign news, although most papers depended upon the news agencies. Peace, prosperity and power did not, however, bring domestic tranquillity. The communist victory in China in 1949 was a shock, as was the invasion of South Korea by the communist North in the following year. The Truman Administration and the State Department were held responsible and pilloried by right-wing Republicans. Senator Joe McCarthy terrorized the American establishment and trampled on the constitutional rights of his hapless victims for four terrible years, and at times it seemed that the press was his closest ally.

There were many reasons for what looked like abject behaviour on the part of the press. The Republicans had been out of office since 1933, and were willing to use any stick to beat Truman in the 1952 election. Most newspaper publishers were Republican, and Colonel McCormick of the *Chicago Tribune* was not alone in abusing the freedom of the press for political purposes. The working press was the victim of its own disciplines. Objectivity, strictly defined, was all. The job of the reporter was to report what the senator said and not try to find out if he was lying. This was more than an article of faith for the news agencies which provided most of the news reports; they serviced thousands of newspapers and radio stations and strict neutrality was essential for their survival. McCarthy also understood the workings of the press. He knew about deadlines and overnighters – stories written and prepared overnight for early morning broadcasts and the afternoon papers – and could be depended upon to provide a new lead even if he had to make it up. He was always available.

Many reporters knew that they were being used, but competition was fierce and whether the story was true or false their editors did not want to be beaten by the opposition. In any case, the rules of objectivity only required stories to be attributed. Whatever McCarthy said was news and had to be reported. In his well-researched book *Joe McCarthy and the Press*, Edwin Bayley quoted a reporter who said: ' "We'd fight to get a two-minute beat on a new name" . . . That simplistic, gee-whiz reporting, with its phoney objectivity, did as much to raise Joe McCarthy from a bumbling unknown to a national menace as the craven behaviour of his fellow senators and the White House.' Douglass Cater, in *The Fourth Branch of Government*, said:

The extent of the communications failure McCarthyism presented can be measured by the fact that few of the reporters who regularly covered McCarthy believed him. Most came to hate and fear him as a cynical liar who was willing to wreak untold havoc to satisfy his own power drive. But though they feared him, it was not intimidation that caused the press to serve as the instrument for McCarthy's rise. Rather was it the inherent vulnerabilities – the frozen patterns of the press – which McCarthy discovered and played upon with unerring skill. 'Straight news', the absolute commandment of most mass-media journalism, had become a strait-jacket to crush the initiative and the independence of the reporter.

Television, then in its infancy, was equally craven. Quickly cowed by McCarthy, the networks operated blacklists of commentators who had offended him and his supporters. There were few heroes. Edwin Bayley's own newspaper, the *Milwaukee Journal* and the *Washington Post* were among the very few newspapers which remained true to the ideal of American journalism. Martin Agronsky of ABC television was a brave opponent, as were Drew Pearson and the Alsop brothers, who suffered through losing customers for their syndicated columns. And yet the tide turned only because McCarthy's attacks continued after the Republican President Dwight Eisenhower had been elected. This the Republican publishers could not stomach. Television also helped in the end, not the chairmen of the networks but the medium itself. It could hold up a mirror to congressional hearings conducted before the cameras. The televised reports of the Army–McCarthy hearings revealed the senator as a bully and character-assassin, and the Senate eventually censured him by a vote of 67–22. It was these hearings which revealed the true character of the Senator to millions of television viewers when he accused the army of shielding communists.

The American press was understandably slow to ease the strait-jacket of objectivity. It had been accepted in the first place because of the excesses of the political press of the nineteenth century (the dark ages of American journalism according to Frank Mott, the press historian); and the news agencies, which did most of the out-of-town reporting, could not change. Moreover, there was a great deal to be said for objectivity, since no self-respecting editor wanted to publish slanted news, but they could not ignore the fact that when rigidly applied objective reporting as practised in the United States made newspapers hostages of politicians, government officials and public relations men as well as demagogues such as McCarthy. Tom Wolfe, John Hersey and others pioneered a new kind of journalism which made good reading and was frequently illuminating. Wolfe's *New York* magazine article on 'Radical Chic' (1970), which described with sly fun the relationship between wealthy white intellectuals and black activists, was a splendid example, but the new style had its dangers. The combination of news reporting and the techniques of fictional writing made for subjectivity; it tended to express the writer's idiosyncrasy rather than transcribing external realities.

James Reston of the *New York Times* said that American journalists should take the British foreign correspondent as a model. He meant that they should report the news as objectively as possible but also provide background information to put it in proportion. Sound advice no doubt, but few Americans believed that they had anything to learn from Britishers. The problem was partly resolved, at least for the better newspapers, by the revival of investigative reporting. As noted earlier (in Chapter 10), it helped papers such as the *New York Times* and the *Washington Post* to broaden the scope of their reporting. The vast majority of the press continued to rely on the news agencies, which tried to provide more background stories. Within their own strait-jacket they did rather well.

The resistance to change by the print unions was less damaging than in Britain. There were punishing strikes in New York, which killed a number of papers. Union power was broken by the *Washington Post* after its presses had been sabotaged, but there was little prolonged resistance elsewhere. The *Los Angeles Times* had never employed union labour, and elsewhere the unions were too weak to hold publishers to ransom as in Britain. The new technology was introduced in the 1960s and 1970s, and helped the press to survive the onslaught of television and the flight of the middle classes to the suburbs.

Television made an impact long before British publishers had to worry about it. The Army–McCarthy congressional hearings were an obvious example, and it was firmly established by 1956 when much of the nation sat up at night to watch the Democratic and Republican national conventions. The impact was all the greater because the United States did not have a national press, and apart from the news agencies and occasional radio hook-ups the country had never been served by a single news organization. Suddenly there were three national television networks, ABC, CBS and NBC, and a few lesser groups. Pro-gramme timings had to be staggered because of the different time zones, but viewers from Miami to Detroit, from Portland, Maine, to Portland, Oregon, could watch the same programmes. The political influences were incalculable. Presidential press conferences, first televised in 1961, further increased the power of the White House. Congressional hearings provided a kind of investigative reporting that no newspaper could ever match. The *Washington Post* broke the Watergate story, but the televising of Senator Sam Ervin's committee hearings sealed the fate of President Nixon and his men. All election campaigns were planned for television, and political commercials earned a fortune for the networks. They also made campaigning financially prohibitive for all except the rich, such as Rockefeller and all the Kennedys, or candidates funded by fat cats. News programmes were extended, in part because they were cheap to make but also because they attracted advertising. They were further extended when individual stations ran their own programmes as well as network news, and breakfast programmes attracted huge audiences. American television suffered from the same limitations as in Britain, but few people noticed. The majority were convinced that television news was more objective and extensive than newspapers.

At the time some futurologist might well have predicted the imminent demise of the press, but it flourished although the advertisement pie had to be shared with television. The circulation of serious newspapers increased as in Britain because they provided a service for a small but influential minority interested in national and international news. They would have been more successful if they could have circulated throughout the United States, but the necessary technology was not then available. Whether or not they wanted to read newspapers such as the *New York Times, Washington Post,* the *Baltimore Sun* or the three or four others which American journalists agreed were the only competent newspapers published in the United States, more than a half of the population could not have them delivered with the local paper. Along with one or two comparable newspapers, the *New York Times* was initially hurt by the flight to the suburbs. The new suburbanites tended to switch to papers such as *Newsday* because they provided local news. Potentially more damaging, downtown departmental stores upon which the *Times* depended heavily for advertising revenue responded to the demographic change by opening branches in the new shopping malls. Seeing many of its readers and advertisers disappearing, the *Times* met the challenge by producing special suburban sections and others devoted to specialized interests. Fortunately it worked. Mr Ochs may have turned in his grave, but the *Times* remained true to its ideals.

The vast majority of the country's newspapers also survived the onslaught of television, and for reasons which are difficult for non-Americans to understand. A great deal was claimed for the American press, mainly by itself, but the average newspaper was, to say the least, not very impressive. At the last count there were 1730 dailies, and very few of them were exposed to competition. To be precise, only about 30 of the country's 1600 communities had more than one newspaper. The United States had become a land of one-newspaper towns, and without the goad of competition few papers tried to give a good news service. Before television, people living in this vast news wasteland had to read the news magazines *Time* and *Newsweek* if they wanted to know what was happening beyond the horizon. (One reason why news magazines were not a success in Britain was that good newspapers were available everywhere.) For such people the arrival of television was like manna descending upon the children of Israel. Which was why the national opinion polls reported that the majority of Americans believed that television news was better than their newspapers. It had to be, there was no comparison.

During my travels in the United States I occasionally read a paper whose publisher or editor obviously tried to do a good job. The *Atlanta Constitution* was one such newspaper and the *South Bend Tribune* of Indiana another, but they were in a minority. The majority were not really in the news business as understood by journalists in New York, London or Sydney. Nevertheless, they flourished, despite television, because they had a monopoly of local advertising, becoming very profitable after the new technology had reduced production costs, and many were taken over by the large newspaper chains.

Newspaper chains or groups were not peculiar to the United States. In Britain they were begun by the old press lords, and by 1930 four groups controlled more than 40 per cent of the provincial press. Hearst and Scripps began much earlier, and by the same year there were more than 30 American chains. They continued to multiply, although many were small, and by 1980 they controlled 71 per cent of the total daily circulation. Whether or not they constituted a threat to press freedom was arguable. Hearst certainly thought that his chain would take him to the White House. Scripps, on the other hand, was concerned to provide his newspapers with services which they could not have enjoyed separately. Some were restrictive in that they closed down opposition newspapers, and others dictated editorial lines which editors were obliged or expected to follow. But the new generation of chain owners were mainly interested in profits. Like Lord Thomson, they read the balance sheets and not the newspapers. Samuel Newhouse of Newhouse Newspapers was typical of the Americans. By 1980 he owned 29 newspapers with a combined circulation of more than three million, and was completely uninterested in informing and guiding public opinion. His editors were more or less free to run their papers as they liked as long as they made a profit. This seems on the surface more commendable but one of his newspapers, the *Birmingham News*, was probably the most rabidly segregationalist sheet in Alabama. He died a very rich man.

Other chains were owned by faceless corporations. Again this was not confined to the United States, but the possibility of a conglomerate or multinational using newspapers for its own commercial or political purposes was disturbing. Many journalists longed for the good old days when a press baron was at least the devil they knew.

The English-language press had come a long way since the days of Barnes, Delane and Bennett. Newspapers were bigger, better printed and provided many more services. The role of the press in public life was still of unique importance, but it had more critics than admirers. There was a widespread assumption that it was an obsolescent medium run by yesterday's men or by companies interested only in profit; that it had been replaced by television, and eventually would be obliterated by further electronic advances. This seemed entirely possible, and in the 1970s Reuters appeared to be taking the next step towards its oblivion.

It seemed an unlikely role for the famous British news agency, which was founded in 1849 by the German-born Baron Paul Julius de Reuter (1816–99). Reuter was always fascinated by communications and more or less stumbled into the news agency business. His first venture was to organize a pigeon post between the end of the new German telegraph line at Aix-la-Chapelle (now Aachen) and that of the French and Belgian lines at Verviers. He then emigrated to Britain, and organized the transmission of commercial telegrams to places still not connected to the telegraph system. Again he used pigeons whenever necessary, but as the telegraph between Britain and the European continent improved he looked about for further traffic and by 1860 was providing London papers with foreign news. The agency was firmly established when he negotiated a cooperative arrangement with the Press Association, which represented the provincial newspapers. The PA received Reuters' foreign news in exchange for its home news, and the combination made Reuters a great international news agency. It had its ups and downs, but was always in the forefront of communications and after the Second World War developed an international system more extensive and flexible than any of its competitors. In the 1970s Gerald Long, a former foreign correspondent, then Managing Director of Reuters, decided to take the agency back to its origins of 130 years earlier as a supplier of prices and business news. At the time of writing 64 different services were available to 15,000 subscribers on 37,900 visual display terminals in 119 cities in 74 countries. It also has a news retrieval service enabling subscribers to extract items from Reuters' worldwide news service. About 90 per cent of the agency's profits are generated by the business information services. The news agency has become the poor relation.

The significance of this success was not immediately apparent. The Newspaper Publishers' Association, which with the Press Association and the press services of Australia and New Zealand owns Reuters, was more interested in profits. Understandable perhaps, but while the new service is limited largely to financial and commodity markets, it obviously has a wider application. An electronic newspaper may not be feasible for the foreseeable future, but the prime role of the press as the purveyor of news, already under threat from television, could be further diminished by the sophisticated computer technology introduced by Gerald Long.

The prospect is disturbing because conventional newspapers are essential to the survival of democracy. The majority may now prefer to get their news from television, but television stations are licensed and ultimately controlled by government, and licences can always be revoked. A few commercial television stations in Britain have had their licences withdrawn, not for political reasons, admittedly, but there can be no guarantee that this will not happen under some future government. An electronic newspaper would almost certainly be liable to some kind of official licensing. The press, on the other hand, has won its freedom and most publishers and editors are determined to defend it. Some newspapers may be considered unworthy of that freedom, but that is for the reader and not the government to decide. As Derek Jameson, the irrepressible one-time editor of the *News of the World,* said when a reader complained to the Press Council about his paper's controversial coverage of Prince Andrew and his girlfriend, Koo Stark: 'You pay's your money, and you takes your choice.' Some press barons, at least, have more guts than television executives, as was proved in the United States when the media were threatened by McCarthy and Nixon. Newspapers, both serious and popular, present different views of the world. They are the watch-dogs of the public interest, and the citizen's freedom is that much more secure as long as they continue to bark.

Many publishers and editors know that newspapers must continue to adapt to meet the competition of the electronic media. The *Washington Post,* for instance, has already spent more than $25 million on new technology, and expects to spend a further $100 million by 1990. Martin Walker, in his book *Powers of the Press,* reports that Chris Burns, the paper's vice-president for planning, wants to transform the *Post* by the end of the decade. The existing paper, with an average of 100 pages a day, fat with small ads and selling 600,000 copies at 25 cents, will probably be reduced to a 40-page paper, only one-third of it advertising, and selling for up to a dollar. Competition from databanks will probably rob the paper of most of its small ads, and it will be required to attract high-price advertisers by providing a more precisely-defined and affluent readership. He believes that sufficient readers will, in the future, want more news, expert comment and analysis, and will be willing to pay for it. The *Post* could still make a profit with fewer advertisements and readers, and could make more with spin-offs such as information packaging, television programmes and software for the information revolution. As Burns says:

> We are in the news centre of the world. There is a growing market for the information and stories we don't even bother to print. Our objective is to be the dominant source of information about the US government, world diplomacy and America. We'll cede stock exchange information to the *Wall Street Journal.* But that's our future.

Burns also seems prepared to cede less affluent readers to television and to drop features such as fashion and cooking. Bascially he is planning to return to the format of the old version of the London *Times* before it added non-news pages to attract more readers. The *New York Times* has other ideas. Despite the failure of its first West Coast edition, it is planning to become a national newspaper by publishing facsimile editions in various parts of the country. The

Wall Street Journal has been doing this for years, and there seems every reason to believe that the *Times* will be equally successful. The *Journal* is striving to become an international newspaper by publishing abroad and the *International Herald Tribune* is also trying to live up to its name. The smaller papers will no doubt survive because of local advertising.

Nor is the British press doomed to wither away. The *Guardian* has demonstrated that the age of expansion has not passed even for a paper of its ancient lineage. Its recent development has been truly remarkable. First known as the *Manchester Guardian*, it was launched as a radical weekly in 1821 and became a daily newspaper after the stamp tax was repealed some 34 years later. Moulded by C.P. Scott, who was editor from 1872 to 1929 and chief proprietor from 1905 onwards, it long reflected his austere and uncompromising character – the teetotal Manchester Non-Conformist who had a cold bath every morning, dined on bread, cheese and fruit, and rode to the office on a bicycle. Scott was an outspoken editor, whose liberalism swung steadily to the left as Manchester and many of his readers moved to the right, but he did not have Delane's nose for news and was not much interested in it. According to W.P. Crozier, who succeeded as editor, he could hardly conceal the view that the editorial writer, the creator of opinion, was superior to the reporter, the mere purveyor of news.

Scott's editorials, nevertheless, made the paper known throughout the world, and to a great extent it became the alternative paper. For instance, when the Fleet Street press supported the Boer war the *Guardian* was against it. His courage and integrity were impressive, but the paper rarely paid for itself and survived on the profits of the *Manchester Evening News*. Laurence Scott, C.P.'s grandson, became managing director in 1947 and decided that the paper would have to be published in London if it were to generate more advertising revenue. It was a bold move, but things went so badly that Scott decided that the paper would have to be merged with *The Times*. Lord Thomson intervened by buying *The Times*, and the *Guardian* had to fight on alone. It succeeded brilliantly, first under the editorship of Alastair Hetherington and then Peter Preston.

They preserved much that was good in the paper. The political reporting was objective in the best sense of the word, and frequently ahead of the competition. The editorials were well-argued, moderate in tone and just left of centre. Good writing was obviously encouraged, although some writers were probably too opinionated for older readers. A good deal of space was given to home and foreign news, and no other newspaper reported the Third World so well. The new editors did not betray the paper's radical past, but C.P. Scott would have been shocked by some aspects of the new radicalism. They took the lead in promoting the women's liberation movement and sexual freedom, and little was left to the imagination. The correspondence columns often seemed to cater mainly for Trotskyists and other groups on the loony left, but it was a very readable paper with an attractive layout. *Guardian* readers must have felt that they were well informed about most of the new political, social and artistic movements. The circulation steadily increased. The closure of *The Times* in 1979 helped, and there were no losses when it resumed publication. The *Guardian*'s circulation continued to rise from what had long been regarded as a plateau of about 330,000 to more than 450,000.

There was a lesson in the *Guardian*'s success for other national papers; not that they, too, should pay more attention to the plight of one-parent families with black lesbian mothers of Jewish persuasion, which one unkind critic said was a feature of the paper, but to changes in British society which were creating new markets for newspapers. One Fleet Street circulation manager said that the *Guardian*'s readership had largely changed. The average reader could once be characterized as a Welsh Methodist schoolteacher but was now a graduate or lecturer of the new polytechnics. Under the cynicism was more than a grain of truth. Posy Simmonds's comic strip was peopled by *angst*-ridden lecturers, and academics were frequent contributors to the correspondence columns. More importantly, many graduates of the new universities and polytechnics did not fit easily into the social groupings whose interests and tastes were catered for by other newspapers. The *Guardian* gave them a home.

The *Sunday Times* also responded to social change, and flourished under the inspired editorship of Sir Denis Hamilton before he was appointed editor-in-chief of Times Newspapers. A grammar-school boy from the North-East who became the colonel of a good fighting regiment in the war, Hamilton nearly doubled the circulation to 1,500,000 within five years. His innovations included investigative reporting, a business news section and a colour magazine, and they were aimed at readers under the age of 35. Most of the *Guardian*'s new readers came from the same age-group, but the *Sunday Times* had a different approach. Judging from the editorial content and the advertisements in the colour magazine, its readers could perhaps be best characterized as middling but upwardly-mobile executives. No doubt that characterization is as misleading as the *Guardian*'s 'black lesbian mothers', but clearly Hamilton had found another new readership.

The competition followed with varying success. There was clearly a limit to this new market, but the *Observer*, one of the country's better newspapers, was given a new lease of life for which its many admirers were duly thankful. The *Sunday Telegraph* was also successfully launched despite the prophets of doom. Hamilton was less successful when, as editor-in-chief of Times Newspapers, he applied his formula to *The Times*. The paper had its ups and downs under the editorship of Sir William Rees-Mogg, and the circulation had dropped to 282,000 when Harold Evans took over. The drop was due to the uncertainty of the paper's future, but a steady increase was expected when Rupert Murdoch bought the company. Evans was a brilliant journalist who had edited the *Sunday Times* after Hamilton's elevation, but when he was suddenly dismissed in March 1982 only 15,000 had been added to the circulation. A year later, under the editorship of Charles Douglas-Home, an old *Times* man, the circulation had reached 335,000 and television advertising and Portfolio attracted more readers. Douglas-Home had yet to find a new role for the paper, but a circulation approaching 500,000 seemed possible.

One thing was certain as 1984 approached, Britain was still a nation of newspaper-readers. Rising cover prices had marginally cut the combined circulation of the national press, but largely because fewer readers were buying two newspapers a day. An encouraging sign for the publishers was that television audiences had fallen by a larger margin than newspaper circulations. One explanation was the growing popularity of videos, and the introduction of cable television was likely to reduce further the audiences of BBC and ITN news programmes. The press – the Gutenberg press as some journalists wryly described their old-fashioned medium – had survived the first onslaught of the electronic press. The provincial and local press had done even better; over a 15-year period the combined circulations had increased by 82 per cent, although a great deal of this was accounted for by freesheets. These were distributed free of charge and depended entirely upon advertising revenue. Some were little more than advertisement sheets, but many had developed into genuine local newspapers. In other words, freesheets apart, just as many newspapers were sold in Britain in 1983 as in any one year before.

The larger provincial newspapers were certainly not in a state of decline, as was proved by Britain's oldest newspaper, the *Glasgow Herald*. Of course, it was published in no mean city, the industrial heart of Scotland, which man for man had produced more engineers, scientists, architects and journalists of repute than any other city in the land. It was a vigorous and often tough city, not unlike Chicago, which had also produced great journalists. Glasgow produced too many of them, and there had long been a thriving export trade to London. One of them, James Holburn, served in Germany, the Soviet Union and India, and as a war correspondent in Spain, Africa and the Middle East for *The Times*. He was that paper's diplomatic correspondent, a very senior appointment in those days, when in 1955 he returned to Glasgow (where he had learned his trade) as editor of the *Herald*. This paper had always looked outwards, but Holburn made it more international-minded, put news on the front page, introduced bylines and promoted women to senior positions. It was a very modern newspaper when he retired, and his deputy, George Macdonald Fraser, was acting editor until he 'discovered' the Flashman papers. (This series of novels based on the further fictitious adventures of the bully, Flashman, from Thomas Hughes's *Tom Brown's School Days* of 1857 was so successful that he had to withdraw to the British tax haven of the Isle of Man.)

One reason why the *Glasgow Herald* flourished in its 200th year, when the circulation was increased despite a rise in price, was the introduction of new technology. The present editor, Arnold Kemp, said that the paper survived and prospered because of the technological revolution. He went on to back it heavily against television as a news medium:

> Sometimes extreme prophecies are heard about the imminent demise of the printed word. The book is said to be dying and the newspaper with it. Tomorrow's citizen, when he wishes to inform or amuse himself, will turn to the magic lantern in the corner of the room. We believe that the prophets are wrong, and that the trusted newspaper will retain its hold on the loyalties and affections of its readers. The printed word, compendious, portable and companionable, remains the supreme medium for detail and intelligent argument.

In fact, the *Herald* was still reliant on the NGA, whose members keyed the journalists' words into the computer, but if the print unions' suffocating grip on production was relaxed or removed the press in general could enjoy another long period of prosperity. Better and cheaper newspapers could be published. More money could be invested in the editorial departments. The histories of newspapers and printing are inter-related, but there could be no newspapers as we know them without journalists. Newspapers will always need men and women with an almost physical urge to report, lone wolves with hungry eyes and the adrenalin in full spate when working on a story. They are the front line troops, whose news reports are the only real power the press can hope to wield. They are the watch-dogs of our democracies, ready to believe but always sceptical; men and women who when dealing with presidents and prime ministers, trade-union leaders and industrialists, yogis and commissars, always ask themselves, 'Why are these lying bastards lying to me?'

The journalists are indispensable, but they cannot run newspapers. They in turn need press barons, not the old megalomaniacs whose lust for power gave the press a bad name, but men and women such as Barnes, Delane, Pulitzer, Ebenezer Syme, Adolph Ochs and Katherine Graham. Even a James Gordon Bennett would do. Barons prepared to seek out the truth; to print all the news that's fit to print; to go on as they began, calling a spade a spade. Barons who love newspapers *and* balance sheets – but in that order.

SELECT BIBLIOGRAPHY

The author is indebted to many authors whose books over the years have extended his knowledge and love of newspapers. They include the following:

Bayley, Edwin R. *Joe McCarthy and the Press* (Madison, Wis., 1981).
Berger, Meyer *The Story of the New York Times* (New York, 1951).
Bernstein, Carl and Woodward, Robert *All the President's Men: Truth About the Watergate Scandal* (London, 1974; Sevenoaks, 1981; New York, 1976).
Bishop, James *see* Wood, Oliver.
Bradlee, Benjamin Crowninshield *Conversations with Kennedy.* (New York, 1975; London, 1976).
Brendon, Piers *The Life and Death of the Press Barons* (London, 1982; New York, 1983).
Cannon, M. *The Australian Thunderer* (Melbourne, 1968).
Cater, Douglass *Fourth Branch of Government* (Boston, Mass., 1959, 1969).
Cudlipp, Hugh *Walking on the Water: Autobiography* (London, 1976). *The Prerogative of the Harlot: Press Barons and Power* (London, 1980; Lawrence, Mass., 1981).
Driberg, Tom *Beaverbrook: A Study in Power and Frustration* (London and Toronto, 1956).
Emery, Edwin and Emery, Michael *The Press and America: An Interpretive History of the Mass Media* (Englewood Cliffs, N.J., 1954, 1978).
Evans, Harold *Good Times, Bad Times* (London, 1983; New York, 1984).
Foot, Michael *Debts of Honour* (London, 1980, 1981; New York, 1981) (US edn subtitled: *Profiles in Autobiography*).
Gretton, Richard Henry *A Modern History of the English People* (London and Boston, Mass., 1913–29; reprint Norwood, Pa).
Halberstam, David *The Powers That Be* (London and New York, 1979).
Koss, Stephen E. *The Rise and Fall of the Political Press in Britain.*
Vol. 1 – *The Nineteenth Century* (London and Chapel Hill, N. Carolina, 1981); Vol. 2 – *The Twentieth Century* (London and Chapel Hill, N. Carolina, 1984).
Leapman, Michael *Barefaced Cheek* (London, 1983).
Mackenzie, Robert Trelford *British Political Parties: The Distribution of Power Within the Conservative and Labour Parties* (London, 1953, 1964; New York, 1955, 1963).
Matthews, Thomas Stanley *The Sugar Pill: Essays on Newspapers* (London, 1957; New York and Toronto, 1959).
Mott, Frank Luther *American Journalism: A History of Newspapers in the United States through 250 years, 1690 to 1940* (New York, 1941).

Pray, Isaac Clarke, Ed. *Memoirs of James Gordon Bennett and His Times, by a Journalist* (New York, 1955; Ann Arbor, Mich., microfilm only, 1956).

Roberts, Chalmers McGeagh *The Washington Post: The First 100 Years* (Boston, Mass., 1977).

Ryan, Albert P. *Lord Northcliffe* (London and New York, 1953).

Salisbury, Harrison *Without Fear or Favor: The New York Times and Its Times* (New York, 1980, 1981).

Schults, Raymond L. *Crusader in Babylon: W.T. Stead & the Pall Mall Gazette* (Lincoln, Nebr., 1972).

Scripps, E.W. *I Protest: Selected Disquisitions*, Ed. O. Knight (Madison, Wis., 1966).

Seitz, Don Carlos *Joseph Pulitzer (Liberator of Journalism): His Life and Letters* (New York, 1924; London and Norwood, Mass., 1926).

Smith, Anthony *Goodbye Gutenberg: Newspaper Revolution of the 1980's* (Oxford, 1980, new edn, 1982; New York, 1980).

Swanberg, William A. *Citizen Hearst: A Biography of William Randolph Hearst* (New York, 1961; London, 1962).

Talese, Gay *The Kingdom and the Power: History of the New York Times* (New York, 1969, new edn, 1978; London, 1971).

Times Publishing Company *The History of the Times* (London and New York, 1935–52).

Van Deusen, Glyndon Garlock *Horace Greeley: Nineteenth Century Crusader* (Philadelphia, 1953).

Walker, Martin *Powers of the Press* (London and New York, 1982).

Whyte, Frederic *Life of W.T. Stead* (Darby, Pa, 1978 – reprint of 1925 edn).

Williams, Francis *Dangerous Estate: The Anatomy of Newspapers* (London and Toronto, 1957, Northamptonshire, 1984; New York, 1958). *The Right to Know: The Rise of the World Press* (Harlow, 1969).

Wood, Oliver and Bishop, James *The Story of the Times* (London, 1983).

GENERAL INDEX

NOTE For Newspaper and Periodical titles, see separate index on pages 207-208.

Index to Newspapers and Periodicals

NOTE Titles are classified under the following groups: **Australia; Canada; Europe; Great Britain; India and Singapore; South Africa and Rhodesia (Zimbabwe); United States of America.**